Programmed Readings For Psychological Skills

Joseph M. Strayhorn, Jr., M.D.

Psychological Skills Press

Wexford, Pennsylvania

Psychological Skills Press

263 Seasons Drive

Wexford, PA 15090

www.psyskills.com

author's email: joestrayhorn@juno.com

Thanks to Rob Kyff for editing this book.

ISBN   1-931773-01-7

Contents

Introduction

This book is unusual because its language is simple enough for beginning readers, yet its ideas are complex and important enough to engage and help adults. This book contains, for example, many ideas that have been used successfully to treat anxiety and depression through cognitive therapy. My hope is that almost no one will find this book either "too hard" or "too easy."

This book is designed to promote two major goals. One of these is to provide practice in literacy. Each brief vignette is followed by a quick question that serves as a comprehension check. I believe that constructing the stories with the goal of character development in mind makes them more interesting. The ones at the beginning are written at an easier reading level; the reading level gradually increases as the book progresses.

Some of the learners who read this book may need no practice in reading skills but may read it to learn psychological skills. The learner practices recognizing concepts that are useful in psychological functioning. The book starts with the basic concepts, which are the names of sixteen psychological skill groups. These concepts organize the answer to the question, "What can people learn how to do in order to be mentally healthy?"

The book gradually provides more specialized ideas.

The concepts illustrated in these readings are abstract. Reading a concrete example of one of these and classifying it according to the more abstract concept give the learner practice in making abstractions from specific examples. This is a very important mental ability. It underlies much of "higher order thinking" or "critical thinking." The act of moving back and forth from the concrete to the abstract is also the best way to understand an idea fully.

Learning to use new words helps people to think in new ways. More than seventy years ago, anthropologists formed an idea that has come to be known as the "Sapir-Whorf hypothesis." This is the idea that the words we know and use, the linguistic structures in our memory banks, do not simply reflect our way of thinking about the world. Learning to use words in new ways also helps us see the world in ways that enable us to cope with it better.

The concepts this book seeks to exercise are meant to empower the student. They enable the student to think about experience in ways that have proven very helpful to many people. The person who has often practiced using these concepts can think more effectively. For example, suppose a situation comes up in which it is very useful to use self-discipline, to do something unpleasant now in order to achieve some greater good later.

Suppose a person has no word he is accustomed to using for self-discipline and no frequently used linguistic concepts having to do with short-term temptations and long-term gains. This person is likely to "default" toward thinking, "This is no fun. Therefore I don't want to do it."

But the person who is used to thinking about self-discipline, temptations, and long-term goals is more equipped to think, "This is less pleasant now, but it will pay off in the long run. So I'll need to use self-discipline." Of course, the second person is still free to give in to the temptation if he wants! For this reason, teaching linguistic concepts is empowering but not coercive.

Here's another example. Suppose a person's sibling acts selfishly on a little matter. Suppose a person has no experience with using concepts such as "How big are the stakes here? How awful is this? Am I getting anything out of continuing to blame my sibling?" This person is more likely to "default" to repetitive thoughts of "It's not fair! I need to get him back!"

On the other hand, the person with lots of practice in thinking about categories of thought is better equipped to come up with thoughts such as "I am not getting anywhere by blaming him. What he did was not a big deal. What

do I want to happen now? What are the possible ways I can make it happen?" These types of thoughts correspond to "not blaming someone else," "not awfulizing," "goal-setting" and "listing options and choosing," respectively.

With these labels in the vocabulary, one is empowered to do "metacognition," or thinking about thinking. Again, the person is still free to blame and seek revenge if that is the choice. But, by acquiring the new concepts, the person is empowered to think in more ways, and in better ways, than he could before becoming fluent in these concepts.

Thus, while practicing reading, the learner comes to acquire and refine a vocabulary of concepts that is meant to help the learner in dealing with life's choice points. These are the goals of these reading exercises. Concepts that have proven very helpful to many people are given numerous concrete illustrations in these little stories.

The questions that come after each paragraph are meant to be easy for the reader who was "tuned in" to the paragraphs preceding them. No one should feel insulted if the questions are "too easy"; that's how programmed instruction is meant to be. Programmed instruction ideally allows nearly errorless performance.

There are various reasons why a learner might need a lower level of challenge. Some learners may be at the beginning stages of reading decoding. Some might have their concentration abilities impaired by depression. Other learners may just want to take it easy and relax. In such cases, someone can read the stories to the learner and give immediate enthusiastic feedback on the answers to the comprehension questions.

For a higher challenge level, the learner can do the "reflections exercise" with each numbered vignette. A reflection is an utterance that paraphrases in your own words what you have just heard (or read) in order to make sure you understood it correctly. You pretend that you have heard the author speak to you, and you speak back. If you start your sentence with one of the following phrases, you can be pretty sure you are using a reflection:

So you're saying _____?
What I hear you saying is

_____.
In other words, _____?
So if I understand you right,

_____?
It sounds like _____.
Are you saying that _____?
You're saying that _____?

One useful way for two people to work together with the *Programmed Readings* is to take turns reading vignettes and reflecting. The student reads the vignette and answers the comprehension question, and the tutor reflects. Then the tutor reads the vignette, the student answers the comprehension question, and the

student reflects. This way the tutor gets a chance to model taking pleasure from reading in an expressive voice, to model doing good reflections, and to model not getting fatigued. You can often get a lot further taking turns than you could if the student read every vignette.

Here are some examples of reflections, for the first several vignettes of this book:

1. So you're saying Jack felt good about persuading Jed not to kill a bug, huh?

2. What I hear you saying is that Peg handled it well and had a good time by herself when she couldn't go to her friend's house?

3. In other words, Sam obeyed his mom and got out of the swimming pool when she asked him to?

4. So if I understand you right, the man was able to use self-discipline to improve his diet.

5. It sounds as if a man was able to enjoy his time while he was waiting for a bus.

6. Are you saying that a rich man felt good about using his money to help people instead of to buy luxuries for himself?

7. You're saying that Rick was honest right away when his dad asked who took the saw, even though his dad was angry.

Doing the reflections exercise with these vignettes accomplishes several things at once. The learner can absorb a lot of information about psychological skills. The learner gets to practice reading fluently and expressively; almost all people can benefit from this skill. The learner gets to practice using reflections; this is a very useful interaction skill that promotes understanding among people. The learner gets to practice language comprehension and language expression each time he hears a vignette and renders it into his own words. The skills of comprehending language and using language to express ideas are probably the two most important goals of academic education.

For the learners who are using this volume to practice reading decoding, it is often helpful for a tutor to read the vignette immediately before the learner reads it. That way the memory traces give some help with the decoding. It is also useful for learners at this stage to read some of the vignettes more than one time, rather than going through the book from start to finish.

Some learners may simply want to read this book on their own, from start to finish, and return to sections to remind themselves of important ideas. My hope is that adult learners will appreciate the simplicity of the language and use the brain energy thus freed up to grasp the complex concepts and ideas more fully.

I believe the best learning experience comes when the learner not only reads these stories but also composes many similar ones. Each section of vignettes can be seen as a set of models demonstrating how to make up many more of the same type. The act of creating examples in fantasy is close to that of creating examples in real life.

Carrying out real-life positive examples of these concepts through your behavior is an activity that will directly make life better. Thus another important way to use this book is to watch carefully for the times in real life when you have done a good example, and to record that in a vignette like the ones included here. Writing down these "celebrations" from your own life and reading them at regular intervals, causes the images of the positive examples to go through your brain repeatedly. This harnesses the power of positive fantasy rehearsal in your service.

If you have any comments on this work, or any needed corrections you would like to point out, or any new vignettes you'd like to submit to Volume 2, you may contact me by email at joestrayhorn@gmail.com.

Sixteen Skills and Principles

1. Work hard. (productivity)
2. Be cheerful. (joyousness)
3. Be kind. Make people happy. (kindness)
4. Tell the truth. (honesty)
5. When you don't get what you want, handle it. (fortitude)
6. Think carefully about what to do. Talk calmly when you don't agree with someone. (good decisions)
7. Don't hurt or kill. (nonviolence)
8. Don't use hurtful talk. (respectful talk, not being rude)
9. Build good relations with people. (friendship building)
10. Choose long term goals over short-term pleasure. (self-discipline)
11. Stick by people who have been good to you. (loyalty)
12. Don't waste the earth's resources. (conservation)
13. Take care of yourself. (self-care)
14. Obey when it is good and right to obey. (compliance)
15. In your fantasy, practice doing good things. Don't have fun pretending people are hurt. (positive fantasy rehearsal)
16. Be brave enough to do what's best. (courage)

Examples of Sixteen Skills

Read each story. Decide which skill or principle each story models.

1. Jack was with his pal Jed. They were in the woods. Jed saw a bug. Jed said, "I will step on the bug."

   Jack said, "No, Jed. Let the bug live. The bug will not hurt us. Let us not hurt or kill when it does no good."

   Jed said, "OK, Jack." Jed did not kill the bug.

   Jack felt good.

A. productivity,
or
B. nonviolence?

2. Peg had a plan. Peg's pal Ann was to come and be with Peg. But Ann called. Ann said, "I am sick. I can't come."

   Peg was sad. But Peg said, "I can take it." Peg did not get too upset. She wrote a note to Ann. The note said, "I hope you get well soon, Ann." Then Peg read a book. The book was fun.

   Peg was glad she had put up with it when Ann could not come.

A. fortitude,
or
B. conservation?

3. Sam's mom let Sam swim. He was glad to swim. He wanted to swim a long time.

   But Sam's mom said, "We must stop swimming now, Sam. We must go."

   Sam was not glad. He did not want to go. But he said, "Yes, mom." He got up to go.

   Sam's mom said, "You did well, Sam. You made your mom glad."

A. compliance,
or
B. self-care?

4. A man liked junk food. He liked candy bars. He liked pop. He liked lots of cake.

   The man read a book. The book said that junk food was not good for him. The man wanted to stay well. The man decided to eat much less junk. He ate more peas and beans and other veggies. He ate more fruit.

The man felt good about what he did for himself.

A. honesty and nonviolence,
or
B. self-care and self-discipline?

5. Two men waited for a bus. The bus was late. The first man got angry. He said, "Why is the bus late?"

The other man had fun. He said, "Now I have a chance to read. Now I have some time to rest. Now I have a chance to think about my plans." He looked at the sky. He felt good.

When the bus came, that man said to himself, "I'm glad the bus is here. But I had fun waiting for it, too."

A. kindness,
or
B. joyousness?

6. A man was rich. Some rich men get lots of big cars. Some rich men get lots of big things. But this man did not spend his money on things. He paid people to help people read. He paid people to

help people grow food. He paid people to clean up the earth. He felt good about how he used his money.

A. self-care and compliance,
or
B. kindness and conservation?

7. Rick had a job to do. He wanted to cut with a saw. He took his dad's saw.

When Rick did the job, he felt glad. But he did not put the saw back.

Rick's dad looked for the saw. He got mad. He said, "Who took my saw?"

Rick felt bad. But he said, "I took it. I will get it for you."

Rick's dad was still mad. He said, "If you take it, put it back!"

Later, Rick's dad said, "Rick, I'm glad you told me the truth. Some kids would not have told the truth. But you did."

Rick felt good to hear this.

A. honesty and courage,
or
B. positive fantasy rehearsal and loyalty?

8. Tom had lots of work to do. He had to do math. He had words to learn to spell. He had lots to read.

A good show came on TV. Tom said, "It would feel good now to watch TV. But the work would not get done. I would feel bad tomorrow."

Tom did the work. He did not watch the show. It was hard. But he did what was best.

A. joyousness,
or
B. self-discipline?

9. Liz loved dogs. Dogs loved Liz. Liz wanted to have a dog. She wanted it all the time.

But her dad said, "We can not get a dog. I know this makes you feel bad." Her dad told Liz why they could not get a dog.

Liz did not cry or scream. She did not get angry. She said, "I can take it." She was nice to her dad.

Her dad said, "Thank you for taking it, Liz."

A. fortitude,
or
B. productivity?

10. Tim had a good friend. A big boy was being mean. The big boy said bad things to the friend. The big boy said, "He is dumb. Isn't he, Tim?"

Tim said, "He is not dumb. He is my good friend."

The big boy said, "You are dumb too."

Tim said, "You can think what you want."

Later, Tim's friend said, "Thanks, Tim."

Tim said, "I wanted to stick up for my friend."

A. loyalty,
or
B. joyousness?

11. A man had some money. But a bad man stole the money. The man could not get it back. Now the man did not have much.

The man had two kids. The man said, "I will work hard to feed my kids." The man worked at two jobs. He tried to do his best. He worked a long time each day.

The man worked so much that he made the money back. He said to himself, "Now I know my kids can eat."

A. honesty,

or

B. productivity?

12. Jan drew pictures. Kim drew too. Jan saw what Kim had drawn. Jan had the urge to say, "That drawing is bad." But then she thought, "I don't want to make Kim sad."

So Jan just said, "It's fun to draw. Isn't it, pal?" Jan smiled at Kim.

Kim felt good. Jan was glad that she had not been rude.

A. respectful talk,

or

B. compliance?

13. Ted was with Mack. Mack said, "Let's watch this."

Ted said, "What is it?"

Mack said, "It's a movie on tape. There's much blood. Lots of men are killed."

Ted said, "I don't want to have fun pretending that people are hurt. I'd rather not see that movie."

They did some other thing with each other.

Ted was glad he did not have fun with the killing in the movie.

A. positive fantasy rehearsal,

or

B. productivity?

14. Bob and Pat were at the river. Bob said to Pat, "I dare you to dive off the cliff."

Pat said to himself, "I want to decide with care." Pat thought, "If the water is deep and safe, it would be fun." But then Pat thought, "If a rock is at the wrong place, I could get hurt or killed."

Pat said to Bob, "The risk is too big. I will not dive."

Later, Pat told his dad what he had done. Pat's dad said, "I am glad that you think before you act. I love my son. I do not want my son to be hurt or killed. You chose well."

Pat felt good that he had made a good choice.

A. good decisions,

or

B. compliance?

15. Min was at a party. Min saw a girl who was alone. The girl did not know the rest of the girls at the party.

Min wanted to help the girl have a good time. She said to the girl, "Hi, I'm Min. What's your name?"

The girl said, "My name is Sal. I'm glad to meet you, Min."

Min said, "I had fun with the game we just played. Did you?"

Sal said, "Yes, I like playing guessing games. What other games do you like, Min?"

Min and Sal talked a lot. They got to know each other.

At the end of the party Sal said to Min, "I feel good that I made a new friend." Min felt good too.

A. honesty and compliance,
or
B. friendship-building and kindness?

16. Pam played the piano. Someone said, "Pam, will you play for our group? Do you like to play for lots of people?"

Pam said, "Yes, that will be fun."

The time came for her to play. There were many people. She looked at them. She felt scared.

She got the urge to run away. But then she thought, "I will try to be brave. I will play even though I am scared."

Her fingers shook. But she played the songs. She kept going until the end. She got less scared.

Pam felt good that she had not run away. She was glad she had been brave.

A. courage,
or
B. friendship-building?

17. Mick wanted to learn to read. One day Mick's mom said, "Mrs. Ling will help you read."

Mrs. Ling asked Mick to work for a long time each day.

At times Mick did not feel like working. But Mrs. Ling said, "We work to make good things happen. If you can work even when you don't feel like it, you've learned a very good thing."

Mick thought about that. He worked, even when he felt like playing.

The more Mick worked, the more work he could do.

One day Mrs. Ling said, "You can do six times more work than when we started." Mick was glad to hear this.

One day Mick was able to read very well. Mrs. Ling said, "You did it by learning to work hard and long." Mick felt good.

A. self-discipline and productivity,
or
B. nonviolence and positive fantasy rehearsal?

18. Ann was at school. At talk time, the boys and girls got to talk. They said what they thought.

Ron said a wrong thing. Ann got the urge to say, "Ron, you don't know a thing." But then Ann thought, "Why make Ron feel bad?" So Ann said, "I have a different idea." She told what she thought.

Ron did not mind this. Ann was glad she had not been rude to Ron.

A. respectful talk
or
B. compliance?

19. Biff was very strong. Biff was very fast. Lunk said to Biff, "I'll fight you. You can't win."

Lots of kids said, "Get him, Biff. Show Lunk he's wrong."

Biff said to Lunk, "Why should I hurt you? Why should you hurt me? That would be dumb."

Lunk said, "You are just scared."

Biff said, "You can think what you will."

The kids were sad. Biff said to them, "To watch a fight should not be fun for you."

The kids knew Biff was right.

A. nonviolence,
or
B. productivity?

20. Jan and her dad went out. They walked in the woods. Jan's dad hurt his leg. He could not walk.

Jan said, "I will run for help." She ran a long way.

Jan got tired. She felt like giving up. She felt like stopping to rest. But she said to herself, "I don't care what I feel like. I need to get that help."

She kept going fast. Then she found people to help! They went to her dad. They brought her dad to the doctor.

Later, Jan's dad was OK. He said, "Thanks, Jan."

Jan thought, "I'm glad I kept on."

A. self-discipline,
or
B. conservation?

21. Pam had to get a shot. The shot would hurt. Pam thought, "I want to be tough."

The doctor stuck the needle in. Pam let her muscles be loose. She played that she was taking a rest.

The shot still hurt. But the needle was out fast.

The doctor said, "You were tough, Pam."

Pam said, "Thanks, Doctor."

A. fortitude,
or
B. nonviolence?

22. Jed liked to play baseball. He wanted a new glove. His mom sent for a glove for him. The glove was to come in the mail. Every day Jed looked. "Maybe it will come today," he thought. But it did not come.

Jed's little brother was Frank. Jed knew that when the glove came, Frank would want to see it.

Frank would want Jed to share it with him.

Jed knew he would feel like keeping the glove to himself. But Jed knew it was right to share with Frank. Jed would be able to use the glove for a long time.

So Jed practiced in his mind. He saw in his mind a box. When the box was open, there was his glove. Frank would say, "May I hold it, please?" Jed saw himself sharing with Frank.

One day it happened, just as Jed had imagined. Jed did share. Frank felt good. Jed used the glove for a long time after that.

Jed was glad he had practiced in his mind. He thought, "That helped me be kind to Frank."

A. kindness and positive fantasy rehearsal,
or
B. self-care and conservation?

23. Brock was on a playground. He saw a younger boy. The boy looked lonesome.

Brock said to his friend, "Let's help the young boy have fun."

Brock said, "Would you like to throw the ball with my friend and me?"

The boy said, "I'm not too good at throwing and catching."

Brock said, "That's OK. I'll stand close."

Brock threw the ball gently. He and his friend said, "Good catch! Good throw!"

After that they talked with the boy. The boy was glad to make some older friends.

A. kindness and friendship-building,
or
B. conservation and loyalty?

24. Mary was at home. Mary's mother started getting supper ready. Mary said, "Mama, may I go outside and play with my neighbor?"

Mary's mother said. "Not now, Mary. It's almost time to eat. I need you to help cook."

Mary said, "OK. I can handle that."

Mary's mother said, "I like what you just did. You didn't get what you wanted. But you didn't let it bother you. You stayed cool."

Mary thought, "I was tough." She felt good.

A. fortitude,
or
B. friendship-building?

25. Sal's mom was tired. She had done a lot of work. She sat down to rest.

Sal said to her mom, "You do a lot of work. It helps me that you do that. Thanks, mom."

Sal's mom smiled. She said, "It means a lot to me that you said that. People can enjoy doing work if there is one person to say, 'Thank you.'"

Sal was glad her words had made her mom feel good.

A. courage,
or
B. kindness?

26. Bob and Rick went to the park. Fred and Sam got there at the same time. Bob said, "Did you guys want to play tennis now?"

Sam said, "Yes, we wanted to play tennis."

Bob said, "That's what we came here for, too. And there's only one court."

Sam said, "Let's think of what we could do."

Bob said, "We could take turns playing one game and resting."

Rick said, "We could flip a coin. The winning pair could play a whole set."

Fred said, "One pair could go and come back later."

Sam said, "We could play doubles. All four could play at once."

They decided to play doubles. All four of them played. They had a good time. They got to know each other, too.

A. good decisions,
or
B. self-discipline?

27. A boy named Rusty was very strong. He lifted weights. But one day Rusty's back got hurt. The doctor said, "Your back will heal. You can start to lift in two months. But do not lift before then."

Rusty did what the doctor said. But the next day, Rusty saw two men. They were carrying a piano. They needed help. Rusty knew he could help with their load. He liked to help with things like this. He got to be kind and to show how strong he was.

But Rusty remembered what his doctor had said. He said, "I'm sorry I can't help you. I have to let my back heal."

The men said, "That's OK." Later, Rusty thought to himself, "I did the right thing for myself."

A. self-care and compliance,
or
B. nonviolence and conservation?

28. A man talked with his wife. He told his wife some things he thought. He talked about laws he thought were bad.

His wife said to him, "You're wrong. Here's why." He got mad when she said he was wrong. He got the urge to yell at her. He got the urge to say, "You're so dumb! You just don't get it." He knew that it would feel good for a short time if he did this.

But he stopped to think about it. He said to himself, "If I talked that way, I would make her feel bad. I would make us not get along well. My goal is to have us love each other. Talking this way would not help us do this."

So the man stopped himself. He said to her, "Tell me why you feel the way you do." He listened to her. He said, "Tell me more." When he had listened a while, he said, "Here is why I feel the way I do." He spoke in a calm tone. He said to himself, "It can be fun to hear ideas, even when someone does not think the way I do."

He and his wife had fun. He was glad that he had decided to speak to her the way he did.

A. respectful talk,
or
B. productivity?

29. A man led his country. He was a brave man.

There was another land next to his. The men there had fought against his men. The men in his land hated those men. They wanted to fight them. But the man knew that to fight more would do no good.

He went to the person who led the other country. He said, "Let's talk about peace." He shook hands with the other leader. They decided not to fight.

He went back to his own land. Many of his own people were mad at him. They hated the other side too much. They did not want peace. But the leader stuck up for peace. He did not let the mad people scare him. He did not have to do what they told him to do.

A. nonviolence,
or
B. compliance?

30. A young woman named Fran was at a party. There were lots of people there. Lots of kids were running around.

Fran had taken care of kids a lot. She saw a boy about three years old. The boy climbed up on a brick wall. The boy stood up. Fran looked for his mom. There was no mom near.

Fran moved fast. She went to the wall. Just as she got there, the boy fell. He fell head first. His head could have hit a hard sidewalk. But Fran was quick and strong. She caught the boy. She put him on his feet.

A man saw what she had done. He ran to them. He said, "You saved that kid's life!"

They found the kid's mom. When she heard about the fall, her face turned white. She stayed close to her boy from then on.

Fran thought, "I'm glad I moved to the right place when I saw him on the wall."

A. friendship building,
or
B. good decisions?

31. Glenn was seven years old. He had a job to do. He was to start a fire. Someone had put gas in a can. Glenn did not know this. He used the stuff in the can to start the fire. The can blew up.

Glenn's legs were burned badly. The doctor said, "Glenn may never walk again."

But Glenn said, "I will not just walk. I will run."

Four months passed. Glenn still could not walk. His mom and dad helped him bend his legs. His brother helped too. After two more months, he could hop around some. He told the doctor, "I will run the next time you see me."

Glenn worked every day. He tried and tried. He did not give up. One day, Glenn did run. Then he ran faster and faster.

When he was twelve, he ran in a race. It was a mile long. He won the race!

He grew up. He kept on running. One day he ran a mile race. He set a record! He ran it faster than anyone else had run it! He was glad that he had kept working and had not given up.

He became a teacher. He worked hard at his job, too. He helped many students by his work. He was glad he had not lost hope and given up after he had gotten burned.

A. fortitude,
or
B. conservation?

32. A man named Carl was a writer. He wrote for a magazine called *The World Stage*. His country got a new leader. This leader wanted to make the army very strong. The leader wanted to get ready to fight.

Carl sensed how bad this leader was. He figured this out before most other people did. He could see that the leader's ideas were wrong.

Carl was not scared to write what he thought. He wrote that his country should work for peace. He wrote that people should choose some other man to lead them.

Some people agreed with Carl. But few were brave enough to write what they thought. Carl wrote very much.

A. courage and nonviolence,
or
B. respectful talk and joyousness?

33. The leader's men did not like what Carl wrote. They put Carl in jail. They said, "We will let you out if you promise one thing. You must stop writing about what your country should do. You must keep quiet about us."

Carl did not want to go along with these men at all. He knew they were very bad men. So his answer was "No." They kept him in jail, as he had known they would.

Every year, some people think, "Who has done the most for world peace this year?" They give a prize to that person. They thought, "Carl should win our prize." He won the prize while he was still in jail.

Carl stayed in jail for the rest of his life. He was not treated well. But he knew he was helping people to find out how bad the leader's ideas were. Because of this, he was willing to put up with lots of pain. He was willing to be locked up in order to help with a cause he knew was right.

A. fortitude,
or
B. self-care?

34. Once there was a man named Dan. He worked with kids. He saw kids hit and kick each other. He saw them call other kids names. Many times kids would do this for no good reason. They just wanted to show their power by picking on someone else.

Dan felt it was not good for kids to be picked on. He also felt that it was not good for kids to bully other kids. He decided to work on this problem.

He used the ways of science. He found out how much it harms kids to be picked on. He found out that they feel bad for a long time.

He found out that lots of bullies grow up to live lives of crime.

Then he worked on ways to get kids to pick on each other less. He worked with schools. He tried out lots of things. He worked at lots of schools.

He kept using science. He found out that, when schools work hard in smart ways to teach kids not to bully, the work pays off. Lots fewer kids get picked on.

He felt good that his work had helped lots of kids.

A. nonviolence and productivity,
or
B. loyalty and self-care?

35. A young girl named Jean was with her dad. They walked by stores. Jean saw some flowers. She said, "They are so pretty! Could you get me some, to give to mom?"

Jean's dad said, "We don't have enough money to spend it on flowers. You can look at them, but we can not buy them."

Jean thought to herself, "I can handle this. I will stay calm. I will find a way to feel good."

She smelled the flowers. She stood and looked at them. She dreamed about ways that she would make some money some day. She planned to buy her mom some flowers when she could. Then they moved on.

Jean's dad said, "You did something good. You did not get what you wanted. But you put up with it. That makes me feel good."

Jean smiled. She said, "Thank you."

Then Jean knew that she had given her dad a gift. She knew that when she had kept cool when she did not get her way, she had helped him. She felt good.

A. fortitude,
or
B. friendship-building?

36. Nan worked at a bakery. She mixed up things to make bread dough. One time she was very sleepy. She dumped things in too fast. Then she said to herself, "Oh, no! I put way too much salt in the dough!"

At first she got the urge to think, "I can get away with this. No one will know until someone tastes the bread. And then no one will know I did it."

But she thought to herself, "I want to do what is right. My boss counts on me to do a good job."

She told her boss what she had done. The boss was not happy. But Nan felt good that she had told the truth.

A. conservation,
or
B. honesty?

37. Nan's boss thought about what Nan had said. She said to Nan, "We could just throw out this whole batch of dough. But let's think some more. Do you know exactly how much salt you put in?"

Nan did know. Nan's boss got a pencil and paper. She sat down and did some math. She said, "Keep this dough. Just add this much of everything else. You will have a very big batch. You will need several more tubs to mix it in. But we will not waste anything."

Nan did what her boss said. When they baked the bread, they

both tasted it. It tasted good, just as it always did.

Nan said to her boss, "I feel proud of you for finding a way to solve the problem."

The boss said, "We can solve most problems, if we can talk about them and think about them and not try to hide them."

Nan's boss used

A. good decisions,
or
B. compliance?

38. Don was at a bus station. He saw an old woman trying to carry a bag. The bag was heavy. The woman stopped to rest. She could not go far before she had to rest again.

Don said to her, "I'd like to help you carry this bag. Just tell me where to go."

He carried her bag to where she was going. She said, "Thank you very much. It makes me feel good to know there are people like you around."

A. courage,
or
B. kindness?

39. A girl was walking away from her house. She looked back. She saw an outside light on, even though it was day. She turned around and went back. She turned the light off.

She thought to herself, "I have saved a little money for my family. I have saved a little energy for the world."

A. nonviolence,
or
B. conservation?

40. A wise man stood outside the gates of a town. A person came walking toward town. The person asked the wise man, "What are the people like in this town? What sort of people are they?"

The wise man said, "What sort of people were there in the place where you came from?"

The person said, "They were mean people. They told bad things about you all the time. They were very stuck-up. They were snobs."

The wise man said, "I'm afraid you will find the people in this town just the same."

The person went away sadly.

Another person came walking toward town. The person asked the wise man, "What are the people like in this town? What sort of people are they?"

The wise man said, "What sort of people were there in the place where you came from?"

The person said, "They were nice people. They were always fun to talk with. They were always willing to help. They were great friends to have."

The wise man said, "I'm happy to say that you will find the people in this town just the same."

The wise man (who could have been wrong) probably thought that the second person was more skilled at

A. productivity,
or
B. friendship-building?

41. A mom thought, "It is time for my boy to eat. I will get him some good food."

But then the boy yelled, "Mom! You get me some food right now! I mean it!"

The mom looked sad. She said, "I was just about to get you some food. But I cannot do it now, because of the way you spoke. We will wait for half an hour. Then you can ask me in a nice tone."

The boy said, "What do you mean?"

She said, "When you speak in a bossy way like that, it would not be kind of me to get you what you want. I would be teaching you to talk like that to me more. And that would be a bad habit for you."

The boy said, "I still don't see why we have to wait."

The mom said, "When you do a certain thing and then get what you want, you tend to do that thing again more often. So it's part of my job to make sure you don't get your food right after you speak as you did."

The boy waited. He did not gripe or whine. Half an hour later, the boy said, "Now may I have something to eat please, Mom?"

The mom said, "That's the type of talk I like to hear. Now we can eat."

The mom wanted to teach her boy

A. courage,
or

B. respectful talk?

42. There was a big flood. Many rescue workers were going to help out. They went in a big truck.

A man drove the truck along a road. He stopped his truck. He was about to go through a tunnel. He thought, "Is my truck too tall to get through the tunnel?"

He drove the truck up close. The truck was just as high as the tunnel. If the man drove the truck through the tunnel, it would get stuck. If the tunnel were half an inch higher, he could drive through.

People gathered around. "People are in danger," the driver said. "I need to get through."

"There's another way to go," said one person, "but you can't go that way today. The heavy rains have flooded that road."

"Maybe we can smash down the roof of the truck," said someone else. But the roof of the truck was very tough.

A little boy said, "I know how to get through! I know how!"

A man said, "Quiet, boy."

Another man just wanted to be nice. He took the boy aside. He said, "I'll listen to you. What is your idea?"

The boy said, "Let a little air out of the tires of the truck."

The man yelled, "This boy has figured it out!"

They did what the boy had said, and the truck got through the tunnel.

The boy did

A. friendship-building,
or
B. good decisions?

43. A woman named Jane lived in a big city. There were lots of poor people there. Jane wanted to help them. She got a big house for people to come to. Poor people could get help there in taking care of their children. People could come there to work together to make their lives better.

Jane worked to help pass laws that would help the poor people. At the time she lived, people sent kids off to work in sweat shops. People made them work all day long, without rest. Jane helped people know that this was not a good idea. She taught people that they should help kids learn and

play, and that kids shouldn't just work all the time.

People loved Jane because of her great

A. self-care,
or
B. kindness?

44. Then things changed in Jane's life. A war started. Jane started to work for peace. She thought the war was a bad idea.

Then her country started to fight in the war. The leaders said, "All of us must be for the war. If you are not for it, you are against your own land!" Jane did not agree. She felt that the war was wrong.

People who had loved her started to hate her. An old friend who was a famous man called her a "silly, vain old maid." She was kicked out of clubs. She got mail from people who told her they hated her.

At last the war was over. Jane got food to give to starving children. She gave some of it to starving children in the land that had fought against hers. This made some people very angry.

They said she was a bad woman. They said she did not love her own land. But she did not care what land kids came from. She did not want to let them starve.

It took many years for people to decide she was right. Not long before she died, people decided that she had done great work for peace. They gave her a prize for her peace work.

A. courage and nonviolence,
or
B. compliance and friendship-building?

45. A man had a flat tire. He worked to fix it. He took the bolts off his flat tire. He took the flat tire off the car. He put the spare tire onto the car. He was just about to put the bolts on.

But he did not look where he stepped. He knocked the bolts. They fell over a cliff. They fell down into a river. Now he could not bolt his spare tire onto the car.

The man was sad and angry at himself. He looked down where the bolts had fallen. It would take him a long time to get down there. Even if he did, the river could

have washed the bolts away. He could not call anyone because there was no phone. He did not know which way to walk. He did not know what to do. He sat down to think.

His little girl was with him. She thought, "I will try to find out how to solve this." She stayed cool. She tried to think of options.

The little girl said, "Dad! I have it! I know how to do it!"

The man thought, "Well, I'll hear what she says." He said, "How can we solve this, my girl?"

She said, "Take a bolt off each of your other tires. Use those bolts to hold your spare tire on. They will work well enough. Then we can drive to where we can get more bolts."

The man said to her, "My smart girl! You have done it! You have a great mind, girl!"

They did what she had said. It worked. The girl felt good that she had helped them out of a mess.

A. nonviolence,
or
B. good decisions?

46. A man had a very bad habit. He would yell mean words when he got angry at people.

He did not like how he got angry at his wife. He would yell at her. He would say very mean things to her. He would get a strong urge to hit her. But later he would feel very bad about this. He would wish that he had been nice.

He had two kids. He loved them. He also loved his wife. He did not want his wife to split up with him.

He read about how to solve this. He read about a plan. He said to himself, "This plan sounds like it may work. I will have to work very hard. But I want to do it."

He made a list of things his wife had done that had made him angry. Then he wrote down what he would like to think and feel and do if she did those things again.

For each one of these, he did a fantasy of staying cool. He did a fantasy of being nice. He did this two hundred times each day. He added more and more to his list each day.

After two weeks of this, his wife said, "I think you've started to change."

After two months of this, his wife said, "I like how you've changed."

The man kept working. After a year, he felt that he had solved the problem of getting angry. He felt great.

A. respectful talk and positive fantasy rehearsal,
or
B. conservation and honesty?

47. A girl learned science and math. She wanted to do something good with what she knew. She read lots of things.

She read about how many people get killed in car wrecks. She knew about people who got killed that way.

She planned a study. She planned to find how many people drive at the speed limit.

She planned how to do her study. She measured how far it was between two signs on streets. She got a video camera. She taped the cars as they drove.

At home, she watched the tapes. She timed how long it took for a car to get from one sign to the next. She did some math. She could tell the car's speed. She did a test. She asked her dad to drive along the road in his car while she taped. She told him how fast he had gone. "Yes," he said, "you got it right." Her way of finding the speed worked very well.

After a while, she had gotten the speed of lots of cars. She found that almost all of them were breaking the speed limit. She found that most were breaking the speed limit by more than fifteen miles an hour.

She wrote up her study. She sent it to a science journal. It got printed! She was happy.

Next the news people talked to her about it. She had fun talking with them and being in the news. She got to talk about car safety.

She felt good to think that what she did might help one person not get killed in a car crash some day.

When she thought about how much good work she did, she felt good about her

A. productivity,

or

B. courage?

48. Mrs. Chen's head hurt. She felt as if she might throw up. Bright light made her feel bad. She took a pill. It helped. But not long later, her head hurt again.

A doctor told her, "There is a way to make this pain come less often. But it is hard. You have to go to bed and get up at the same time each day. You have to run or swim or work out in some other way at the same time each day. You have to eat your meals at the same time each day. When your body gets used to doing these things at the same time each day, there is a good chance you will have much less pain."

Mrs. Chen read about this in books. She thought, "I will give it a good try." She started doing what the doctor had said. It was hard. There were times when she did not feel like going to bed, but she did. There were times when she did not feel like running or swimming, but she did. When she had to be out at the time for her meal, she would take a meal with her and eat it wherever she was.

After two months, she looked at the charts she kept. She said, "I got the pain about two times a week before I started this. And now I only get the pain about once every four weeks. That is lots better!"

So she kept on. She was glad she had been able to help herself.

When she did the things she didn't feel like doing, to make her own health better, was that

A. self-discipline and self-care, or
B. nonviolence and friendship-building?

49. Mr. Kep thought, "I am too much alone. I want to have more friends." Mr. Kep talked to a wise man about this. He said, "How can I have more friends?" The wise man asked him lots of things. The wise man listened to how the man spoke.

At last the wise man said, "I want you to try one thing. Try it with the men and women you know. When you see them, greet them with a fun tone of voice. Say 'Hi' to them with a tone in your voice that lets them know you are very glad to see them. When they tell you things, let your tone of voice tell them you are very glad to have heard what they said to you."

Mr. Kep went home. A man who lived next door was working outside. Mr. Kep said, "Hi! Looks like you're doing some good work!" He said it in a nice tone.

The man said, "Yes, but it's hot out here."

Mr. Kep said, "You're right on that one! It's very hot!"

The man said, "But I found out a way to keep cool outside when it's hot."

Mr. Kep said, "Is that right!"

The man said, "I get my shirt and hat wet. As they dry out, they keep me cool."

Mr. Kep said, "That's really smart! I'm glad you told me that! How did you get that idea!"

They kept on talking. Soon Mr. Kep had gotten to know the man. They had begun to like each other.

A. honesty, or
B. friendship-building?

50. Jan was in love with a man named Ben. She wanted to stay with Ben. She wanted to be his wife. When she was with him, she felt great. She thought he was the best man in the world.

One day, Ben said to her, "I don't want to see you any more. I have met someone else. I want to be with her. I am sorry. We must break up."

Jan was very sad.

Jan's grandmother saw her. Her grandmother said, "Why are you so glum?" Jan told her grandmother what Ben had said.

Her grandmother said, "I went through the same thing. In fact, I went through it four times!"

Jan said, "How did you take it?"

Her grandmother said, "I knew I could have fun in ways that did not need a man. And my own mom would tell me, 'There are more fish in the sea.' Of course she meant, 'There is some other man for you if you want one.' I did not think it was true at the time. But in a while, I learned she was right. And now I'm glad about how it came out. If I had stayed with any of those men, I would not have met your grandfather. And I wouldn't have had your mom, and she would not have had you!"

Jan hugged her grandmother. She still felt sad. But she said to herself, "I can take it, just as my grandmother did." She found lots of ways to have fun without Ben.

When Jan took it well, that was

A. compliance,

or

B. fortitude?

51. A woman had a task to do. She wanted to write a book. But it was hard to sit down and do it. Other things kept coming up. Months went by. She had no book.

She read about ways to get herself to work. She said to herself, "Here is a plan. I will reward myself for work. I will not eat any junk food unless I write. Each time I write an hour, I will have one fourth of a cookie."

She did what she had planned. She got lots of work done.

One day there was lots of stress. She was tired. She was hungry. She got the urge to go to her cookies and eat a bunch of them.

But then she thought, "I have been using a good plan to help myself write. If I eat the cookies when I have not done my work, I will spoil my plan. This is a big choice. I want to do the best thing."

She did not get the cookies. She ate some soup. She rested and relaxed. She felt good about her choice.

Later that day, she wrote some more of her book. Then she had part of the cookie. She thought, "I am glad I stuck to my plan."

A. nonviolence,

or

B. self-discipline?

52. A man looked at himself in the mirror. He thought, "I need to lose some weight. I want to work out more. Maybe I should join a health club. I could drive there and work out."

He looked at how much it cost to go to the health club. He thought, "It costs a good bit of money, but if it makes me get in shape, it is worth it."

Then he looked at his house. He thought, "This place is a mess. I need to get it cleaned. Maybe I should hire a maid to clean it." He found out how much it costs to hire a maid. He thought, "If my house gets so clean that I don't feel shame when I ask people to come over, it will be worth it."

But then he got an idea. He thought, "I can run in place while I clean up my house. What if I could make myself do that for half an hour a day?"

He got his feet moving. He ran in place while he cleaned dirty dishes. It was a little hard to do it while he ran in place. But he got used to it.

Then he ran around his house and picked up things and put them away. Then he swept his floor. He did not stop running. He kept on while he washed his clothes. He kept on while he put his clothes away.

At the end of the time, he was tired. He could feel sweat on his skin. He thought, "I got a good work out. And my house looks a lot better. And I did not spend money on a gym or a maid!"

He did this every day. It was hard to make himself do this. But he felt good. He took the money he had saved and used it in a good way.

When he did things he didn't feel like doing, to save money, that was

A. loyalty and respectful talk,
or
B. conservation and self-discipline?

53. Three boys lived with their mom. They spent lots of their time getting angry at each other. They would not do what their mom said. She got angry at them. They got angry at her. All of them stayed very poor.

A man came to visit the mom. He watched her and her boys. After a while she said to him, "What are your thoughts, when you watch us?"

He said, "I was just thinking of an old tale."

One boy said, "Tell it to us."

The man said, "It is a sad tale. Once the parts of someone's body had a fight. The arms and legs said to the belly, 'You are always wanting some new thing to eat. We are sick and tired of getting what you want. You can't make us do what you want.' The belly got angry and yelled at them. But they did not listen to the belly. They did not get the belly any more food. After a while, the arms and legs got too weak to move. They thought, 'We worked against the belly, but we beat ourselves as well. We did not know that we are all in this game together.' But by the time they learned this, it was too late."

The boys sat and thought. The oldest one said, "I think I know why you thought of that tale when you watched us. We work against each other, too, don't we?"

The man said, "I'm glad you can see that. Maybe there is some hope for you."

The man's lesson had to do with

A. courage and conservation,
or
B. compliance and good decisions?

54. A boy had a job. He was to watch some sheep. If wolves

came, he was to yell, "Wolf! Wolf!" The people nearby would run to help.

One time the boy was bored. He wanted to see something happen. He yelled, "Wolf! Wolf!" The people nearby all ran to him. They carried hoes and rakes. They were ready to chase the wolf away. The boy just laughed. When they saw that they had been tricked, the people were angry. They told the boy's dad.

The boy's dad was scared. He knew that if the people could not trust his son, they would not help him again. He knew that if the wolves came, his son might get killed.

The dad said to the people, "I will help my son. I will teach him not to lie to you again."

The dad said to his son, "If they can not trust you, you may get killed by wolves. It is time for you to learn not to lie. You must practice twenty times each day for thirty days."

The dad taught his son how to practice. When the boy did it, he sounded like this. "I am in the field. I am watching the sheep. I feel bored. I think about how one

time I cried 'Wolf!' But then I think some more. I want to make a good choice. I want the people to trust me. I do not want to get killed. I will think of another way not to be bored. I can sing a song. I can make up a story. I can run and walk while I watch the sheep. Now I am doing all those things. I feel good that I made a good choice. I feel good that I did not lie."

The dad made the son talk like this twenty times a day for thirty days. The son did what his dad told him to do. He did not lie to the people again.

One night, a long time later, a bunch of wolves did come. The boy cried, "Wolf! Wolf!"

The people thought, "Is he telling the truth?" But they came running with rakes and hoes. They chased away the wolves. The boy thanked them. He felt glad to be alive.

The boy learned

A. productivity and joyousness, or
B. honesty and positive fantasy rehearsal?

55. Larry had a birthday. He got some money.

His friend Dick said, "I would use the money to buy cards to trade."

His brother Alf said, "I would use the money to buy candy."

His friend Ned said, "I would use the money to buy really cool shoes."

Larry thought, "I don't need any of those things. I don't even want them. For me, they would be a waste."

Larry bought some seeds for birds to eat. Every winter day he put out seeds. He watched the birds eat his seeds.

He was glad he had spent his money in this way.

A. self-care and positive fantasy rehearsal,
or
B. conservation and kindness?

56. Once, long ago, there was a king. The king listened to his people. He also watched them. They did not like to work. They thought other people should do the work for them.

One day the king got up early. Everyone was still asleep. There were no horses or riders on the road. No one was walking on the road. The king put a big rock in the middle of the main road.

Later, people passed by the rock. They were angry that the rock was there. They said, "Someone should move that rock." But no one moved it.

The end of the week came. The king called the people to the rock. They all came.

The king said, "I put this rock here. I also put something under it."

The king moved the rock out of the way. Under the rock was a box. The king opened the box. It had a lot of money in it. There was also a note. The note said, "If you are the one who moved this rock out of the way, you get this money."

The king said, "I am sorry that I could not give the money away. Since I was the one who moved the rock, I will take the money home." The king left with the money.

The people learned something from this.

The people learned about:

A. productivity,

or

B. nonviolence?

The next story is from a fable by Aesop.

57. A man had seven sons. They argued with one another too much. They didn't help one another enough.

Sometimes people acted mean to one of them. That son had to face the problem alone. The others didn't help out. The man wished his sons would stick up for each other.

The man called them together. He said, "I have a lesson for you. It is about how you should act with one another."

The sons gathered around. The man showed them seven sticks. He said, "Please try to break these sticks." The sons broke the sticks. It was easy.

Then the man said, "Here are seven more sticks. They are the same size. But this time it will be different." The man put the sticks together in one bundle. He tied a rope around each end of the bundle. He said, "Now who can break the sticks?"

Each of the sons tried. But no one could break the whole bundle of sticks.

The man said, "That's the end of the lesson." He walked away.

The man's lesson was about

A. loyalty,

or

B. positive fantasy rehearsal?

58. A boy had a problem. He hated his math homework. It took him a long time to do it. Other people could get it done quickly. But he had to work for hours. He told a friend. The friend said, "Let me watch you work." The boy worked some math problems.

The friend said, "You took a long time just then. What were you doing in your mind?"

The boy said, "I was counting up in my mind, to add the numbers."

The friend said, "That's your problem. You need to be able to add numbers without counting up. You need to know the math facts cold. Things like six plus four. Eight times nine. Twelve minus seven."

The boy said, "I can figure those things out in a while."

The friend said, "You need to make them automatic. That way your brain can think more about the other stuff. Get so fast at them that you don't have to think about them."

The boy said, "How do I do that?"

The friend said, "Take a few facts every day. Practice with them over and over. Time yourself. Keep going. Don't stop until you can say each answer in less than a second."

The boy got a stop watch. He wrote down 20 math facts. He started the watch. He said the answers as quickly as he could. He stopped the watch. It had taken him 200 seconds.

He did it again. This time it was only 100 seconds. He felt excited. He was on his way.

He did it again and again. Finally one time he looked at his watch, and it was nineteen seconds!

Every day he did the same thing with another batch of math facts. It was very hard to make himself do this. But he made himself do it every day.

A few months later he saw his friend. He said, "It worked!"

The friend said, "What worked?"

The boy said, "I learned to do the math facts very quickly. And now I get through my math homework very fast. And I don't hate it any more."

The friend said, "Hooray! I'm glad you did that! Not many people are as tough as you are, though. Not many can make themselves work like that."

The boy felt good.

The boy used

A. self-discipline,

or

B. nonviolence?

59. There were two families. One family was not happy. The other family was happy. In both families there were two boys. All the boys liked to go to swimming races.

The unhappy family went to a race. The older boy came in second for his age group. The younger boy came in first for his age group.

They were coming home. The younger boy said, "You came in

second, but I came in first. I did better than you, ha ha."

The older boy said, "No you didn't. I swam faster than you. And the people I swam against were better."

They kept on talking like this.

Their mom and dad listened to them talk. Their mom said, "Quit talking like that!" But the boys didn't quit. The mom and dad felt sad.

The happy family also went to a race. The older boy came in second for his age group. The younger boy came in first for his age group. This happened just as in the other family.

On their way home, though, it was different. The older boy said, "Wow, you did great! You came in first! I'm really proud of you!"

The younger boy said, "But you swam lots faster than I did. And you swam against lots faster people. You did great. I hope I can swim like you some day."

They kept on talking like this.

Their parents listened to them talk. They felt good that their boys said nice things to each other. Their mom said, "I like how you give credit to each other."

These parents were glad the boys were good swimmers. But they were even more glad that the boys helped the family to be in a good mood.

A. productivity,
or
B. respectful talk?

60. Once there was a turtle. People came to the land where he lived. They took away his food supply. They drained the pond he lived in. He knew he had to move.

But it was a long and dangerous journey. A bird was going far away also. The turtle got an idea. He said to a big bird, "Please carry that stick with your feet. I'll hold on with my jaws. You can fly me with you."

The bird said, "I'll help you in that way." So the bird held the stick, and the turtle bit it. They took off.

What did the bird do:

A. kindness,
or
B. fortitude?

61. On the way, another bird said, "Look at that. Who thought up

that smart way to move the turtle?"

The turtle got the urge to say, "I did. Wasn't it smart?" But the turtle heard a voice in his head. The voice said, "Think before you act." He thought. He decided that he had better keep his mouth clamped onto the stick.

What did the turtle do:

A. joyousness,
or
B. good decisions?

62. The turtle thought, "I'm glad I have strong jaws. But I want to be safe." So the turtle grabbed the stick with both his front legs. Then he pulled up his back legs. He wrapped them around the stick too. He didn't let go with his mouth, either.

It was a good thing he did this. There was some wind. It made the ride bumpy. He might not have been able to hold on with just his jaws.

What did the turtle do:

A. loyalty,
or
B. self-care?

63. Finally they reached the new land. The bird flew down over a pond and dropped the turtle in. The turtle yelled, "Thanks, bird! You were kind to me!"

A long time later the turtle still lived in the pond. The same bird came down to drink. An alligator went after the bird. The turtle said, "Fly, friend!"

The bird flew. He saw the alligator. He yelled, "Thanks, turtle," as he flew away.

The alligator said, "Why did you do that? I thought you were on my side."

The turtle said, "That bird flew me here a long time ago. If the bird hadn't helped, I probably wouldn't be alive. I couldn't let you eat that bird."

A. loyalty,
or
B. compliance?

64. The alligator said, "I was pretty hungry. That bird would have made a good meal. But I know how you feel, turtle. I would have done the same thing. I can handle being hungry a while longer." And he ate some plants

instead. They didn't taste nearly as good as bird.

The turtle said, "Thanks, friend."

What did the alligator do:

A. fortitude,
or
B. self-care?

The following is a retelling of the Hans C. Andersen story, "The Emperor's New Clothes."

65. Once there was a king. He loved new clothes. He spent all his money on clothes. He wasted lots of time on clothes, too. He changed clothes very often. He wore different clothes each hour of the day.

This was a bad example of:

A. courage,
or
B. conservation?

66. One day two strangers came to town. They said they could make pretty clothes. They said people who were smart could see the clothes, but people who were not smart could not see the clothes. They said people who were not

good at their jobs could not see them and that clothes would tell who was really smart. The two men were really telling lies.

The strangers did bad examples of:

A. joyousness,
or
B. honesty?

67. The king thought, "That sounds good. I can tell who is smart. I can tell who is good at a job." The king asked the men to make clothes. He paid them lots of money.

The king did a bad example of:

A. productivity,
or
B. good decisions?

68. The two men put on an act. They moved as if they were working. But they were not making clothes. They just kept the money. They kept the fine cloth. They did bad examples of:

A. productivity,
or
B. courage?

69. All the people in the town heard about the clothes. They wanted to find out how smart the other people were. They wondered who could see the clothes.

A man worked for the king. The king sent this man to see how the work was coming. The man could not see any clothes. But he did not say what he thought. He thought, "I'm scared to let anyone know I'm not smart. I won't say that I can't see the clothes."

The two weavers said, "Do you like the clothes?"

The man was scared to tell the truth. He said, "Oh, they are very pretty. I will tell the king." And he did tell that to the king.

The man did bad examples of:

A. courage and honesty,
or
B. productivity and friendship-building?

70. The king sent another man. The other man thought, "I cannot see the clothes. I must be bad at my job. But I don't want people to know." So he pretended to see the clothes too.

Then the king himself went to see. He thought, "The others could see. I don't want them to know I'm dumb." So he pretended to see, too. He said, "These clothes are great! I will give you weavers a prize! When you are done I will go on a parade through the town."

Having the parade was a bad example of:

A. self-discipline,
or
B. good decisions?

71. The weavers kept on acting. They moved the scissors. They moved the needles. Then one day they said, "The clothes are now done!"

They moved as if putting the clothes on the king. The king went on a parade through the town. All the people acted as if they could see the clothes. They all said, "Oh, the clothes are so pretty!" Nobody wanted anyone else to think he was dumb.

But one child was not scared. He did not care what people thought. He said, "The king has no clothes on!"

The child did an example of:

A. honesty,

or

B. compliance?

72. The other people talked to each other. They told each other what the child had said. Finally they all yelled, "He has no clothes on!"

The king's face turned red. He was ashamed. He was angry at the two men. But they were gone, with the king's money.

To handle this, the king would need:

A. fortitude,

or

B. compliance?

73. A girl was asleep. She woke up. She couldn't get back to sleep. She thought, "What should I do?" She thought, "I could watch TV."

But then she thought again. She said to herself, "No, I'll do something useful." She went to the kitchen. She put away the dishes. She mopped the floor.

She still was not sleepy. She thought of her aunt. She thought, "My aunt is lonely. She would

like a letter from me." So she wrote the letter.

Then the girl was tired. She went back to bed. She thought, "I'm glad I did useful things." She went to sleep.

A. productivity,

or

B. compliance?

74. A boy was happy. He was set to go to a science museum. He loved the science museum. His mom drove him a long way. He was very excited when they got there.

But then they saw a sign. It said the museum was closed. It wouldn't be open that day. The boy felt bad. He felt like yelling very loudly.

But then he thought, "Here's a chance for me to get tough. I want to be strong. This is not the end of the world."

He said to his mom, "I can take it, mom. Thanks anyway for driving me. We can find something else fun." He stayed cool.

A. honesty,

or

B. fortitude?

75. A boy had a sister. She was four years old. She came to her brother. She had a big smile. She said, "Guess what! I can count to five! One, two, three, four, five!"

The boy was not in a good mood. He felt like putting her down. He felt like saying, "So what. You're not so great. Other four-year olds can count to 100."

But he stopped himself. He thought, "I don't want to hurt her feelings. I want to do what's right." So he said to her, "That's great. You're really on your way! You're learning how to count well."

She smiled even more. He felt good about his choice.

A. self-care,
or
B. respectful talk?

76. Long ago some people were slaves. There were bad laws. The laws said people could own other people. They could do with them what they wanted. But many people knew this was bad. They helped slaves run away. They helped them escape to a land where no one could own slaves.

A woman named Jan lived in the land where people could have slaves. Jan thought that having slaves was wrong.

One day a man came to Jan. He said, "Can you keep secret what I say to you?"

She knew the man. She knew he was good. She said, "Yes."

The man said, "I am part of a group. My friends and I are helping slaves get free. We help them run away. We help them get to the free land. We find houses where they can stay. We hide them if people come to look for them. We tell them how to get to the next house. We give them food. Will you be one of us, Jan? Will you let these good people stay with you? Will you hide them?"

Jan thought. She thought about the dangers. She knew that many slave owners were mean. They got angry at people who helped free slaves. They would kill Jan if they found out. Jan knew that there was a law against helping slaves escape. She knew she could be locked up in jail.

But Jan thought, "I want to do something good with my life. I want to take a risk. I will help the people get free." So she said to the man, "Yes, I will help." And she did it. She was very careful. And she helped many slaves get free.

A. courage,
or
B. compliance?

77. Mandy was selling her house. A man came to look at it. He looked at the basement. It was dry. The man said, "Does water leak into the basement?"

Mandy thought, "It looks dry now. I could get away with a lie. Maybe I could sell the house for more money. But it wouldn't be right."

Mandy said, "Yes. When there is a lot of rain, the walls get damp. Sometimes a little bit of water gets on the floor. If you want it very dry, it will need to be fixed."

A. honesty,
or
B. joyousness?

78. Tom did not feel like getting out of bed. He felt grumpy. His mom saw him. She said, "Good morning, Tom!" He felt like just looking away. He felt like frowning. He felt like saying nothing back.

But then he thought, "I want my family to be happy. I can help by being cheerful. My mom is being nice." He smiled at her. He said, "Good morning to you. How are you today?" When he did that, he felt better.

A. joyousness,
or
B. nonviolence?

79. Lana was a young lady. She met a young man at a party. His name was Ken. Ken was very good-looking. He was smart and rich. He also knew how to talk well. Lots of ladies liked to talk with him. They all wanted him to love them and marry them.

But Ken wanted Lana. He took her to nice places to eat. He took her to big parties. He wanted to marry her.

She felt like saying, "Yes. I do want to get married!" But she thought some more. She thought,

"Getting married to the right person is very important. I want to get to know Ken better." She decided to spend more time with him.

She soon found out more about Ken. When he didn't get what he wanted, he would yell and scream. Sometimes he would slap people. He drank way too much alcohol. He got drunk often. He was very selfish. He always needed to have his own way.

So Lana decided not to marry Ken. She said good-bye to him.

Lana's friends thought she was crazy. But Lana knew she had done the right thing.

A. good decisions,
or
B. compliance?

80. Zack was eating out. He got his food. But he had gum in his mouth. He got an urge to stick the gum on the bottom of the table.

But then he thought, "Wait a second. That would mess up this table. Someone will have to clean this up. I want to respect that person. Other people who eat here may touch the bottom of the table. I want to respect them, too." So

Zack wrapped the chewing gum in a napkin. He put it in a trash can.

A. nonviolence,
or
B. kindness?

81. Rick and Seth were friends. Rick played with Seth a lot. They built a fort. Seth was nice to Rick. He let Rick decide how the fort should be.

Seth showed Rick how to play chess. Seth played chess well. If Rick made a bad move, Seth would not laugh. Seth would sometimes say, "You can take that move back if you want, Rick."

Seth's dad and Seth took Rick on hikes. Rick loved to walk in the woods with them.

Then Rick and Seth started going to school. Kids started to make fun of Seth. Kids would chant, "Seth is fat. Seth is fat." Seth would get upset. This just made the mean kids have more fun.

When Rick had started school, he had wanted friends. He had wanted the boys to like him. He could see that most of them were mean to Seth. He knew that if he stuck up for Seth, the boys might be mean to him too. But he decided he couldn't let down his friend.

One day the boys were chanting, "Seth is fat." One of them said to Rick, "Join us, Rick. Don't you think he's fat, too?"

Rick said, "He's been my friend for a long time. He's been nice to me. I'd rather have one friend who's nice than a bunch of friends who are mean. Please stop being cruel and mean to him."

The boys yelled mean things at Rick. But Rick did not care. He was glad he had been a true friend.

A. loyalty,
or
B. compliance?

82. Ben had a lot of work to do for school. But he had a new game. He thought, "I don't feel like doing the work. I feel like playing with the game."

But then Ben thought, "I will make a deal with myself. I will do my work. When the work is done, I will give myself a reward. I will let myself play the game then."

Ben did what he had planned. He was glad he had worked first and played second.

A. loyalty,
or
B. self-discipline?

83. Chet was in college. Chet had to write a report. It was about why there is crime. But Chet put off his work. It was the night before it was due. Chet felt scared. He thought, "How will I get it done on time?"

Then Chet looked on the Internet. He saw a report there. It was called, "Why Is There Crime?" It was a good report. Chet wished it were his report. Chet got the urge to turn it in and say it was his. But then he thought, "That would be cheating. I need to write my own report." He read a lot more. He got ideas from lots of places. He wrote his own report. It took him all night. He was very tired. But he was proud to turn it in.

A. honesty,
or
B. friendship-building?

84. Jon was reading a book. His sister came to him. She was going to a party. She said to Jon, "How do you like what I'm wearing?"

Jon did not like what she was wearing. He got the urge to say, "I think you look like an idiot in that outfit." But he did not say that. He thought, "I don't want to hurt her feelings."

So Jon said, "I like some of your other clothes much better. You look much better in those."

His sister was not hurt. Jon was glad about this.

A. respectful talk,
or
B. courage?

85. Ann had lots of friends at school. One day she went to the lunch room. At one table were lots of her friends. At another table was a new kid in school. The new kid was sitting by herself. She looked lonely.

Ann sat down with her. She said, "Hi. I'm Ann. What's your name?" Ann found out lots about the new girl. The new girl found out lots about Ann. Ann thought, "I want my friends to meet her, too."

A. honesty,
or
B. friendship-building?

86. A boy got a present from his grandma. It was a video game player. It cost lots of money. The boy knew he wouldn't use the present much. He didn't want to waste the money it had cost. He wondered what to do. He didn't want to hurt his grandma's feelings. He talked with his mom about it.

The boy took the gift back to the store. The store gave him the money back. The boy used the money in another way. He helped a child in a poor country. He wrote letters to the child. He felt good that he was helping. He was glad he had used the money well.

A. conservation,
or
B. fortitude?

87. Ralph was writing. He was using his computer. All of the sudden the power went off. The lights went out. Ralph's computer went off. Then the power came back on. Ralph checked what he

had written. He had lost half an hour of work.

Ralph had the urge to stamp his foot and scream. He had the urge to stop what he was writing. But then he thought, "I need to stay cool. What should I really do?"

Ralph decided to keep working. He wrote again the part he had lost. It took him only twenty minutes this time. He was glad he wrote it again before he forgot it.

A. fortitude,
or
B. kindness?

The next story is based on a play by Henrick Ibsen called *An Enemy of the People.*

88. In a town there were warm springs. People liked to take baths in them. Lots of people came to bathe in the springs. People in the town made money from renting rooms. People in the town made money from selling food. And they made money when the people paid to use the baths. The people in the town thought the baths were very good for people's health.

A doctor lived in the town. He found that some people got sick after being in the baths. He studied the water. He found that the water was bad for people. The water had bad things in it. It would cost a lot of money to clean up the water.

The doctor told the leaders of the town. They didn't thank him for finding the truth. They got angry at him. They told him to keep quiet. They thought, "We will just not tell people. We can keep making money."

These people did bad examples of

A. honesty,
or
B. joyousness?

89. The doctor told more people. They acted the same way. They didn't want to lose their money. They didn't care very much if people got sick.

He wrote about what he had found. A science journal printed what he wrote. Then newspapers wrote about it. The people in the town got madder at him. But he knew he was right. He knew it was wrong not to tell people that the baths were not healthful.

It was scary for him to have so many people angry at him. But he kept telling the truth about the baths.

A. friendship-building,

or

B. courage?

90. Nick was in high school. Nick had a friend named Joan. Nick and Joan had been friends for a long time.

There was a dance. Nick asked Joan to go with him. She said, "Yes." They went, and they were having a good time.

Joan was talking with her friends. Nick and his friends saw another girl. She was very good-looking. One of Nick's friends said, "Wow, look at her!"

This girl came up and started talking to Nick. She gave Nick lots of playful smiles. She stood very close to him.

The girl said, "Why don't you spend the rest of the dance with me? I'm not with anyone."

Nick thought that would be fun. But he knew it would hurt Joan. He did not want to hurt her. She

was a good friend. He explained this to the new girl. He said, "You are not with anyone at this dance, but I am."

The new girl was angry. She called Nick a wimp. Nick did not change his mind. She walked away. Nick learned later that she had a strange problem. She liked to play unhappy games with people. She liked to steal boys away from other girls. Then she would drop them. Then she would go on to someone else.

Nick had a good time at the dance with Joan. He was glad that he had not hurt his friend.

A. conservation,

or

B. loyalty?

91. Ted had a lump on his hip. The doctor said, "We'll have to cut it off. We will numb your hip with a drug. That way it won't hurt when we cut."

But Ted could not take that drug. He had taken a shot of it before. It had made him very sick.

The doctor said, "There are other drugs we can use."

Ted told the doctor, "I have read some good things in books.

Some people have used their minds to handle it when they are cut. I would like to try this."

The doctor said, "You would like to get the lump cut off with no drug to numb it?"

Ted said, "Yes, please."

The doctor said, "You can try. We will be ready with a drug if you need it."

They planned the day when the lump was to come off. Every day before that, Ted practiced in his mind. He imagined lying down relaxed. He imagined telling himself he was safe. He practiced relaxing his muscles. He practiced feeling peaceful.

The day came. The doctor cut the lump off. He sewed the skin back up. Ted did not use a drug. He did all the things he had planned. He could feel some pain. He just did not feel scared. He said, "If you can get rid of the fear, the pain is not so bad."

A. kindness and friendship-building,
or
B. positive fantasy rehearsal and courage?

92. Ned ran for office. He got elected. He went to Congress. Every day he voted on laws. He talked with other Congress people. They talked a lot about what was best to do.

Some people in another country got angry. They did some bad things. The people who voted for Ned wanted to fight them. They wanted a war.

The leader of the country also wanted war. Other people in Congress said, "We must go along with him. We must all agree. If we don't, we are hurting our country."

But Ned did not agree. He thought war was a bad idea. He thought there were other, better ways of working things out. He thought lots of people on both sides would get killed for no good reason.

The day came for a vote. Ned knew that if he voted against the war, people would not elect him again. He knew that people would say he did not love his country. He knew they would call him a coward.

They did the vote by a roll call. One by one the leader called their names. "Do you vote for the war?"

"Yes," said the first one. "Yes," said the second and third. Every one of them said, "Yes."

But then they got to Ned. "Do you vote for the war?" said the leader.

Ned took a deep breath. "No!" he said.

Everyone in the room was quiet. They all looked at him. Then the leader went on. Ned was the only one who voted "No."

They fought the war. Ned was not elected again. Ned got a different job.

Many people were killed. Years passed. The war went on.

Finally the war ended. People asked each other, "What did we get from this?" They decided that it had not been smart to get into the war.

Ned felt good that other people now knew he had been right. But he had always felt good that he had done what he thought was right.

A. self-care and compliance, or
B. courage and nonviolence?

93. Rod said, "I hate doing chores."

Mike said, "Do you really? I like it a lot."

Rod said, "I would have to see that to believe it."

Mike said, "Come over to my house tonight. We'll be doing chores from seven to seven-thirty."

Rod showed up at Mike's house at seven. Mike said, "First we sing while we clean up the kitchen. Do you know "'The Ash Grove'?"

Mike and his mom and dad and sister all sang. It sounded great. While they sang, they washed dishes. They swept the floor. They mopped the floor. They wiped the table. Rod learned the song and sang with them. He helped mop the floor.

Mike said, "We tell stories while we clean up the dust." They all went from one room to another, sweeping and mopping up dust. They took turns telling a story.

Rod thought, "What a good story!"

Mike said, "We're going to tell jokes while we put laundry away." Rod thought of some jokes too. He helped fold the clothes and hang them up.

After that they did a few more chores. They just chatted with each other. They had a good time with this too.

Rod said, "Thanks for having me over, Mike. I really enjoyed it! I'd like to do it again with you!"

A. courage and nonviolence,
or
B. joyousness and productivity?

94. A man named Tim taught math. He figured out some new ways to teach math. He tried out those ways. They worked really well. He taught other people to use the same method. It worked well for them too.

Tim decided to write a book. That way, lots of people could use the method.

But it was hard to find time to write. Tim had other things to do. Tim thought, "This book is a big goal. I want to do it very much."

Tim started getting up in the morning at five-thirty. He started writing each morning. At first this was very hard. He did not feel like getting out of bed. But Tim got used to it.

Tim finished the book. And the book helped lots of people to learn math.

A. self-discipline and productivity,
or
B. loyalty and respectful talk?

95. Fred was trying to lose weight. He planned what he would eat each day. He planned not to starve himself. He planned a healthy diet. But he found that it was hard to stick to his plan. Sometimes he ate other things.

He decided to practice in his mind. He imagined getting the urge to eat too much. Then he imagined himself being strong and sticking to the plan. Then he imagined himself feeling good about being strong. He did a lot of this practice.

This sort of practice let him stick to his plan. He got to a good weight. He felt proud of himself.

A. self-discipline and positive fantasy rehearsal,
or
B. kindness and respectful talk?

96. Jack was at a party. Other teen-aged kids were there. One boy said, "Hey, take this pill. It makes you feel really good."

Jack said, "What is it?"

The boy said, "I don't know. But I tried it. It made me feel good."

Jack said, "It must be a drug of some kind. I don't do drugs like that. And do you want to know something? I think it's not smart to take a drug when you don't know what it is."

The kid said, "Who cares what you think?" He looked angry. He walked away.

Jack did not care that the kid looked angry.

A. self-care,
or
B. productivity?

97. Kurt learned how to drive a car. Kurt's dad told him, "When I was your age, I had a good friend. Her name was Lisa. She went out with a guy. He drove the car too fast. They had a wreck. Lisa was killed. I was very sad. I tried to make sure I never did the same thing. That's why I drive slowly."

Kurt was smart. He could understand articles with a lot of math. He found out the danger of going very fast. He found out how many more people get killed when cars go very fast. Kurt decided he would not drive too fast.

One night Kurt was driving. Some friends were with him. They teased Kurt for driving slowly. One said, "You drive like a grandmother." But Kurt was not scared of what they thought. He told them what he had learned. But they just put him down more.

Just at that time, a car pulled out of a side street. The car stalled right in front of Kurt's car. Kurt slammed on the brakes. The tires screeched. Kurt stopped. He was one inch away from the other car. If he had been going faster there would have been a bad wreck.

Kurt looked at his friends. He said, "Are you OK?"

One of his friends said, "Uh, Kurt. I think I changed my mind. I think I like the way you drive."

Kurt smiled at him. He said, "Thanks."

A. joyousness and conservation,
or
B. self-care and courage?

98. Laurie was a good actress. She was the star in school plays. She acted in other plays in her town. She loved acting. She was good at acting partly because she worked so hard. She worked hard on every play she did.

A. productivity,
or
B. kindness?

99. One night Laurie was in a play. After the play, a man came up to her. He said, "I'd like to talk with you. I work for people who make movies. Would you like to try out? I think you might be the star of it."

Laurie thought, "Wow! I don't believe I'm hearing this! I'd love to be in a movie! This is so cool!" She felt great.

A. honesty,
or
B. joyousness?

100. The man said more nice things to her. He said how well she could act. They set up a time for her to try out. She felt good.

Then she said, "Please tell me more about the movie."

She listened to the man talk. The movie sounded like a "slasher" movie. It sounded like a horror show. Lots of people would get killed in a gory way.

Laurie thought, "I want to make a good choice about whether to do this. How can I learn some more?" Then she got an idea.

Laurie asked the man, "May I see a copy of the script, please?" The man told her she could pick up a copy. She thought, "I'm glad I figured out this way of finding out more."

A. compliance,
or
B. good decisions?

101. She picked up a copy of the script the next day. She read it. Laurie felt a bad feeling in her gut. At first she didn't want to admit the truth to herself. But she kept thinking. Then she said to herself, "This will be a very, very bad movie."

Laurie read some books she had. They talked about how violent movies make some people hurt other people in real life.

Laurie did a lot more thinking. She decided that being a star was not so important. It was more important to act in a way that did good for people. She could do this by picking good plays. She knew she did not want to do anything that got people to practice hurting other people in their fantasies.

A. positive fantasy rehearsal,
or
B. fortitude?

102. Laurie called the man on the phone. She said, "I'm sorry. I can't be in the movie."

The man was angry. He said, "Why not?"

She was ready for this. She told him the truth. She said, "I think this movie tries to make it fun to watch killing and hurting. I don't believe in that. I don't want to be a part of it."

The man got madder. He said, "Well, aren't you so good. Listen to this. You'll never make it as an actress. You are passing up such a good thing. You are throwing money down the drain. You could have been famous. You are making a dumb mistake."

Some girls would have been scared by this type of talk. But Laurie was ready for it. Laurie spoke back to him. Her voice was calm, but firm. She said, "Maybe I am throwing money away. But at least I'm not making the world a little meaner. At least I'm not making money by selling violence. This movie will be a piece of trash."

The man was so angry that he hung up on her. Still, she felt good. She said to herself, "Being rich or famous is not so important. Doing things I can feel good about is important."

A. courage,
or
B. compliance?

103. Bob got into his car at the parking lot. He backed up his car. He heard a scrape. He stopped and got out. He had scraped against another car. There was a little dent in the other car. He thought, "I could drive away. But that would not be right."

He took out his pen. He wrote a note. The note told his name and phone number. It told the person that he had dented the car. He left the note on the windshield. Then he drove home.

The man who owned the other car called him up. Bob had to pay lots of money to get the car fixed. But Bob still felt good. He knew he had done the right thing.

A. productivity,
or
B. honesty?

104. Ruth and Larry were married. They had a problem. Larry would go and get something to eat. Ruth would say, "I was saving that! It was for the picnic. Now I will have to go and get more." She would get angry.

Larry would get angry, too. He would say, "How could I know you did not want me to eat this?"

This happened a few times. They decided to sit down and think. They listed options. They thought about having two refrigerators, one for each of them. They also thought about having a special box. This would be the box for food that no one should eat. They thought about taping a note on the food if it should be saved.

They chose the option of using a note. It worked well for them. Now they did not get angry about this.

A. good decisions (conflict resolution)
or
B. joyousness?

105. Sandra said to Jill, "May I borrow your book?"

Jill said, "Yes. But I need it back in two weeks."

Sandra said, "OK."

Sandra had borrowed books before. She thought about those times. There were times when she did not give the book back on time. She felt bad about those times.

Sandra thought, "This time I will give it back on time."

Sandra had a little notebook. In it, she wrote down the things she had to do. There was one page for each day.

She looked at the page for two weeks from today. She wrote down, "Jill needs her book back" on this page. She turned back a couple of pages. She also wrote, "Give Jill her book back" on this page.

Two weeks had almost passed. Sandra looked at her notebook every day. She saw what she had written. She said to herself, "Oh, yes! I need to take it back."

Sandra took Jill's book back. Jill said, "Thanks, Sandra."

Sandra said, "Thank you for lending it to me."

Sandra was glad she had decided to use the notebook. She was glad she had kept her word to Jill.

A. fortitude and courage,
or
B. good decisions and honesty?

106. Jane loved dogs. So did her mom. So did her dad. So did her brother Pete. Pete said, "Let's get a dog."

They did not rush to decide. They sat down and talked.

Jane said, "Here's a big problem. We are all gone all day, almost every day. Pete and I are in school. Mom and Dad are at work. The dog would have to stay home alone. We live in the city. He could not run around outside while we are gone. I don't think the dog would be happy."

Dad said, "Here's another problem. We are all very rushed. We do not have enough time to clean up the house. We do not have time to keep up with close friends. Where will we get the time to take care of a dog? It takes a lot of time."

They decided they could not do a good job of taking care of a dog. They felt sad.

Then Jane said, "Let's list some other options."

Pete said, "Mr. Smith next door is our good friend. He has a nice dog named Cody. Cody does not get out enough. Maybe we could help Mr. Smith with his dog."

They talked to Mr. Smith. He said, "I feel bad that I cannot take Cody out as much as he wants. I cannot play with him as much as he wants. I would love to share him with you."

Mr. Smith was out a lot in the evening. Mr. Smith gave them a key. He told them the times when he was out. They took Cody for walks when Mr. Smith was out. They played with Cody. Cody was very happy to see them. They got to be with him a lot. They felt good about their choice.

56

A. self-care,

or

B. good decisions?

107. Jeff wrote a book. He started selling it. People would send money to him. He would send them his book.

Jeff found out there was a tax. For each book he sold, he had to pay his state some money. He did not mind paying the money. But he hated keeping all the records. He hated adding up all the numbers. He hated filling out the forms. He did not like paper work.

Jeff got the urge to forget about the tax. But then he thought some more. He thought, "I need to obey the law. I don't want to get myself in trouble."

So he made himself add up the numbers. He made himself fill out the forms. He did not like it. But he was glad he had done it.

A. compliance and self-discipline,

or

B. conservation and loyalty?

108. Matt was a doctor. He worked at a hospital. A man came in late at night. Matt saw him in the waiting room. The man could not breathe well. The man's lips had turned blue.

Matt knew this was not good. The man was not getting enough air. Matt decided to go straight to work. He knew there was no time to lose. He put the man in a wheel chair. He pushed him to a room where he could help him.

A. productivity,

or

B. compliance?

109. A woman was at the front desk. She said to Matt, "Wait! He is not on the right payment plan. He should go to a different hospital."

Matt said, "He needs help quick." Matt kept on helping him.

The woman went to get her boss. Her boss came to Matt. Her boss said to Matt, "You should not be doing this. He does not have the right papers. The hospital will not get its money."

Matt spoke quietly. But he spoke in a mad voice. He said, "If you want him to go, you'll have to drag me away from him. And he might die. If he does, I will tell the court it is your fault."

The boss was very mad. But he walked away. Matt was glad he had stood up to him.

A. compliance,

or

B. courage?

110. Matt helped the sick man. The man did not die. The man did well. But the man could not pay the hospital.

The next morning, Matt got a call. It was from the boss. The boss said, "You are fired. You can't work here any more."

Matt went home. At first he was so angry he could not think well. He just walked and ran. Then he sat down. He made a plan. He said, "I will not put up with this. I will not let bad men have their way."

Matt got on the phone. He called up other doctors. He asked, "Did anything like this happen to you?" Lots of other doctors said, "Yes."

Matt made a plan with them. They would work together. The doctors met together. They wrote down the things that had happened. They got a lawyer. They talked to the group of people that ran the hospital. They worked very hard. Matt kept making plans.

In the end, the hospital boss was fired. Matt got his job back. The new hospital boss said, "Here is the new rule. If someone needs help quick, try first to get him or her well. We will worry about money later."

Matt thought to himself, "I think I made the right choices from start to finish."

A. loyalty,

or

B. good decisions?

111. Sara loved to be with people. That was not a problem. But she hated to be alone. That was a problem. She had work to do by herself. She needed to do her homework. When she tried to do it, she would get lonesome. She would come out of her room. She would find someone to play with or talk to. It was hard to get schoolwork done.

Sara was a good writer. She had some good things she wanted to write. But she could not get it done. It was too hard for her to be alone.

One day Sara decided, "I am going to work on this. I am going to learn something new. I will learn to enjoy being alone."

Sara had read that if you want to change something, you should keep track of it. So she kept track of how much time she spent alone each day. She made a chart. She also rated how good or bad it felt to be alone. At first it felt bad.

Sara tried to spend some time alone every day. She worked at this even when she did not feel like it. When she got some good work done, she said to herself, "Hooray for me!" When she had a good time alone, she was glad. She kept working.

A few months passed. Now she was spending lots more time alone. She was getting lots of work done. And she was having a good time doing it! She felt good about what she had done.

A. kindness and friendship-building,
or
B. self-discipline and joyousness?

112. Judd had a problem. He put off his work. He could not get started on it. He felt bad when he did it late. He felt worse when he did not do it at all. But still he could not change.

One day he talked to his friend Max. Max said, "Why don't you do something about it?"

Judd said, "Like what?"

Max said, "I don't know anything about this problem. But here is a way to work on any problem. Go to the library. Look up books on how to solve this problem. Do the same thing at bookstores. Read the books with great care. Write down the best ideas you find. Read that list of ideas every morning and every night. Try to use those ideas every day. Every day, rate yourself on how well you did. Pat yourself on the back when you do well."

Judd said, "That sounds like a good plan. It will be a lot of work. But I think I need to do it."

Many times Judd did not feel like doing this work. But he did it anyway. He found books. He read them. The ideas were good. He wrote them down. It was hard to read them every day. It was hard to rate himself every day. But he did it. And when he did it, he said to himself, "Good for you, Judd."

Months passed. Judd spoke to Max again. Judd said, "Max, I've been working on the problem. I don't put things off nearly as much now!"

Max said, "Wow, Judd. I'm surprised. Since I talked with you, I learned more about putting off work. It is a very hard problem to solve. Good for you!"

A. self-discipline,
or
B. respectful talk?

113. Rashad wanted to go to college. Rashad knew that people who finish college get better jobs. But then he found out how much college costs. Rashad thought, "I wonder if there is a way to save some of that money."

Rashad went to the library. He looked at books in the bookstore. He looked on the Internet. He learned many things. He worked hard to learn more about the problem.

A. productivity,
or
B. kindness?

114. Rashad learned that you can take college courses by mail and over the Internet. Some of these cost much less than courses at college.

He learned about a way that you can take tests to get credit for college. He thought, "This costs even less money. If I can study and learn on my own, I can get credit for it."

Rashad knew he was smart. And he knew he could make himself work hard. Not many other people could do this. But he felt he had it in him. Rashad studied hard. He took tests. He got credit for courses.

He did some courses by mail. He wrote papers and sent them in. The teachers read them. They liked what he wrote. He passed more courses that way.

After a lot of work, he had enough credits. He got a piece of paper he wanted very much. The paper said that he had finished college. He had saved many thousands of dollars. He had learned very much.

He decided to go for more school. He got into graduate school. He had written such good papers that the graduate school paid for him to come.

A. loyalty and kindness,
or
B. self-discipline and conservation and thrift?

115. Jill was playing a game. In this game you moved along a path. You spun a spinner when it was your turn. You moved the number of spaces that your spinner pointed to. If you landed on a good square, you would get to go ahead. If you landed on a bad square, you would have to go back.

Jill spun the spinner. It landed on six. She knew that six would set her back. She spun it again very quickly. She hoped no one would see.

She was playing with her dad. Her dad said, "I think you spun twice, to get the number you want. You can't do that. That's cheating, Jill."

Jill had the urge to say, "No, I did not do that." But she knew that was not true. She had the urge to run away. But she said to herself, "I can be strong."

She said to her dad, "You're right. I cheated. I will try not to do that again." She moved her piece six squares. She landed on the bad square. She moved her piece way back. Now she was close to the start of the path.

Later, Jill's dad said, "I'm proud of you, Jill. When you said, 'I cheated,' you did something very brave and truthful. Not many people can do that."

A. honesty and courage,
or
B. positive fantasy rehearsal and self-care?

116. Jane loved her husband. One day he got shot. The bullet did not kill him. But it kept him from walking. He rode in a wheel chair. He would have to do this for the rest of his life.

Jane was very angry. She was very upset. For a while she could not do much of anything.

Time passed. Jane said to herself, "Something very bad happened. But I need to handle it. I need to do something good with the energy from these bad feelings."

Jane read and studied a long time. She thought about how to prevent violent crimes. She quit her job. She started a group to prevent violence. She worked long and hard. She thought, "I think I am keeping some people from being shot. That makes me happy."

A. honesty and conservation,
or
B. productivity and fortitude?

The following is a retelling of the folk tale, "Beauty and the Beast."

117. A man was rich. He had many ships. But then his ships were lost at sea. He felt bad. But he did not just mope around. He did not just wail about his loss. He thought a lot about what to do. He did lots of things. One of them was to sell his big house. He moved to a small house in the woods. He lived there with his three daughters.

A. compliance and nonviolence,
or
B. good decisions and fortitude?

118. The man got some news. It said one of the ships had landed. The things in it were safe. The man thought, "Hooray! I can go and get those things! Then I can sell them. I've been luckier than I thought!"

A. joyousness,
or
B. respectful talk?

119. He said to his three daughters, "I'm going on a trip. What would you like me to bring back to you?" The first wanted fine gowns. They would cost a lot of money. The second wanted fine jewels. They would cost even more. The youngest was called Beauty. She did not want things that cost a lot. She asked for one flower.

A. conservation and thrift,
or
B. courage?

120. The man got to his ship. He found that the news was wrong. Bad men had taken all the things on the ship. Now they were gone. He thought a lot about what to do. He thought, "I don't like this. But

I can handle it. I have done all I can do here. Now I'll go home. Maybe I can find something for my daughters on the way home."

A. joyousness,
or
B. fortitude?

121. It was the middle of winter. He rode toward home on his horse. He was in the middle of the woods. It was cold. There was a snowstorm.

He came to a big and pretty house. It had all the lights on. The door was wide open. He wanted to get out of the cold. He went inside.

He could not find anyone. He saw a big dinner. It seemed to have been made for him. So he ate it. He thought, "I want to thank the person who gave this to me." So he went looking for someone so that he could say, "Thank you."

A. friendship-building,
or
B. self-discipline?

122. He came to a fine garden. It had flowers blooming, even in winter! He picked one rose. He thought, "I'll take this to Beauty." He was trying to be nice. But the rose was not his.

So this is not such a good example of:

A. loyalty,
or
B. honesty?

123. He heard a scary voice. It seemed to growl at him. It said, "How dare you pick my rose!" The man turned around. The person he saw was very scary. He looked half man and half animal. He had fur on him. He had sharp teeth like a wolf. He was called the Beast.

The man said, "I'm sorry. I was just picking this to take to my daughter, Beauty."

The Beast said, "Then you must send her to me. If you don't, you will lose your life!"

To make this threat was a bad example of:

A. nonviolence,
or
B. conservation?

124. Beauty was scared. But she wanted to save her father. So she

went back to the big house where the Beast lived.

A. self-care and respectful talk,
or
B. courage and loyalty?

125. The Beast was very nice to Beauty. He always spoke kindly. He got her all she wanted and needed. At the end of the day, she would get supper. He would come to be with her. They would talk. He would listen well. He always tried to make her happy.

He gave examples of:

A. self-care and courage,
or
B. friendship-building and kindness?

126. At first, the way he looked scared her. Then she got to know him better. He kept on being very nice. She got over being scared. Soon she even liked to be with him.

One day he asked her, "Do you love me?"

She thought, "I must tell the truth. I will, even if it is not what he wants to hear." She said, "No."

A. honesty,
or
B. compliance?

127. One day the Beast said, "You seem sad. Please tell me why?"

Beauty said, "I miss my father."

The Beast was quiet a long time. Then he said, "You are free to go."

Then he said, "I told your father he would lose his life if you did not come. But that was a lie. I never would have hurt him. I just wanted to be with you."

He was quiet some more. He said, "I fear that you will never come back. That will make me very sad. But I want you to be happy."

A. productivity,
or
B. kindness?

128. He gave her a magic ring. He said to her, "If you ever want to come back to me, turn the stone on the ring. Say, 'I want to go back to my Beast.'" He gave her gifts for her father and sisters. He gave her a magic horse to ride home on.

A. kindness,
or
B. self-care?

129. She got back home. Her father and her sisters were very happy. They said, "Thank goodness you're home with us!" They sang and danced. They felt joy just to look at her.

A. joyousness,
or
B. self-discipline?

130. They felt so good to have her home that she did not leave. But she found that she missed the Beast. She missed the way he listened to her in such a kind way. One night she had a dream that he was dying. She thought, "I want to stand by him. I don't want to leave him to be sad all by himself." So she turned the stone on her ring. She said, "I want to go back to my Beast."

A. loyalty,
or
B. conservation and thrift?

131. She saw him before he saw her. He sat in the garden. He held his head in his hands. He was not dead. But he was very sad. He looked like his reasons for living were gone. She spoke, and he turned around.

He said, "You came back! Is it true? Do you love me?"

She said, "Yes! I do love you!"

In front of her eyes, he then changed from a Beast into a prince. Beauty's love had freed him.

Beauty's father was amazed to see the prince. So were her sisters.

Beauty and the prince were married. They lived happily ever after.

People who choose to marry someone with whom they can live happily ever after have used the principle of:

A. self-care,
or
B. good decisions?

132. A boy saw a movie. The movie was about a scary monster. The monster did bad things.

After the movie the boy had a problem. The thought of the monster kept coming into his mind. He tried not to think of it. But the more he tried this, the less it worked.

He told his big brother about his problem. His big brother thought, "I know something about this type of problem. I want to make my brother happier." And the big brother said, "I think I can help you, if you can understand the things I will say."

A. kindness,
or
B. self-discipline?

133. His big brother said, "When you try not to think of something, it's very hard. I read a story once. A person was trying not to think of a white bear. When he would try not to think of it, it would come into his mind. You might try it now. Try not to think of a white bear."

The boy said, "You're right. I'm trying not to think of it. I check to see if I did think of it. And that brings the bear to my mind."

The big brother said, "Think of the scary monster on purpose. Let yourself get used to it. You can change what he does, in your

mind. You can put him in a dancing dress. You can make him clean up the house. You can see him being too scared to go off a diving board. You can put him on a very little TV screen far away. You can magically make him nice. After a while, you will get used to thinking about him. Then the thought won't be a problem any more."

The boy did those things. After a while, the thought of the monster didn't bother him any more. He said, "Thank you, big brother!"

His brother said, "I have more advice."

The boy said, "What is it?" The brother said, "Don't watch monster movies. Watch movies about people doing good things."

The boy said, "That's good advice too. Thanks."

The big brother advised:

A. positive fantasy rehearsal,
or
B. honesty?

134. A boy had a problem. He could not wake up in the morning. At night, he couldn't get to sleep.

When Saturday came, he slept till noon. He stayed up late Saturday night. On Sunday he slept till one. On Sunday night, he tried to go to sleep early. But he just lay in bed. He tossed and turned. On Monday morning, he hated to hear the alarm ring. He felt that he had only begun to sleep. It went on like this, week after week.

The boy thought, "I might feel embarrassed to talk about this with my doctor. But I have nothing to lose. I could end up getting some help. I will give it a try." So he decided to ask his doctor.

A. nonviolence,
or
B. good decisions?

135. He told his doctor about this problem. His doctor said, "I know what you can do." The boy said, "What can I do?"

The doctor said, "Your brain has something like a clock in it. That clock tells you when it's time to get sleepy. It tells you when to wake up. Your clock is set for going to bed late and getting up late. You need to set it earlier."

The boy said, "How do I do that?"

The doctor said, "Buy a very bright light. Get an exercise bike. Get up at the same time each morning. When you get up, ride the bike and use the light. Do this for at least half an hour. The light tells your body that it's day. The exercise helps your body know it's time to be awake."

The doctor said, "The light and exercise will help you get sleepy earlier. Soon you'll be able to get to sleep early."

The doctor had found out about these things by reading lots of books and articles. He had worked very hard to keep up with good things to know.

The doctor had done

A. positive fantasy rehearsal,
or
B. productivity?

136. The boy did what the doctor had said. At first it was very hard. He did not feel like getting up. He did not feel like getting exercise. He did not feel like being in bright light. He just wanted to sleep. But

he did what he was told. He thought to himself, "I can be strong."

Soon it got easier. Then it got to be a habit. He would bounce out of bed with lots of energy. He felt much better.

He thought, "It was very hard. But I'm glad I made myself do it."

A. self-discipline,
or
B. kindness?

137. A woman had a problem. She was scared of elevators. When she was not on them, she knew they were safe. But when she got on one, she thought, "I'm going to die." She would think, "Let me out of here!"

For a long time the woman was scared to tell anyone about this. But one day she thought, "I have a good friend. I can tell her things about myself. Nothing too bad will happen." It was scary, but she talked with her friend about it.

A. courage,
or
B. joyousness?

138. The friend said, "This is amazing! I had the same problem! I solved it. Do you want to know how?"

The woman said, "Yes. Please tell me."

The friend said, "You have to stay on the elevator for a long time. Don't get off quick. That doesn't work. If you get off quick, you feel much better in the short run. But you'll want to get off quick the next time. You'll stay scared. You have to stay on a long time. That way you have time to get used to it. That way you'll be less scared the next time."

The woman said, "I see. You're saying I should stay on the elevator a long time. But I don't think I can do that. I'm too scared. If I could stay on a long time, I would not have this problem."

The friend said, "That's what I thought. You can do more than you think you can. Have you ever tried? It might help if first you practice in your fantasy. Just pretend you're on an elevator. If you practice that a lot, it will be easier to stay on the elevator in real life."

The woman said, "I'll think about these things. Thank you.

You have been very nice to tell me what you know about this."

The friend had used

A. conservation,
or
B. kindness?

139. The woman decided to try what her friend had said. She started by closing her eyes and trying to see in her mind what it would be like to stand in the elevator for a long time. At first this was scary. But after she did it more and more, she got used to it.

There was an elevator where she worked. She went there on a weekend. Not many people were there. She got on the elevator. She felt her heart pound. Her hands shook. She thought, "I'm scared eight on a scale of ten. It's good that I practiced in my mind first. If I had not done that, maybe I could not have stayed on."

But she stayed on. She rode up and down. She said, "I'm going to keep staying on." She did it, even though she did not feel like it.

A. self-discipline and courage,
or
B. kindness and respectful talk?

140. After a few minutes, she felt a little better. She thought, "Now I'm only scared six on a scale of ten." She stayed where she was.

She rode the elevator for half an hour. At the end of the time, she was scared only one on a scale of ten.

She said to herself, "Hooray for me! I did it!"

When she said, "Hooray for me," that was an example of:

A. joyousness,
or
B. kindness?

141. The next day, she remembered what it felt like to be on the elevator without being scared. She went over it in her mind. Then she really rode the elevator. At first she was scared four on a scale of ten. After twenty minutes, her fear went down to zero.

She kept riding the elevator every day. She also kept practicing riding it in her fantasy. Pretty soon the elevator didn't scare her at all.

She told her friend. Her friend said, "You were really brave and strong!"

The woman said, "Thanks for telling me how to do it."

The woman felt great about what she had done.

When the woman got on the elevator in her fantasy, to practice being on it, that was an example of:

A. positive fantasy rehearsal, or
B. respectful talk?

142. Tom was in high school. The end of school was near. On the last day, someone would give a speech. Tom's class voted to choose a speaker.

The class chose an actor. The actor had been in lots of movies. All the movies were very violent. All of them had much killing. In the movies the actor seemed to have fun killing.

Tom read lots of books. Some of these told about why people hurt and kill. Tom read lots of studies. The studies showed that movies about killing caused real-life violence. Not every person who sees the movies will hurt someone. But some people do copy things they see in movies.

Tom wrote for his school newspaper. Tom wrote why the class should have chosen someone else as speaker. Not many people felt the same way. But a few did.

Tom wrote more. When the actor came, Tom passed out leaflets. His leaflet had facts about violence. The leaflet said, "Hurting and killing people should not be fun. This man's movies should make us sad. Good movies help us to practice good things in our minds."

A. positive fantasy rehearsal, or
B. compliance?

143. Lila was like most of her friends. She bought lots of things. She spent lots of time shopping. The things she bought got in her way. She spent lots of time trying to arrange her clutter.

Lila read a book. The book told about the earth's resources. It told about how making lots of things creates waste. Some of the waste goes into rivers or into the air. Making more things creates more garbage.

The book also told about how much time people spend on things they don't really need. It told about how people could use that time better in really helping each other.

Lila said, "I'm going to try something. I'm going to see how little I can buy and still be happy."

Lila stopped eating at fast-food places. She saved a lot of money from this alone. She ate food she cooked at home. The food was better for her anyway. It did not cost nearly as much. She could invite friends over to eat it with her.

She stopped buying new clothes. She found that the clothes she already had were just fine. Every once in a while, she bought clothes at a used clothing store. They looked fine.

She stopped spending lots of money to have fun. She looked for ways to have fun for free. And she found them. She invited friends over and played games with them. She sang songs and played music with a couple of her relatives. She got friends together to play volleyball at the park. She spent a lot of time talking and listening to

people. She went on long walks. She read books from the library.

She found that she needed very little money to be happy. This made her feel freer.

A. compliance,

or

B. conservation?

144. Edna had a younger sister named Jenny. Edna felt she had to "one-up" Jenny. For example, Jenny would show her mom a drawing she had made. Then Edna would say, "Look at my drawing." Edna wanted to show that hers was better.

Sometimes Jenny would say, "I can add some numbers."

Then Edna would say, "I can add bigger numbers."

One day Jenny said, "Guess what? I know three horses."

Edna got the urge to say, "Well, I know five horses." But then she stopped and thought.

Stopping and thinking before saying something are skills more helpful for

A. good decisions,

or

B. conservation?

145. Edna said to herself, "Why can't I just let her be proud of something? Why do I always have to one-up her?"

So Edna said to Jenny, "You do? Tell me about the horses you know!" And Jenny told her. She had fun.

The next day Jenny said to her mom, "Look, mom, I can read a word!"

Her mom looked. Her mom said, "That's great, Jenny." Her mom expected Edna to tell how she could read a whole book.

But Edna just smiled at Jenny. She said, "Wow, Jenny. What a good job." Jenny felt good. Their mom was surprised.

That night, their mom and dad talked. Their mom said, "Edna is growing up. She's learning she doesn't have to one-up Jenny!" Their dad felt good to hear this.

A. nonviolence and compliance, or
B. respectful talk and kindness?

146. Jeb was a doctor. He was the kind that made people look better. He fixed the parts of people's bodies that didn't look good.

Jeb was a very good doctor. Lots of people wanted him to fix their bodies. They would have paid lots of money.

But Jeb spent a lot of time helping poor people. He went to a poor country. Most people there did not have money for a doctor. Lots of people there needed his help. Some had gotten hurt. Their hurts had healed in ways that looked very ugly. Other people had been born with ugly things on their bodies. Some of these people felt very ashamed.

Jeb fixed their bodies. He did not ask them for any money. People heard about this. Many people came to him for help. Jeb worked many hours. But he was happy.

A. kindness and productivity, or
B. self-care and compliance?

147. The next few questions have to do with the titles of imaginary self-help books. Self-help books are the sort that people read to learn how to do something well. Guess which skill or principle each book has to do with. The first book is:

How To Get People to Like You

A. courage,
or
B. friendship-building?

148. How To Eat What Is Best So You'll Live a Long Time

A. self-care,
or
B. joyousness?

149. The Handbook for People Who Want To Prevent War

A. compliance,
or
B. nonviolence?

150. How To Buy Less Junk So You'll Need Less Money

A. conservation and thrift,
or
B. respectful talk?

151. How To Stay Married to the Same Person for the Rest of Your Life

A. loyalty,

or
B. productivity?

152. How To Be Tough and Strong and Resist Temptations

A. self-discipline,
or
B. compliance?

153. How To Get Over Your Need To Disobey All Authority

A. compliance,
or
B. positive fantasy rehearsal?

154. How To Practice Things in Your Mind To Achieve Your Goals

A. positive fantasy rehearsal,
or
B. kindness?

155. How To Do What You Need to Do, Even When You're Afraid

A. courage,
or
B. compliance?

156. How To Get More Work Done in Less Time

A. productivity,
or
B. kindness?

157. The Key To Taking Pleasure from Living

A. joyousness,
or
B. kindness?

158. Lessons in Following the Golden Rule

A. fortitude,
or
B. kindness?

159. How To Become a Promise-Keeper

A. honesty,
or
B. fortitude?

160. How To Handle It When Disaster Strikes

A. friendship-building,
or
B. fortitude?

161. How To Make Smart Choices, Even When You're Uncertain

A. nonviolence,
or
B. good decisions?

162. How To Use Tact When You Speak With People

A. good decisions,
or
B. respectful talk?

163. How To Talk out Problems that Come up between People

A. fortitude,
or
B. good decisions?

164. You, Too, Can Stop Smoking

A. self-care,
or
B. compliance?

Self Discipline, Temptations and Long-term Goals

165. This section has to do with self-discipline. Self-discipline means doing things that let you reach your goals, even when you're tempted to do something else that would feel better in the short run. Using self-discipline is one of the best ways of being tough and strong. The stories that come next ask you to decide whether the person used self-discipline or not.

Self-discipline means doing

A. what feels best now,
or
B. what lets you reach goals?

166. A person was trying to lose weight. But when he saw some nuts and potato chips and buttered popcorn, he ate all that he could hold. They tasted so good that he couldn't stop. Then he thought, "Tomorrow I will start to lose weight." But the next day, the same thing happened.

A. self-discipline,
or
B. not self-discipline?

167. A person was trying to stop smoking. She said to herself, "I am done with smoking. I have had my last one." For a few days she felt very bad. She could not keep her mind on what she was doing. She felt sick. She had a very strong urge to smoke many times each day. But she said to herself, "I must be strong. My life is at stake." She did not smoke. In time, she began to feel better. One day she found out that she did not feel like smoking any more.

A. self-discipline,
or
B. not self-discipline?

168. A boy wanted to play baseball with other kids. But he found that he was not skilled at baseball. He could not hit well. He could not catch or throw very well either.

He started practicing. He threw the ball against a wall, and he caught it when it bounced back. He practiced throwing the ball up and hitting it with his bat. Whenever he could find someone to pitch to him, he would practice hitting that way. He practiced over and over, every day. Some days he did not feel like practicing. But he did it anyway.

He got lots better at baseball. He still did not get to be a great player. But he got good enough that he could have lots of fun playing with his friends.

A. self-discipline,
or
B. not self-discipline?

169. A girl wanted to learn to play the piano. One of the main things she had to

learn was to read music. She wanted to be able to look at notes of music written on paper and play the right note on the piano. She had a hard time remembering the notes. She would look at a note on her page of music and think, "Is that G or B, or what?" When it took her so long, she could not play well.

One day she decided, "I want to learn to name notes very fast." She took some of the music she was trying to play. She got a watch. She started timing. She named all the notes in one of her songs. She wrote down how long it had taken her. Then she did it again. She wrote down how long it had taken her this time. She kept doing this. When she could name the notes very fast, she went to a different song.

Every day, for several months, she drilled like this. She did it even when she didn't feel like it. She got faster and faster at naming the notes. She found that this helped her to play the piano better.

A. self-discipline,
or
B. not self-discipline?

170. A boy was very restless; he could not sit still very long. He did not try to make himself sit down when he didn't feel like working. Instead, he got up and walked around whenever he felt like it. Sometimes he felt like handling something that belonged to someone else, without asking that person. When

he felt like this, he would just do it. He thought to himself, "I can't help it. This is just the way I am."

A. self-discipline,
or
B. not self-discipline?

171. A boy had a hard time keeping his mind on things. It was hard for him to pay attention to what he was reading. He decided he wanted to learn to concentrate better. In a book, he read about a way of teaching himself to do this.

He tried out the method he had read about. Every day, he set a timer for five minutes. He read a hard book during this time. When the bell went off, he rated how well he had kept his mind on his task. He used a scale where zero meant not keeping the mind on the task at all, and ten meant keeping the mind on the task perfectly. Then he read again for another five minutes, and again he rated himself when the timer went off. He kept doing this until he had read for a whole hour.

When he had kept his mind on task well, he would think to himself, "Let's see if I can remember what I did with my mind, so I can do it again." He kept working for many weeks. He taught himself to concentrate very well.

A. self-discipline,
or
B. not self-discipline?

172. A man started to take guitar lessons. He said to himself, "I'll practice when I get the urge to. I won't do it when I don't feel like it." After the first couple of weeks, he never got the urge to practice. When he got to his lesson, he could not play what he was supposed to learn. He felt bad about this. But more and more lessons came, and he still did not practice. In the end he decided he had wasted his money on his guitar and the lessons.

A. self-discipline,
or
B. not self-discipline?

173. A girl wanted to get to school on time. But every morning, when it got to be time to get up, she was still sleepy. She did not feel like getting out of bed. So she turned over and went back to sleep. She kept doing this. She was late almost every day, and some days she did not show up at school at all.

A. self-discipline,
or
B. not self-discipline?

174. The same girl got some advice. Someone told her that she should be in some bright light for at least half an hour as soon as she wakes up. The person also said that she should exercise hard soon after she wakes up and that she should also go to bed and wake up a little earlier every day. But she did not feel like doing any of these things. So

she did not do them. In the end, she was kicked out of school.

A. self-discipline,
or
B. not self-discipline?

175. A boy had a bad habit in school. The rule was to raise your hand and get called on before talking. But when this boy wanted to talk, he would just go ahead and talk. He would not raise his hand and wait. The teacher and the other students became angry with him.

Someone said, "I'll tell you how to solve that problem. Practice in your fantasy. Imagine getting the urge to talk. Then imagine holding up your hand and waiting. Imagine feeling good about this."

But the boy did not find that this sort of practice was fun. So he did not do it. He kept on making people angry. They did not like him as much.

A. self-discipline,
or
B. not self-discipline?

176. A girl went to a new school. On the playground, all the girls jumped rope. But she did not know how to jump rope. She felt bad. She went home and started to practice. She could not jump over the rope even one time. But she did not give up.

First she practiced jumping up and down without even using a rope. Then she practiced swinging the rope over her head and just stepping over the rope. She learned to do this faster and faster. After a long time, she learned to jump over the rope one time. She did this many times.

Day after day she kept practicing. Then she learned to jump two times. She kept practicing for many hours and many days. Finally she learned to jump rope well. She had fun with her friends on the playground. She felt proud of herself.

A. self-discipline,
or
B. not self-discipline?

177. A man had an office with papers and books and letters and other things all over the place. He could not find things easily because they were on top of one another. He thought to himself, "This place is too much of a mess. I need to get organized."

So he picked a certain half hour of time every day to work on organizing himself, and he wrote down that time in his appointment book. When the time came, he usually did not feel like organizing. But he did it anyway. He liked being able to get a lot more work done. He liked being able to find what he needed easily.

A. self-discipline,
or
B. not self-discipline?

178. A man wanted to get good at playing chess. But when it was his turn to move, he did not feel like thinking and planning for very long before he moved. He felt like moving right away. He got beat in chess just about every time he played.

A. self-discipline,
or
B. not self-discipline?

179. The same man had a chess coach. The coach told him to study a book and to do a few chess problems every day. The man started working with the book. After a few minutes, he said, "This is boring." He put the book down. He did not do any more problems. He did not learn to win at chess.

A. self-discipline,
or
B. not self-discipline?

180. A man read an ad about a computer kit. The ad said that you could save lots of money by putting together a computer from its parts. The man bought the kit. But there were lots of directions to read. He put together a few of the parts. But then the man said to himself, "I don't feel like this right now." He kept putting it off. He never put the parts together. He did not have a computer that worked. He wasted the money he had spent on the kit.

A. self-discipline,

or
B. not self-discipline?

181. A woman bought a treadmill to exercise with. At first she did not feel like exercising. For a while the treadmill just sat without being used. But then she decided that she would make herself exercise whether she felt like it or not. She decided to walk on the treadmill for half an hour each morning, while she studied a book. On many mornings she did not feel like doing this. But she did it anyway. After a while she got into much better shape. She was proud of herself.

A. self-discipline,
or
B. not self-discipline?

182. A man signed up for a college course at a school. This was the sort of course that you take by mail. You read a book, write the answers to questions, and mail your answers in to your teacher. The course cost a lot less to take this way than in a school. The man thought he was going to save lots of money. But he found that he did not feel like doing his work. He said to himself, "I'll do it later." He never got around to doing it. He wasted the money he had spent on the course.

A. self-discipline,
or
B. not self-discipline?

183. A man had a bad habit. If there was a picture on someone's wall that was just a little crooked, he would have to make it straight. He had to do this even at other people's houses. Sometimes he would think he had not got it right and would do it over and over many times. The man felt bad about spending so much time on this.

He read about a way to get over it. He made some pictures a little crooked on purpose. He sat and stared at them. He felt a very strong urge to straighten the pictures. But he did not let himself do it. At first he felt very bad. But after about half an hour he got used to it. He did this for several days. After a few days he did not feel he needed to make the pictures straight.

A. self-discipline,
or
B. not self-discipline?

184. A woman was afraid of being on elevators. She felt she had to take the stairs. But she got a job where she needed to go places with other people. It made her feel bad to have to tell them she was scared to ride with them on the elevator.

So she read about how to break herself of the fear. She read that she should get on an elevator and stay on it a long time. She decided to do it. At first she felt very scared. But she had read that if she got off when she was most scared, she would not get over the fear. She knew she had to stay on. So she stayed on, even though it felt really bad.

Finally she began to get used to the elevator. She found herself getting less scared. She stayed on a long time every day for several days. Finally she was able to ride elevators without feeling bad.

A. self-discipline,
or
B. not self-discipline?

185. A man had a lot of work to do. He had to figure out how much tax he had to pay his country. He said to himself, "I don't feel like doing this. I feel like watching something good on television." Each time he thought about doing the tax, he thought, "I feel more like watching another show." So he never did the tax. He had to pay a lot of money to the government as a fine.

A. self-discipline,
or
B. not self-discipline?

186. A boy set a goal of learning to type. He decided he would practice typing for at least half an hour each day. He got a book on typing. He made sure to use the right fingers on the keys. He practiced the typing drills that the book told about. Some days he did not feel like practicing, but he did it anyway.

After three weeks of doing this, he was ready to use a computer program where he would practice typing spelling words. He did this for three more weeks. Then he practiced copying some good writing that other people had done.

After a few months, he was a pretty good typist. Now he could type his own ideas without having to concentrate too much on the typing.

A. self-discipline,
or
B. not self-discipline?

187. A man set a goal of getting a lot stronger. So he bought some barbells and dumbbells. But as soon as he started to lift them, he got a little tired. He thought, "I don't feel like lifting any more." On another day, he said to himself, "I'll lift them some time later." He never used the weights, and he never got any stronger.

A. self-discipline,
or
B. not self-discipline?

188. A boy set a goal. There was a dance contest, and he wanted to win it. Every day he practiced the dances many times. Most of the time his partner could not practice with him, so he imagined that his partner was there and imagined what his partner was doing, while he practiced his part. On many days he did not feel like practicing. But he did it just the same.

On the night of the contest, his partner got sick. He danced in the contest with another girl who had never practiced with him. But he did well enough to get third place in the contest, anyway.

A. self-discipline,
or
B. not self-discipline?

189. A mother set a goal of teaching a child to comply or obey well. But most of the time, when the child disobeyed the mother, the mother thought, "I just don't feel like doing anything about this." When the child did obey, the mother thought, "Now I don't have to do anything." The mother ended up doing nothing to teach the child to be obedient.

A. self-discipline,
or
B. not self-discipline?

190. A girl wanted to be better at math. Someone suggested that she study her math book. She picked it up and started to read it, but then she thought, "I feel like reading something else. Come to think of it, I feel even more like watching television." So she watched television instead of reading the math book.

A. self-discipline,
or
B. not self-discipline?

191. A boy wanted to make better grades. Someone gave him some advice. The person said, "Make up a practice test before each test you take. Try to make it like the real test, but even harder. Practice taking your own test until you can do it perfectly." The boy got his book and started writing down questions. But then he said to himself, "I don't like this, because I can't daydream as much while I'm reading the book." So he didn't make up his own test or take it.

A. self-discipline,
or
B. not self-discipline?

192. A girl wanted to learn to concentrate better on things she was listening to. She read about an exercise to help her keep her mind on her task. She found someone who was willing to do the exercise with her.

The person would read her a few sentences from a book. Then the person would stop. The girl would reflect what the person said. She would say, "In other words, you're saying . . .," and she would fill in the blank. The person would give her a rating that told how accurate she was. She would try for a 10 on a scale of 10 rating.

She did this exercise every day for a half an hour. Gradually she got to be very good at keeping her mind on what she was hearing.

A. self-discipline,

or
B. not self-discipline?

193. A man set a goal of being nicer to his wife. He wanted to get along better with her. But every time she did something he did not like, he yelled at her in a very mean way. Later he always thought to himself, "I can't help it. I just don't feel like being nice to her when she does things I don't like."

A. self-discipline,
or
B. not self-discipline?

194. A girl had a habit of sucking her thumb. She set a goal of breaking that habit. She tried to keep her thumb out of her mouth, even when she felt very much like sucking it. A couple of times a day she would try to go for half an hour without sucking her thumb. She counted how many times she put her thumb in her mouth. Even when she got a very strong urge, she would keep the thumb out of her mouth.

To help herself more, she painted her thumbnail with some stuff that had hot pepper in it. When she forgot and put her thumb in her mouth, the pepper taste would remind her to take it out. She remembered to put the pepper stuff on her thumbnail every day, even though she felt like sucking her thumb.

Finally she broke the habit. After a few weeks she did not feel like sucking her thumb any more.

A. self-discipline,
or
B. not self-discipline?

195. Self-discipline means choosing to do what it takes to meet a long-term goal, instead of doing something that gives short-term pleasure. The short-term pleasure is a "temptation." It tempts us to do something that does not serve the long-term goal. The next few stories will ask you to tell what is the temptation and what is the long-term goal.

A man loved to go to horse races. He would bet on a certain horse to win. He got a real thrill out of watching the race. When he won some money, he would have lots of fun. But often he would lose a lot of money. When he added up the numbers, he found he had lost a great deal more money than he had won.

He said to himself, "I want my family to have enough money. I want to quit betting on horse races." But this was very hard for him. It took a lot of self-discipline.

The thrill of betting was the

A. temptation,
or
B. the long-term goal?

196. A person went in to work. He had many reports to write. He had many forms to fill out. When he went in, he thought, "This will be a great day. I will have lots of time to do this paper work.

I need to do these things if my business is to succeed."

But he went on the Internet. He found something that was very much fun to read about. This led him to other sites that taught him all sorts of good things. But he did not get his work done.

Making his business succeed was the

A. temptation,
or
B. the long-term goal?

197. One night, a woman was talking on the phone with a friend. It got to be time for her to go to bed. She knew that she had to get up early the next day. She wanted to wake up having some energy. She wanted not to be tired all day. But to chat on the phone was great fun for her. It was hard for her to get off the phone.

Not being tired tomorrow was the

A. temptation,
or
B. the long-term goal?

198. A man drank too much alcohol. When he drank too much, he acted very angry. He made people angry at him. He did things that were not smart. He lost some jobs. He lost friends.

One day, he stopped drinking alcohol. He said, "I don't want to mess up my life any more."

He went to a party. His friends were drinking beer. One of them said, "Come

on, have a beer." He wanted to fit in with his friends. And he knew the beer would taste good.

Fitting in with the friends and the good taste of the beer were the:

A. temptation,
or
B. the long-term goal?

199. A woman spent too much money. She spent much more than she made. She liked fine clothes. She liked jewels. She borrowed lots of money. But she had to pay money to use borrowed money. She had to borrow more and more. People called her up very often and said, "Please pay us what you owe."

She thought, "I need to change. I need to spend less. I want not to owe people money. I want to have money saved up."

But when she saw a pretty dress she liked at a store, it was very hard for her not to buy it.

The dress was the

A. temptation,
or
B. the long-term goal?

200. A man had a bad habit. It happened when he and someone else were talking. The other person would be talking. The man would have a thought that he wanted to say. So he would interrupt the other person. He would start talking before the other person stopped. He almost never let the other

person finish. This often made the other person angry. The man lost some friends this way.

The man wanted to have friends. But he got such strong urges to say what he thought. It was hard to hold back and wait.

Having friends was the

A. temptation,

or

B. the long-term goal?

201. A man wanted to exercise more. All the books he read about health told him that exercise would help him live longer and be healthier. But when he got some free time, he enjoyed playing with his computer and surfing the Internet. It was hard to exercise instead.

Surfing the Internet was the

A. temptation,

or

B. the long-term goal?

202. A man worked at a store. His job was to deal with people who had a gripe about something they had bought. Sometimes the people acted very mean. Sometimes they acted very spoiled. The man sometimes thought about how good it would feel to tell them off. He got the urge to say, "You think you know it all, don't you? You are just a spoiled brat."

But the man knew that it was his job not to make the people angry. He

wanted to do his job well. He wanted not to get fired. So he used great self-discipline. He was calm and nice to all the people.

Doing a good job and keeping his job were the

A. temptation,

or

B. the long-term goal?

203. A boy wanted to ride his bike. He got on and started pedaling. But then he thought, "I forgot my helmet." His helmet was in the house. It would take a couple of minutes to get off the bike and find it and come back out. It would feel much better to go on the ride right away. But he wanted to protect his head if he fell. And he wanted to stay in the habit of following the rule.

Getting to ride, right away, was the

A. temptation,

or

B. the long-term goal?

204. A woman was going to have a baby. She had read that drinking alcohol while expecting a baby was not good. The alcohol could harm the baby's brain. It could make the baby less smart. She wanted her child to be smart. But she went out to eat. The place where she ate had great wine to drink. She thought, "I may never again have the chance to drink such good wine."

The good wine was the

A. temptation,

or

B. the long-term goal?

205. A man had ants in his house. He knew that he could use ant poison to get rid of the ants right away. But he read that people who used more of the ant poisons got a brain disease more often when they were old. He wanted to be well when he was old.

Being healthy when he was old was the

A. temptation,

or

B. the long-term goal?

206. In a certain country, there were two religions. The people often did not get along with the people in the other religion. They often fought with each other. Sometimes they killed people from the other side.

A group of young men had a friend who was killed in this way. Some of the young men said, "We must get revenge. It will feel good to make them pay for his death. It will feel good to make them pay the price."

A wise old man told them, "This will only make their people want to have revenge on us. Someone who has done nothing wrong may get killed because of your revenge. If you want peace to come, you should give up the good feeling you would get from having revenge."

Having peace come is the

A. temptation,

or

B. the long-term goal?

207. A man was driving to a ball game. He wanted to get there soon enough to see the game start. He wanted to get a good seat. But he had left too late. He was on a big highway. He had the urge to put his gas pedal to the floor. He had the urge to go very fast. "I do want to get there quickly," he thought. But then he thought, "I also want to stay alive. And I don't want to kill someone else in a wreck."

Going fast to get there quickly is the

A. temptation,

or

B. the long-term goal?

208. A mom was with her little boy all day. The boy kept wanting his mom to talk to him and listen to him and look at him. When she tried to be alone, he would try to get her attention.

She got tired of this. She got the urge to scream at him. She got the urge to yell out, "Go away and leave me alone!" She knew he would be so scared that he would leave her alone for a while. And she knew it would feel good for a short time to let her emotions show.

But then she thought, "I want him to be good. I want him not to scream at me. If I would scream at him, I would be teaching him by my example. I would be teaching him to scream at me and other people. I want him to be calm. I will show him how to do this. I will ask him to play by himself for a while. I will be alone. But I will do it in a very kind way."

Having her son act calm and kind was the

A. temptation,
or
B. the long-term goal?

209. A woman was at a party with her husband. Another man came up to her. This man thought she was very pretty. He said, "You look really nice." He looked at her as if he wanted to fall in love with her.

The woman thought that it was fun to see that the man liked her. But she wanted to have a happy marriage. She did not want her husband to feel that she wanted this man. She decided to go and talk with someone else.

The fun of getting attention from the other man was the

A. temptation,
or
B. the long-term goal?

210. A dad was at a store with his daughter. The girl saw a toy. She began to whine. She said, "Please, I've got to have it! I'll be sad every day until I get

it!" The dad said no. She cried. She wailed very loudly.

The dad thought, "I could get her to quit wailing by spending just a little money and getting her what she wants. It would feel good to stop the wailing."

Then the dad thought, "If I got her the toy, that would teach her that she can get what she wants by wailing. I don't want her to learn that. I want her to learn fortitude."

So he said, "When you wail like that, I cannot get you what you want. That would teach you the wrong thing." She kept wailing for a while. Then she stopped.

Getting the girl to stop wailing right away was the

A. temptation,
or
B. the long-term goal?

Kindness and Selfishness

211. We have lots of chances each day to be either kind or selfish. It's good to notice those choice points when they come. Making kind choices makes people happier. Many of the big problems of the world could be solved if more people did more kind acts.

Chances to choose between kindness and selfishness come

A. often,
or
B. not often?

212. It was holiday time. A girl got a present from her aunt. She hoped it would be a toy. Instead, it was a shirt. The girl didn't even like the shirt. But she did not want to make her aunt feel bad. She wanted to be grateful for the gift. So she said to her aunt, "Thank you for giving this to me. I'm really glad you thought of me on this holiday."

A. kindness,
or
B. selfishness?

213. There was a boy named Jack. Jack invited a boy named Ted to play at his house. When Ted came over, Jack started to play on a video game. Jack liked doing this. But Ted did not like doing this. Ted wanted to do something else. But Jack kept on playing his video game anyway.

A. kindness,
or
B. selfishness?

214. Emily had a cough. But she did not want other people to catch the sickness she had. She knew other people would not like it if she coughed on them. So when she coughed, she always turned her head away from other people. She also covered her mouth with her arm.

A. kindness,
or
B. selfishness?

215. Lauren was sitting at a lunch table. A girl named Sara sat next to her. Sara did not have any lunch. Lauren said, "Don't you want any lunch today, Sara?"

Sara said, "I forgot to bring my lunch, and I also forgot to bring some money to buy lunch."

Lauren said, "I have more lunch than I need. You can have half of mine." So Lauren and Sara shared Lauren's lunch.

A. kindness,
or
B. selfishness?

216. A man had done a lot of work. He was very tired. He got to take an afternoon off without working. He went home. He lay on his bed and went to sleep. His daughter wanted to know where to find the screwdriver. She went up to him and said in a loud voice, "Dad, do you know where the screwdriver is?"

A. kindness,
or
B. selfishness?

217. There were two brothers, named Lunk and Pete. Lunk ate very loudly. He smacked his lips. He made slurping noises when he drank. Pete said, "Lunk, could you please not make those noises? They bother me."

Lunk thought it was funny that Pete was bothered by this. So he made the noises even louder than before. He laughed each time Pete asked him to stop.

A. kindness,
or
B. selfishness?

218. Caleb was very interested in maps. He did not want to stop talking about maps. His uncle visited him. Caleb talked to him about maps. He did not stop to let his uncle talk. His uncle was not interested in maps. His uncle yawned and looked away and looked at his watch. But Caleb kept talking about maps. He did not care whether his uncle was interested or not.

A. kindness,
or
B. selfishness?

219. A boy named Zack noticed that Nick had put his shoes on the wrong feet. He started to tell Nick. But then he noticed there were several other kids who would hear what he was going to say. Zack thought it might embarrass Nick for the other kids to hear. So Zack waited until he could be alone with Nick. He told him then.

A. kindness,
or
B. selfishness?

220. A girl promised to feed her dog and to give it water. But a friend called her on the phone. The friend told her about a very fun thing they could do. The girl was very excited. She did not want to think of anything else. She did not feel like thinking about boring things such as chores to do. She ran off to visit her friend. They were together for a long time. In the meantime, the dog was very hungry and thirsty.

A. kindness,
or
B. selfishness?

221.A boy sat next to a friend on the bus. The friend looked very upset.

Every once in a while it would look as though he were about to cry. The boy looked at him and didn't say anything. He pulled out a hand-held video game and played it while his friend looked very sad.

A. kindness,
or
B. selfishness?

222. Duke was at his friend's house. They were playing with the friend's father's computer. Duke knew how to change the settings on the computer. He set the computer to make the screen look different when the computer came on. When they got through playing, Duke left the computer set in the new way.

A. kindness,
or
B. selfishness?

223. A girl at school worked very hard. She made a very complex building out of plastic blocks. When she finished, she felt good about her work of art. She went to find someone to show it to.

A boy wanted to use some of the blocks himself. He saw the girl's building. He took her building apart so that he could get the blocks.

The girl was upset. She said, "Why didn't you use the blocks in the box over there? No one is using them."

The boy said, "I would have had to walk across the room to get them. Your blocks were closer."

A. kindness,
or
B. selfishness?

224. Rick took a shower at his house. He got some water on the bathroom floor. He started to leave the bathroom. But then he thought about the next people who would be in the bathroom. He spent some time mopping up the water off the floor. He left the floor dry.

A. kindness,
or
B. selfishness?

225. Tom wanted to practice playing his tuba. He knew he would make some fairly loud noise. He learned that his sister was studying for a big test in her room, next door to him. So he took his tuba down to the basement to practice, so he would not disturb his sister.

A. kindness,
or
B. selfishness?

226. There were lots of people waiting in line to get on a ride at an amusement park. Someone was too impatient with waiting in line. So he broke in line near the front.

A. kindness,

or
B. selfishness?

227. Two friends met. The first said, "How are you?"

The second said, "I'm feeling sad. Something bad happened to me."

The first said, "Well, I'm going to see a neat movie today. It's about some people who live on a different planet. A friend of mine saw it and said it was really good." Then the first person went on talking about fun things he was planning to do.

A. kindness,
or
B. selfishness?

228. Two friends met. The first said, "I've been doing a lot of thinking lately about something very unusual."
The second said, "That sounds interesting. Tell me about it, please."

A. kindness,
or
B. selfishness?

229. Sam got together with two of his friends who did not know each other. Sam said, "I'd like to introduce you two to each other. Pat, this is Lee, who goes to school with me. Lee, this is Pat, who is in my class at Sunday school."

A. kindness,
or
B. selfishness?

230. Zeke was in a grocery store. He saw a very young child who was walking around crying. The child was calling, "Mommy! Mommy!"

Zeke thought, "That crying is an annoying sound." He walked away from the child, so that he would not have to hear the sound that he didn't like.

A. kindness,
or
B. selfishness?

231. Boys and girls were playing on a playground. A girl fell down on some pavement. She skinned herself. Other boys and girls ran past her. They paid attention to their own games, and they did not pay attention to her.

A. kindness,
or
B. selfishness?

232. Boys and girls were playing on a playground. Ralph noticed that a little boy was having trouble getting his shoe tied. He said, "Could I help you tie that?" The boy nodded. Ralph tied his shoe and smiled at him and said, "There you go!"

The boy said, "Thanks."

A. kindness,
or
B. selfishness?

233. Some kids got to school. They found out that their regular teacher was sick. They had a substitute teacher. They thought to themselves, "Good. We can get away with anything we want, today."

At the beginning of the school day, the kids were talking to each other. The substitute teacher said, "May I have your attention, please?"

The kids went right on talking and ignored what she had said.

A. kindness,
or
B. selfishness?

234. Anne was invited over to Jane's house. They played for a while. They walked through the kitchen. Anne thought, "I am hungry." So she opened Jane's family's refrigerator and looked around for something good to eat. She found something that looked good and she started eating it.

A. kindness,
or
B. selfishness?

235. John was watching television. His great aunt came into the room. She said, "I seem to have lost my glasses. I wonder where I could have put them." John's great-aunt could not see very well without her glasses. That made it hard for her to find her glasses.

John kept watching his show. He thought, "I hope she doesn't speak any more. I don't want her to interrupt my show."

A. kindness,
or
B. selfishness?

236. Tara was sad. She said to Amanda, "My family is short on money. We're not going to be able to have a vacation this year."

Amanda said, "My family is going to have a great vacation. We're going to Yellowstone National Park. And we're going to get to see the Grand Canyon, too. I think the Grand Canyon is so awesome! I can't wait." And then Amanda talked some more about her fun plans.

A. kindness,
or
B. selfishness?

237. Greer was playing tennis. He was getting ready to make his next serve. He saw a ball bouncing over toward him. The ball had been hit by someone a couple of courts away from him. Greer thought, "That person would have to walk a long way to get the ball. But I can get it with only a few steps." So he took a few seconds and got the ball and threw it back to the person.

A. kindness,
or
B. selfishness?

238. Two kids were playing with toy people. One had a toy person say, "Hey, we need to go to the grocery store. Here we go!"

The second one said, "That's not a grocery store; that's a light house."

A. kindness,
or
B. selfishness?

239. Someone used the bathroom in her house. She used the last bit of toilet paper. She thought, "When the next person comes in here, I don't want them to be without toilet paper." So she went to a cabinet, got a new roll of toilet paper and put it on the rack.

A. kindness,
or
B. selfishness?

240. Someone got a drink of water. When he had finished the water, he left the glass on the floor in the living room of his house. The place he left it was where someone else in the family was likely to knock it over and break it, if someone didn't pick it up and put it away.

A. kindness,
or
B. selfishness?

241. A man shared a car with his wife. He was driving the car home at night. His wife planned to drive it to work the next morning. The gas tank was nearly empty. He thought, "I wonder if I will have enough gas to get home?" When he made it home, he thought, "That was lucky that I had enough gas to get home. The gas gauge is right on empty." Then he did not give it another thought.

A. kindness,
or
B. selfishness?

242. A girl came home and took off her coat. She started to leave it on the stairs. But then she thought to herself, "If I leave it there, it will clutter up the place for the other people in the family. People could trip on it as they walk on the stairs." So she hung it up in the closet instead.

A. kindness,
or
B. selfishness?

243. A kid built something out of Legos. He was very proud of what he had built. He ran to show his brother. He said, "Look what I built!"

His brother looked at it and said, "I built one three times bigger and better than that one."

A. kindness,
or
B. selfishness?

244. Zack was in kindergarten. He had learned to read really well. He could read hundreds of words. One day his friend Joe came up to him looking very proud. Joe said, "Guess what! I can read five different words!"

Zack smiled at Joe. He said, "Hey, that's good! Congratulations, Joe!" Zack did not talk about how many more words he could read.

A. kindness,
or
B. selfishness?

245. Judy asked Betsy to go swimming with her. Judy knew how to swim very well. But Betsy did not know how to swim well enough to go into the deep water. Betsy said, "Go ahead to the deep water if you want to, Judy. I'll stay here."

Judy said, "No, that's OK. I'll stay here with you. I'll enjoy being here with you more than I'd enjoy being in the deep water."

A. kindness,
or
B. selfishness?

246. Three people were together. One of them whispered something in the second one's ear. The second one whispered back to the first in the same way. The third felt left out.

A. kindness,
or

B. selfishness?

247. Some people were having a party. A two-year-old boy picked up a paper clip. He was playing with the paper clip near an electrical outlet. A ten-year-old boy saw what was happening. He thought, "I'm going to go into a different room. If that little kid gets hurt, I don't want to be blamed for it."

A. kindness,
or
B. selfishness?

248. A boy and his mom and dad were asked to eat supper with another family. At supper time, the boy was given a plate with a few different types of food on it. He called out to his mother, "Mommy, I don't like this food. I don't have to eat it, do I?"

A. kindness,
or
B. selfishness?

249. A girl had a new toy. She was proud of it. She showed it to a boy. The boy said, "That's the old version. I have the new version. It's ten times better than that."

A. kindness,
or
B. selfishness?

250. Tom and Ben sat next to each other on the bus. They were riding home from

school. Tom was proud. He said, "Guess what? I got an A on a test! I got 96 per cent right!"

Ben had gotten 100 per cent right on the same test. But Ben did not mention this. He just said, "Congratulations, Tom! It feels great to get an A, doesn't it?"

A. kindness,
or
B. selfishness?

251. Rachel had been playing at Mary's house. When Rachel's mom came to pick her up, Rachel said to Mary and her mom, "Thanks for having me over. I had a good time."

A. kindness,
or
B. selfishness?

252. Ted's group took a hike along a trail through the woods. A boy named George was not in good shape. He could not walk as fast as the other boys. Ted noticed that George was getting left behind. Ted did not want George to feel left out. So Ted slowed down and walked with George. They talked with each other a lot along the way.

A. kindness,
or
B. selfishness?

253. Mack was in the hospital. Mack was almost well. Another boy moved into the room with Mack. This boy felt very sick. He hurt very badly. He was tired.

Mack turned on the TV. A basketball game came on. Mack watched it. When the team that Mack liked did well, Mack clapped and cheered loudly. When that team did badly, Mack shouted out how angry he was.

A. kindness,
or
B. selfishness?

254. A man had a dog that shed lots of hair. The man got dog hair all over his clothes. He went to a friend's house. When he was about to leave, he noticed that he had gotten dog hair all over the chair where he had been sitting. As he left, he thought to himself, "Well, that's one way of getting some of the dog hair off myself."

A. kindness,
or
B. selfishness?

255. A boy had some toy animals. They did not break easily. If they got dirty, they could be washed off easily. The boy was working on his homework. His younger sister said, "May I please play with your toy animals?"

The boy said, "No, you can't. They're mine."

A. kindness,
or

B. selfishness?

256. A man went to play paintball. He got lots of dirt and mud on his shoes and clothes. Playing the game made him tired. When he got home, he thought, "I don't feel like taking off these clothes. If I get things muddy, my wife can clean it up." He went to the couch and took a rest.

A. kindness,
or
B. selfishness?

257. A man was in a car. He was drinking some soda he had gotten from a fast food place. When he finished, he thought, "I don't want to clutter up this car." So he threw the cup out the window.

A. kindness,
or
B. selfishness?

258. A man got a present. After he unwrapped it, he left the wrapping paper on the floor. He thought to himself, "My wife will throw the wrapping paper away sooner or later."

A. kindness,
or
B. selfishness?

259. A girl got a snack. When she finished, she left her glass and her plate on the kitchen table. She thought, "It's my mom's job to clean this up."

A. kindness,
or
B. selfishness?

260. A man came home from work. He was tired. As soon as he walked in the door, his wife started talking to him about something that was on her mind. She did not stop talking to hear what he had to say. She kept talking for twenty minutes without stopping to let him say anything back to her about what she had said. She did this every day.

A. kindness,
or
B. selfishness?

261. A woman spent all day taking care of her young children at home. When her husband came home from work, she wanted to chat with him. She told him some of her thoughts and stopped to let him say something back. He didn't answer. He hadn't even listened. She asked him how his day had gone. He said, "OK," without looking at her. He just turned on the TV and started watching it. He did this every day.

A. kindness,
or
B. selfishness?

262. Sara went to play with Jill. They got out many toys. They played with

them all over the floor. Sara was about to leave. Sara said, "Before I leave, may I help you put these toys away, or do you want to leave them out?"

Jill decided that she would not play with them after Sara left. So Jill said, "I think it's time to put them away. Thank you, Sara." And they put them away together.

A. kindness,
or
B. selfishness?

263. At school, a girl was reading out loud. She could not read as well as most of the other kids in her class. She tried to read "electric eel," but instead she said, "electric seal."

A boy in the class figured this was his chance to make people laugh. So he said, "I'm an electric seal!" He clapped his hands together and went "Arf! Arf! Skkkk!" sounding like a seal bark and an electric spark. People laughed at him.

A. kindness,
or
B. selfishness?

264. Lunk went to play with Jake. When Lunk came in, Jake said, "Hi! How have you been doing?"

Lunk didn't feel like answering. So he didn't say anything. He looked around for interesting things in the house.

A. kindness,
or
B. selfishness?

265. Two people were playing with puppets together. It was time for them to finish. The person who owned the puppets said, "Would you like to help me put them back in the box?" The other person said nothing. He looked around at other things in the room while the owner put the puppets back in the box and put the box back on a shelf.

A. kindness,
or
B. selfishness?

266. Jean went to a playground with her friend Alice. Jean saw a group of her friends. Alice did not know these friends. Jean got the urge to run off and play with the group and let Alice fend for herself. But then she thought, "I want to make sure that Alice does not feel left out." So she went around to her friends and said, "I want you to meet my friend Alice." Jean made sure that she stuck by Alice so that Alice would have someone to play with.

A. kindness,
or
B. selfishness?

267. A girl and her mom went to visit a woman. The woman said to the girl, "I forget. What grade of school are you in now?" The girl did not feel like talking

about this. She preferred to play with
the woman's kids' toys. So the girl said
nothing to the woman. She just played
with the toys.

A. kindness,
or
B. selfishness?

Entitlement

268. Entitlement is the feeling that you deserve to have someone else do something for you. Sometimes people feel "too much entitlement." This means they expect too much from other people. Feeling too much entitlement sometimes makes people act spoiled. They think that people should do just what they want.

Sometimes people feel "too little entitlement." This means they expect too little from the other person. Sometimes people have "reasonable expectations." This means they expect something that is fair and just.

The stories that come next let you practice thinking about how much to expect of other people.

Too much entitlement means

A. expecting too much,
or
B. expecting too little?

269. When you make joint decisions with other people, it is very good to know what's reasonable. If each person expects too much from the other, the two people will not be able to agree well on some option. But if both people know how much to give and how much to take, they will be more able to decide on something that suits both of them.

Having reasonable expectations is really useful for the skill of

A. conservation,
or
B. good decisions?

270. A boy was at a restaurant. He wanted some ketchup. The waitress walked by. She carried a big tray full of food. The boy said, "Excuse me" to the waitress. He wanted her to stop and listen to him tell her that he wanted more ketchup.

She said, "I'll be with you in a moment." She went to the other table. She put the heavy tray down.

The boy felt angry. He thought, "She should have just stopped for a second and listened to what I wanted! I'm going to leave a very small tip."

The boy had

A. too much entitlement,
or
B. reasonable expectations?

271. A man got drunk a lot. He sometimes beat up his wife. He hurt her badly. People said to his wife, "If I were you, I'd leave him and not come back. Or, at least, you should not come back until he has done something to change himself."

The wife answered them by singing a song. The song went, "As long as he needs me, I know where I must be." She thought, "It's my duty to give him what

98

he needs. I can't expect him to be anything that he's not."

The wife had

A. reasonable expectations,
or
B. too little entitlement?

272. A man was playing with his one-year-old daughter and his three-year-old son in his driveway. A couple of boys from next door started riding their bikes into his driveway and back out again. Each time, they came fairly close to the one-year-old girl. The man said to them, "Could you please not ride in our driveway right now?

The boys said to each other, "It's not fair. We're not hurting anyone. We didn't do anyone any harm."

The boys had

A. reasonable expectations,
or
B. too much entitlement?

273. A man bought a musical instrument called an omnichord. The woman at the store said, "If anything goes wrong, bring it back within ninety days. If you bring it in by that time, it can be fixed for free."

Right away, the man noticed something wrong with it. It made strange noises when it was set a certain way. But the man did not take it back. A year later, he got around to taking it back. He said, "I know the ninety days

were up a long time ago. But it didn't work right from the start."

The woman at the store said, "I'm sorry. Once the ninety days are up, you have to pay for the repair." The man thought this was very unfair. He thought that they should fix it for free.

The man had

A. reasonable expectations,
or
B. too much entitlement?

274. A mom had a ten-year-old son. She said to him, "You're old enough now to do your own laundry. I'm going to show you how to do it. From now on, you can do it for yourself. This will be one way that you can help in the family."

The boy said, "That's unfair. None of my friends has to do his own laundry."

The boy had

A. reasonable expectations,
or
B. too much entitlement?

275. A girl's mom took the girl swimming. They were there for two hours. Then the mom said, "It's time to get out now. We must leave."

The girl said, "No, not right now. Give me just ten more minutes."

The mom said, "No, we have to leave now."

The girl said, "OK, five minutes."

The mom said, "No."

The girl said, "You're being unfair. I was willing to give in a little and compromise, but you were not."

The girl had

A. reasonable expectations,

or

B. too much entitlement?

276. A girl's mom left to go on trips very often. The girl stayed with her aunt and uncle at those times. One time the mom went for a trip to the beach. The mom was gone for two weeks. At the end of the time, the mom came to get the girl. The girl hugged her aunt and uncle. She looked sad and said, "I'll miss you."

The girl and her mom walked out the door.

The mom was angry at the girl. The mom said, "You should not have acted sad. I'm your mom. You should be happy to come with me. You will get punished."

The mom had

A. reasonable expectations,

or

B. too much entitlement?

277. Sal went to visit Ann. Sal was hot. Sal asked, "Do you mind if I open a window or turn the heat down? I'm a little hot."

Ann said, "I'm sorry. I have to keep it warm here. My grandmom who lives here gets very uncomfortable when it's

cooler. And the windows in this apartment don't open."

Sal said, "I see. I'll just put up with it, then."

Sal had

A. reasonable expectations,

or

B. too little entitlement?

278. A ten-year-old boy went to work with a tutor for an hour each week. After the first fifteen minutes, the boy said, "Now we've done what you want to do. Now I should be able to play a video game."

The tutor said, "Playing video games doesn't help us reach our goals."

The boy said, "That's not fair."

The boy had

A. reasonable expectations,

or

B. too much entitlement?

279. A girl had a favorite toy. One Sunday, when her dad didn't have to go to work, he said, "Do you want to go to my office? We can talk and play there." They had a good time. They went home. When they were back at the house, the girl said, "Oh no! I left my toy at your office!"

The dad said, "No problem. I'll bring it back home tomorrow after work."

The girl said, "No, I want it now. Please drive over and get it."

The dad said, "I don't want to take the time to do that now. You'll be fine without it for one day." The girl thought this was very unfair. She sulked, and she looked very angry.

The girl had

A. reasonable expectations,
or
B. too much entitlement?

280. Todd bought a tablet of paper. He stored it at school in the rack under his desk. Lunk sat behind Todd. Lunk ran out of paper. Lunk reached into Todd's rack and took some paper from the tablet. He did not bother to ask Todd if it was OK.

This went on for a week or two. Todd thought, "Oh, well, it's just a little paper. I guess I don't have the right to gripe."

Todd had

A. reasonable expectations,
or
B. too little entitlement?

281. A woman was in the hospital. Two doctors came into her room. The older doctor was talking to the younger one. They hardly spoke to the woman. They started to put a tube down the woman's nose. The woman said, "Hey, wait a minute. Before you just stick a tube down me, aren't you going to tell me what's going on?"

The doctors looked angry. They said, "We don't have much time."

The woman had

A. reasonable expectations,
or
B. too much entitlement?

282. A boy checked out a book from the library. He dropped it into a mud puddle. It was ruined.

The woman at the library said, "All you have to do is to pay us the price of a new copy. We'll order it and put the codes and tags on it."

The boy said, "That's not fair. The book had been used a little bit. A new book will be better. Plus, I didn't drop it in the puddle on purpose. It was an accident."

The boy had

A. reasonable expectations,
or
B. too much entitlement?

283. A dad was taking care of his four-year-old girl. He watched a sports game on TV. Then he went to his computer and surfed the Internet. Then he talked to a friend of his on the phone for a long time. He did things like this all day long. He did not talk or play with his daughter at all.

His daughter thought, "I don't like this. I wish he would play with me or do something with me, at least a little bit."

The dad thought, "She should be able to entertain herself."

The dad had

A. reasonable expectations,

or

B. too much entitlement?

284. A boy got some soup and corn and beans for supper. He did not eat much of them. For dessert he got a little ice cream. He asked for some more ice cream. His mom said no. He said, "But I'm still hungry."

She said, "If you're still hungry, you can eat more of the soup, corn and beans you didn't eat for supper."

The boy said, "That's not fair."

The mom had

A. reasonable expectations,

or

B. too much entitlement?

285. A boy had a friend over to play. A friend named Lars called up. Lars wanted to come and play. The boy wanted to keep playing with the friend who was already at his house. He wanted just the two of them to be together.

The boy said to Lars, "Today isn't a good day. How about tomorrow?"

Lars said, "Why can't I come over today?"

The boy said, "I have another friend here today."

Lars said, "Well, I have just as much right to come over today as he does, don't I?"

Lars had

A. reasonable expectations,

or

B. too much entitlement?

286. Jane had Ashley over to visit. They got some cereal to eat. Jane said to Ashley, "What kind of cereal would you like?" Ashley picked one. Jane gave it to her.

They poured milk on it. After Ashley had eaten a few bites, she said, "I changed my mind. I had this cereal yesterday. I'd like to throw this out and get a different kind."

Ashley had

A. reasonable expectations,

or

B. too much entitlement?

287. A woman started work for a company. When she was hired, her boss said, "You will get paid every two weeks." This was very important to her because she was almost out of money.

After she had been working for a week, a different boss said, "We've decided to pay you every month. You'll get your paycheck after three more weeks."

The woman was out of food. But she did not say anything to her boss. She thought, "I'm just lucky to have a job at all."

One of the her friends said, "What do you have to lose by asking for some pay ahead of time, for one time only?"

The woman said, "No, I don't want to look too pushy."

The woman had

A. reasonable expectations,

or

B. too little entitlement?

288. A doctor prescribed a drug for a man. The man called the drug store on the phone. He said, "I'd like you to get this drug ready for me now. That way I can pick it up without waiting."

The person at the drug store said, "I'm sorry. The way we do things is to get it ready once you are here. You'll have to wait about ten minutes at most."

The man said, "But I don't want to wait. I want to just walk in and pick it up right away."

The person at the drug store said, "We make sure people are here for a reason. Lots of people who call on the phone do not show up. If we get the drug ready and someone does not show up, we lose a lot of time and money."

The man said, "That's stupid. You should know that I'm going to show up. I'm telling you right now that I'll be over in half an hour."

The pharmacist had

A. reasonable expectations,

or

B. too much entitlement?

289. Sam was driving his car. Sam drove at the speed limit. The speed limit was fifty-five miles an hour. But no one else seemed to go that speed. Most cars were going at least seventy miles an hour. Mick got behind Sam. Mick could not change lanes right away, because

too many other cars were coming. Mick thought that Sam should speed up. He shook his fist at Sam and yelled at him.

Sam thought, "If you want to go over the speed limit, that's up to you. But I don't feel a need to speed up. And I don't feel a need to pull off the road to get out of your way."

Sam had

A. reasonable expectations,

or

B. too much entitlement?

290. Kids were playing on a playground at school. It was a hot day. There was only one water faucet at this school. Kids were waiting in line to get water to drink.

A girl cut her foot. The teacher took the girl to the head of the line, in front of the children who had been waiting. The teacher got some water to wash off the girl's cut.

A kid in line said, "That girl should wait her turn like the rest of us have to. We were here first. This isn't fair."

The teacher had

A. reasonable expectations,

or

B. too much entitlement?

291. Kate went to a birthday party. She played games. She got some cake and ice cream to eat. She had a good time. As she left, she thought to herself, "Hey! Usually I get a bag of party favors with candy or little toys in them.

I didn't get that this time. That's no fair!"

    Kate had

A. reasonable expectations,

or

B. too much entitlement?

292. Mrs. Brown was in her front yard. She was playing with her daughter Susie. A girl from down the street was walking by. She picked Susie up. Mrs. Brown said, "Please don't pick her up." The girl from down the street thought, "I should be able to pick her up. I'm not hurting her. I won't drop her."

    Mrs. Brown had

A. reasonable expectations,

or

B. too much entitlement?

293. Lana went out to eat. The host at the door said, "Would you like the smoking or the nonsmoking section?" Lana asked for the nonsmoking section. The host took Lana to a seat next to the smoking section. Someone about two feet away from her was smoking. Lana said, "Could I please have a seat farther from the smoking section?"

    The host thought, "These nonsmokers think they own the place."

    Lana had

A. reasonable expectations,

or

B. too much entitlement?

294. A man called a doctor's office to make an appointment to see a doctor. The person he talked to said that he should come at two o'clock. The man got there a little before two o'clock.

    At five minutes after two, the man went to the lady at the front desk. He said, "I was told to come at two. I should be seen at two. My time is worth just as much as the doctor's time."

    The lady said, "I'm sorry. Some very sick people came in. The doctor is a little behind."

    The man said, "I don't care who came in. A promise is a promise."

    The man had

A. reasonable expectations,

or

B. too much entitlement?

Guessing the Feeling

295. The stories that come next ask you to guess how someone is feeling – what emotion the person is having. The list below is a list of "feeling words." This list tells some of the ways the people in the stories might be feeling:

Angry (Mad, Irritated)
Scared (Frightened, Afraid, Fearful)
Sad
Guilty
Ashamed or Embarrassed
Disappointed
Bored
Jealous
Impatient
Lonely
Worried
Discouraged
Tired

Admiring
Calm
Determined
Happy (Joyful, Glad)
Proud
Patient
Grateful
Relieved
Confident
Interested
Liking or Loving
Compassionate
Fun
Energetic

The words in this list are words for

A. thoughts,
or
B. emotions?

296. You'll notice something in these stories. If you want to guess the feeling, you will need to know what the person thinks about what is going on. Two people can have the same thing happen to them, and they can feel two very different feelings. How you feel about something depends on what you think about it.

A girl ate supper. Her mom said, "You can have some ice cream for dessert."

The girl said, "Could I have chocolate sauce on it, please?"

The mom said, "I'm sorry; we have no chocolate sauce."

The girl thought, "No problem! I'm just happy that I get some ice cream! I love it!"

This girl felt

A. happy,
or
B. worried?

297. Another girl had the same thing happen. Her mom said, "I'm sorry, we have no chocolate sauce."

This girl thought, "That bad mommy of mine! She should have gotten some at the store! It's all her fault!"

This girl felt

A. lonely,

or

B. angry?

298. Some parents took their kids to a water slide. One parent thought, "Yahoo! This looks really neat! I want to do it too!"

This parent was

A. having fun,

or

B. feeling sad?

299. Another parent went to the same water slide. This parent thought, "Those guard rails don't look high enough. I think someone could fall off. I don't think this place is safe."

This parent was

A. feeling angry,

or

B. feeling worried?

300. You feel guilty when you feel bad about doing something wrong. You feel ashamed or embarrassed when you think other people have seen you do something stupid or bad. You feel impatient when you have to wait for something, and you don't like waiting.

A little boy was waiting in line at a park. He wanted to go on a ride. He

thought, "I wish this line would hurry up! I feel like I've been standing here all day! This is no fun."

He felt

A. ashamed,

or

B. impatient?

301. The little boy's mom was standing in line with him. She thought, "I blew it. I made a bad choice. My boy is too young to enjoy this place. I wasted a lot of money to get in here. I ruined his day, too."

She felt

A. guilty,

or

B. lonely?

302. A boy knocked a vase over. It broke. He thought, "I should have been more careful. By not being careful I broke something my mom liked a lot."

He felt

A. guilty,

or

B. impatient?

303. Someone went to a party. She spilled grape juice all over her lap. People laughed at her. She thought, "I wish no one could see me right now. I wish I could disappear."

She felt

A. embarrassed,

or

B. loving?

304. You feel admiring when you think, "Wow, that person did something really good."

Grateful is another word for thankful; feeling grateful is feeling like saying, "Thanks!"

Jon slipped while ice-skating. He was about to fall. His older friend, who was a very good skater, caught him by the arm and kept him from falling. Jon said, "I was about to get hurt, and you helped me! Thank you!"

Jon felt

A. grateful,

or

B. sad?

305. Then Jon said to his friend, "I can't believe how quick you are! Most people wouldn't have thought to catch me until I was flat on the ice!"

Jon felt

A. bored,

or

B. admiring?

306. Relieved means you're glad something bad didn't happen. Confident is feeling, "I can do it!"

A little girl got sick in the middle of the night. She had a very hard time breathing. Her father was a doctor. He knew what to do for her. After he did it, she was able to breathe easily. Her dad

thought, "I know what to do. I've studied this type of sickness very carefully."

He felt

A. admiring,

or

B. confident?

307. His wife had watched what happened with their little girl. She thought, "Thank goodness she's better! I was afraid she was going to die! Phew!"

She felt

A. relieved,

or

B. sad?

308. Interested means you feel the urge to pay attention to something – you're not bored by it. Compassionate is the way you feel when you get the urge to take care of someone or to protect or comfort someone.

Two students watched while a doctor did an operation. One of the students thought, "Isn't this something! I can see the big artery that goes right through our bellies! Wow!"

That student felt

A. bored,

or

B. interested?

309. The second student had different thoughts. She knew the person the

doctor was operating on. She thought, "This poor guy. He has had so much pain. I hope this helps him. I want to comfort him when he is in pain after this."

This student felt

A. compassionate,

or

B. guilty?

310. Two people saw a dog. One thought, "Oh no! It's a big dog. Maybe it's mean! I hope it doesn't kill me!"

This person felt

A. scared,

or

B. bored?

311. The second person saw the dog too. This person thought, "Aw, poor thing. He looks like he has no owner. Maybe he's hungry! I want to take him home and feed him and give him a bath."

This person felt

A. compassionate,

or

B. grateful?

312. Some people's house had a big window. A bird was flying. The bird must not have seen the big window. The bird rammed against the window, hard. The people in the house heard the noise. They looked outside. The bird was on the ground. It had knocked itself out. It

was not dead. The mom thought, "Oh, phew, I'm so glad that it wasn't killed. Now at least there's a chance it will live."

This mom felt

A. relieved,

or

B. interested?

313. When the dad saw that the bird had hurt himself, he thought, "It's our fault. We should have put some stickers or something on the window so the bird would have known not to fly into it. Our being lazy caused this bird to get hurt."

This dad felt

A. lonely,

or

B. guilty?

314. When the big sister saw the hurt bird, she thought to herself, "Aw. That poor thing. I want to help it. How can I take care of it?"

This sister felt

A. admiring,

or

B. compassionate?

315. They watched the bird. They made sure that the cat who belonged to the people next door did not eat it. After a while, the bird got better. It stood on its feet for a while. Then it flew away. The little brother said, "Aw. I was hoping

we could keep it for a pet. I'm sorry it's gone."

He felt

A. disappointed,
or
B. happy?

316. The dad thought, "How could my son be so selfish about this? He does not sound happy that the bird got well. He seemed to think only of himself. Maybe we are not raising him right. Maybe he is watching too much TV. Maybe he is not going to be a compassionate person."

He felt

A. proud,
or
B. worried?

317. A man went to his car. All over the windshield were little crystals. They looked like snowflakes. When the man saw them, he thought, "Wow! Aren't they pretty! Isn't it wonderful that nature makes such pretty things for our eyes to see!"

He felt

A. happy,
or
B. disappointed?

318. Then the same man reached into his car to get his scraper. He wanted to scrape the crystals off so that he could see to drive. He found that the scraper

was gone. He thought to himself, "I'll bet that wife of mine took it to use in her car. Why can't she ask me before she does things like that? She is sometimes so selfish!"

He felt

A. proud,
or
B. angry?

319. A girl and her younger sister were eating out with their mom and dad. An old woman walked past the table. As she passed, she looked at the younger sister and said, "Aren't you a pretty one!"

The older sister thought, "She's nice. I'm glad she said something that made my younger sister feel good."

She felt

A. grateful
or
B. relieved?

320. Another girl and her younger sister had just the same thing happen. This time, the older sister thought, "Why does my younger sister get this nice talk from that woman, when I get nothing? It's not fair!"

She felt

A. compassionate,
or
B. angry?

321. A person was about to give a speech to a large group. He looked at their faces. He thought, "I really know what I'm going to say. I have planned this very well. They are going to learn a lot from me."

He felt

A. confident
or
B. worried?

322. Another person was about to give a speech to a large group. He looked at their faces. He thought, "What if I mess up? They will think I'm stupid. I may not get a chance to give another speech. That will be awful."

He felt

A. impatient,
or
B. scared?

323. A person woke up in the middle of the night. He lay in bed. He did not go back to sleep. He thought, "Oh no. What if I don't go back to sleep? Maybe I won't be able to do anything right tomorrow. Maybe I'll be too tired for anything. That will be awful. Oh, I hope I get back to sleep!"

He felt

A. scared,
or
B. confident?

324. Another person woke up in the middle of the night. He also did not go back to sleep. He thought, "Hooray! I have some time to get some work done. I'll work on that story that I have been trying to find time to write." Then he got up and did the work. After he had done it, he thought, "Hooray for me! I used the time to do something good!"

He felt

A. proud,
or
B. compassionate?

325. A man listened to a friend. The friend told about something very sad that had happened to him. The friend sometimes was so sad that he stopped talking. He just stared into space for a while. Then he would say something else.

The man who was listening thought, "Why don't you just come on out and say it? Why do you have to wait so long in between saying things?"

He felt

A. sad,
or
B. impatient?

326. Another man had just the same thing happen. This man thought, "He's staring off into space a lot and not speaking. I think that's because he feels so sad. I feel sorry for him. I'd like to be able to help him. Maybe I can do that by being a good listener to him."

He felt

A. compassionate,
or
B. grateful?

327. A woman was going to get into a car with a man she worked with. The man walked to her side of the car and opened the door for her. She thought, "He probably just thinks I'm a weak woman. He thinks I can't even open the door for myself. But I can open it without the help of you or any other man."
   She felt

A. angry,
or
B. bored?

328. Another woman had just the same thing happen. She thought to herself, "How nice that he is being polite. I'm glad he is not just wrapped up in himself. He did something thoughtful for me."
   She felt

A. compassionate,
or
B. grateful?

329. A teacher said, "Here is your math homework for tonight. It is lots of problems. We have not been working very much lately. We need to catch up."
   One student thought, "So many problems! I don't see how I can do

them all. Maybe I'll be up all night. Oh, my. What if I can't finish them?"
   This student felt

A. relieved,
or
B. worried?

330. Another student in the same class thought, "It's not our fault that we have not been working much lately. It's the teacher's job to keep up the pace of work. To give all this work at once is not right. The teacher is doing something wrong!"
   This student felt

A. angry,
or
B. admiring?

331. Another student in the same class thought, "OK, so it's time for me to get tough! If I work fast and stay on task, I should be able to finish these in an hour. I'm not going to whine. I can be strong and do it!"
   This student felt

A. compassionate,
or
B. confident?

332. A woman was at home. She did not have any plans for the day. She thought, "I wish I were with someone. But here I am, all by myself."
   The woman felt

A. loving,

or

B. lonely?

333. Another woman was at home too, with no plans for the day. She thought, "Ah. I have a chance to rest today. No big jobs are pressing on me today. I can read a book if I want. I can take a quiet walk. How nice it is to have some time off."

This woman felt

A. calm,

or

B. impatient?

334. Someone played his first game of chess, against a computer. He got beat. He said to himself, "Oh! Why can't I do better? I'm so dumb! I should not have gotten beat! This game must not be for me."

This person felt

A. embarrassed and impatient,

or

B. admiring and scared?

335. Another person also played his first game of chess, against a computer. He also got beat. He said to himself, "I remembered how to move all the pieces! I'm beginning to catch on to how to play this! I've done something good by learning to play such a hard game! It will take lots of time to learn to play very well. No one can do that right away."

This person felt

A. ashamed and sad,

or

B. proud and patient?

336. A student worked with a math tutor. The tutor said, "We need to do more practice on the math facts. I want you to be able to add and subtract and multiply and divide very fast. It's not enough to be able to get the right answer. I have a goal that you will be able to say the right answer within two seconds. We will practice 400 facts each day."

The student thought, "Oh, no. This will not be fun. My tutor should be doing fun things with me. My tutor should not get me to do things I don't feel like doing."

This student felt

A. angry,

or

B. admiring?

337. Another student had the same thing happen. This student thought, "This tutor is doing his job. There are other things that we could do that he would surely enjoy more himself. But he is getting us to do the tough stuff. If I get faster, all the math I do from now on will go faster. I have a good tutor."

This student felt

A. grateful,

or

B. lonely?

338. The word *determined* means that you feel a strong wish to reach your goal. The word *discouraged* means that you feel like giving up on your goal.

A girl started in a new school. This school was harder than the one she had been in before. She was working to get good grades. She got her first test back. She got a C on it. Other people she knew in the class got A's. She thought to herself, "I guess I'm just not smart enough to make it in this school. I don't know what I'm going to do. I should never have come here."

She felt

A. discouraged,
or
B. determined?

339. Another girl had the same thing happen. She thought to herself, "At least I passed this test! I'm on my way. I'll have to work even harder. I want to see an A soon. Maybe I can do it on the test coming up tomorrow!"

She felt

Λ. discouraged,
or
B. determined?

340. A young woman started on her first job. She did not know where she could find something she needed. She asked another worker. The other worker did not know it was her first day at work. The other worker was in a bad mood. She said, "I've got enough work to do for myself, without telling you things."

The young woman thought to herself, "I can tell this job isn't going to work out. I feel like going home."

She felt

A. discouraged,
or
B. jealous?

341. Another young woman had the same thing happen. This woman thought to herself, "Hey, it takes more than one rude person to get me down. I'm going to make this job a success. If she won't tell me where this thing is, I'll just ask someone else."

She felt

A. grateful,
or
B. determined?

342. A boy was starting to learn to play tennis. Someone threw a ball to him. He swung the racket. He missed the ball. He tried again. This time he hit the ball into the net. He tried again. He hit the ball into the net again.

He said to himself, "I can tell I'm not cut out for this game. I'll never be any good at it."

He felt

A. discouraged,
or

B. confident?

343. Another boy had the same thing happen. This boy said to himself, "Hooray! At least I'm able to hit the ball. As I practice more and more, I'll be more able to hit the ball where I aim it. I'm going to keep working!"
He felt

A. guilty,
or
B. determined?

344. A teenaged boy wanted to invite a girl to go to a dance with him. He called her on the phone to ask her.

As he spoke with her, he thought to himself, "I'm sure I sound silly to her. If she says no, it will mean she thinks I'm a dumb person. People will laugh at me that I asked her. People will all think I'm dumb."
He felt

A. embarrassed,
or
B. admiring?

345. Another teenaged boy also called a girl on the phone to ask her to go to the dance.

He thought to himself, "If she says yes, it will be fun to go with her. If she says no, then at least she may feel good that I wanted her to go with me. Either way, it will be fine."
He felt

A. calm,
or
B. angry?

346. A boy lay in bed. He had not gotten to sleep yet. He thought, "What if some bad man comes into my house? What if he has a gun? Could he break the window?"
He felt

A. bored,
or
B. scared?

347. Another boy lay in bed. He had not gotten to sleep yet either. He thought, "This is a great time to have a nice fantasy. I can see it in my mind. I am swimming in a nice cool pool of water, in a river that flows through the hills. There are woods all around. The water is so clean that I could drink it. My best friend is with me. We have a nice lunch that is ready to eat when we get done."
He felt

A. sad,
or
B. calm?

348. Alana went over to Jean's house. Jean said, "Come on, Alana! Please listen to my little sister play the piano! She has learned her first song!"

Jean's little sister played a very simple song. Alana thought, "She can't play well. This isn't good music. They should not waste my time on this. Why did I have to listen to this?"

Alana felt

A. angry,
or
B. guilty?

349. Another girl named Betsy went to Jean's house. Jean's little sister played the same song for Betsy.

Betsy thought, "Wow, this is really neat. I have to hand it to that little girl. She is not scared to show what she can do! It looks like she has been working hard, too! I'll bet before long she's going to be playing all sorts of other songs!" And Betsy said those things out loud.

Betsy felt

A. lonely,
or
B. admiring?

350. The word *jealous* means that you have seen something good happen to someone else, and you feel bad that it didn't happen to you instead. You feel bad about someone else's getting what you wanted.

Cindy went with her mom and dad to watch her sister Ann compete in a spelling bee. Ann won first place! Cindy thought, "Hooray for my sister! She worked hard, and it paid off! She is bringing honor to our family!"

Cindy felt

A. jealous,
or
B. admiring?

351. Mandy went with her family to watch her sister in a spelling bee. Her sister won first place, too. Mandy thought, "Why does she have to get all the praise? Why can't people clap for me? I deserve to be in the spotlight instead of her."

Mandy felt

A. jealous,
or
B. worried?

352. A teenaged girl looked at her room. There were things all over the place. She could not find anything. It was a mess.

The girl sighed. She thought, "This is hopeless. I can never get this stuff put in order. I would not know where to start."

She felt

A. discouraged,
or
B. angry?

353. Another teenaged girl looked at her room. It was a mess, too.

This girl thought, "All it takes to get this room in order is work. I can do it. It may not be fun, but it will pay off. I will be able to find things after I do it. I'm going to do it right now!"

She felt

A. grateful,

or

B. determined?

354. A boy heard his alarm clock go off. He was still very tired. He did not feel like getting out of bed. He said to himself, "I can move my muscles. I can start walking. I want to get my day started. I am using self-discipline!"

He felt

A. fun,

or

B. determined?

355. Another boy heard his alarm clock go off. He also was tired. He did not feel like getting out of bed. He said to himself, "I'm too tired to get up. I just can't do it. It's no use."

He felt

A. discouraged,

or

B. jealous?

356. A boy was home. He did not have anything to do. He thought, "Yay! I have some free time! I can read the book I started a few days ago! Or I can work on the story I started writing! It's so nice to have free time!"

He felt

A. compassionate,

or

B. joyful?

357. Another boy was at home. He did not have anything to do. He thought, "What is there to do? I can't think of anything. This won't be fun."

He felt

A. bored,

or

B. impatient?

358. A girl sat down to do her science homework. It was about electricity. She thought, "Maybe I'll learn how the electric things in my house work! Maybe I'll learn what light switches do. Hey! I see something here about switches! I'm curious about what electricity really is. Maybe this will tell me. Let's see!"

She felt

A. interested,

or

B. compassionate?

359. Another girl sat down to do her science homework. It was about electricity. This girl thought, "How long, I wonder, will it be until I'm done with this? Maybe when I'm through I can call up a friend. I wish we didn't have so much to read. I don't care about electricity."

She felt

A. worried,

or

B. bored?

360. A boy was walking down the aisle of a bus to his seat. He stepped on someone's foot. He thought, "I should have been more careful. My carelessness led someone to get hurt a little."

He felt

A. guilty,

or

B. relieved?

361. Another boy had the same thing happen. He thought, "Why did that person have to have his foot out in the aisle? He should have known better!"

He felt

A. confident,

or

B. angry?

362. Another boy had the same thing happen. He thought, "Uh oh. It looks like the person whose foot I stepped on is a big and mean-looking man. And he looks angry. What's he going to do to me?"

He felt

A. impatient,

or

B. scared?

363. A teenaged boy was going out with some friends. His mom said, "Be sure to be back by eleven o'clock. And please call me when you get to the place you're going."

The boy thought, "She treats me like a baby. She should just mind her own business and let me live my own life."

He felt

A. angry,

or

B. worried?

364. Another teenaged boy was going out with his friends, and his mom said the same things. This boy thought, "It sounds like she is worried about me. It must be hard to be a mom and to worry about whether your son is safe. I feel sorry for her when she feels bad. I want to keep her from worrying as much as I can."

He felt

A. proud,

or

B. compassionate?

365. A man bought a kit to make a bookcase. Some words printed on the box said, "You put it together yourself. It's so easy!"

The man got his tools and worked on the bookcase. He found out that it was very hard to put the bookcase together. Things did not fit unless you lined them up just right. And, if you got something wrong, you had to take things apart and start over.

The man got something wrong. He saw that he would have to take things apart again.

He thought, "I hate this stupid bookcase! What a piece of junk!"

He felt

A. angry,

or

B. jealous?

366. Another man had the same thing happen. But this man thought to himself, "OK. I think I see what I did wrong. I think I'll be able to get it right next time. Let me make a careful plan. I'll take my time and make it work this time."

He felt

A. grateful,

or

B. patient?

367. A boy played in a tennis match. Lots of people were watching. The boy swung at the ball. He missed it. He lost the point.

He waited for the other boy to serve the ball to him for the next point. As he waited, he thought, "Everyone saw me miss that. I looked like a klutz. I'll bet people laughed at me."

He felt

A. embarrassed,

or

B. proud?

368. Another boy played in a tennis match. He had the same thing happen.

He waited for the other boy to serve the ball to him for the next point. As he waited, he told himself, "Watch the ball. Move quickly. Aim it. I want to win this point."

He felt

A. interested,

or

B. determined?

369. A girl loved her dad very much. Her dad got a bad type of cancer. He said to her, "I will probably die before long. I don't fear dying very much. Everyone does that. But what I mind is that I won't be able to do all I can to make sure you are happy. Will you do something for me? Will you use your head, and do the things that make you lead a good and happy life?"

The girl said, "Yes." She cried some. A few weeks later, her dad died. The girl was very sad.

A few days later, the girl thought, "I can't ever be happy without my dad. I don't see how I can go on."

She felt

A. discouraged,

or

B. angry?

370. A few weeks later, the same girl thought, "My dad's wish was that I lead a good and happy life. I want to do it for him. I want to do it for myself, too. It will not be easy. But I want it. And I can do it."

She felt

A. glad,
or
B. determined?

371. The word *energetic* means that you
have lots of energy; you are not tired.
A man had a lot of work to do. He had
to write reports and fill out forms. He
sat down and did the work. It took a
very long time. But the man finished the
work.

He said to himself, "I'm drained. I
worked so hard. I don't have any energy
left."

He felt

A. tired,
or
B. worried?

372. Another man did the same thing.
He finished the work too.

He said to himself, "Hooray! I
finished! I did what I set out to do! I
want to celebrate!"

He felt

A. lonely,
or
B. energetic?

Danger, Fear and Ways of Reducing Unrealistic Fear

373. This section asks you to think about danger. When you feel scared, it's good to figure out if you are really in danger. If you are in danger, you will want to try to protect yourself. If you are not in danger, you will want to try to get over feeling scared.

The more likely it is that something really bad will happen to you, the more danger you're in.

One of the ways to get over fear, when you are not in danger, is to remind yourself that you are not in danger.

Someone lived in a country where there was war. A bomb hit the house next door. The house was blown up. The person felt very scared.

A. much danger,
or
B. not much danger?

374. Someone was away from home. He was scared of what he would find when he got back. He was scared that his house would be broken into. He was scared that a bad person would have stolen things.

In the neighborhood where he lived, people's houses almost never got broken into. He had lived in this house for many years. He had been out many times. No break-ins had ever happened.

A. danger,
or

B. not much danger?

375. Jake signed up to fight in a boxing match. He was not good at boxing. The man he was supposed to fight had knocked out the last ten men he had fought. Jake felt scared.

A. danger,
or
B. not much danger?

376. Someone was in a car. The driver was going very fast, far over the speed limit. The tires were screeching. The car was just missing running into other cars. They scraped against a telephone pole.

A. danger,
or
B. not much danger?

377. Someone walked by a building. The building was fairly new. It looked like it had been made well. The person felt scared that the building would fall over on him.

A. danger,
or
B. not much danger?

378. Someone felt scared that at least one person in his school would have a birthday party and not invite him to it.

He said, "I'm almost sure this is really going to happen!"

A. danger,
or
B. not much danger?

379. A boy was out in the woods. Several hunters were shooting their guns a lot. They were shooting at deer. They had a lot of beer with them. They had drunk a lot of it. Some of the hunters were so drunk they could not even walk straight. The boy felt scared that he might get hit by a bullet.

A. danger,
or
B. not much danger?

380. A man hurt his back. His doctor warned him, "Don't try to lift heavy things for a while. If you do, you'll make your back worse." His doctor knew this, and he was right.

Someone said to him, "Can you help me move my piano?"

The man said, "Sure, I'll help you." But then he remembered his back. He felt scared that he would hurt his back again.

If he were to lift the piano there would be

A. danger,
or
B. not much danger?

381. Let's talk about two types of danger. Danger of getting hurt or killed is physical danger. Danger of losing friends or of having people think you are bad is social danger.

A boy was to give a speech in front of his whole school. He had forgotten to get his speech ready. He didn't have anything to say. He felt scared.

A. physical danger,
or
B. social danger?

382. Four or five of a boy's best friends said to him, "We dare you to jump off that bridge into the river. We'll all think you're a coward if you don't do it. We won't like you any more unless you do."

The boy started to do it. But then he looked down. He saw how far it was to the water. He wondered whether the water had rocks or big logs just under the surface. He was scared that his friends would not like him, but he was more scared of getting hurt or killed.

The chance that his friends would not like him was

A. physical danger,
or
B. social danger?

383. A girl was about to play in a basketball game. She thought, "What if I make a mistake? What if I miss a really important shot? Maybe people won't like me as much."

She was thinking about

A. physical danger,
or
B. social danger?

384. If you're in danger, try to protect yourself. This is especially true if you're in physical danger. What if you're not in danger, but you still feel scared? In that case, it's good to try to get used to whatever is scary. You do this by staying in the scary situation for a long time. That way you can get used to it.

A person was on a golf course. He was on a high hill. It started to rain. Lightning started to strike. He knew that lightning had struck the golf course before.

Should the man

A. protect himself,
or
B. try to get used to it?

385. A girl had done her homework well. She knew the lesson well. But she was afraid her teacher would ask her a question, and she would miss it. She felt very large fear.

Should she

A. protect herself,
or
B. try to get used to it?

386. A girl lived near people who had a big dog. The dog was also fierce and

mean. The girl walked along the street. The big dog came running toward her, growling and showing his teeth. She was scared.

Should she

A. protect herself,
or
B. try to get used to it?

387. Another girl had a fear of dogs. This girl had a friend who had a lazy and cute little cocker spaniel dog. This dog was nice. He had never bitten or growled in his life. When the girl saw the dog, she was scared.

Should the girl

A. protect herself,
or
B. try to get used to it?

388. A boy was watching TV. All of a sudden he remembered that a science project was due the next day. He had not finished it yet. He knew he would be called upon to show it to everyone. He felt scared. He did not want to look silly in front of the class. He thought he might try to just get used to the idea of looking silly and not finish the project. Then he thought he might protect himself from this danger. He could do this by finishing the project. He could also practice giving a talk about it.

Is he worried about

A. physical danger,
or

B. social danger?

389. A woman had the chance to get a good job. She would enjoy the job very much. This job would pay her lots of money. It would let her do lots of good for the world. There was just one problem. For this job, she would have to ride in airplanes a lot. She was scared of riding on planes.

She looked up some facts about planes. She found that the chance of a flight having a crash was very, very small. She decided that she would be safe.

But she was still scared. She was partly scared the plane would crash. But she was mainly scared she would get scared during the flight and look foolish in front of the other people. She was scared that people would look at her and think, "She's got something wrong with her."

Worrying about looking foolish was worrying about

A. physical danger,
or
B. social danger?

390. A girl opened a jar of pineapples. She expected them to taste good. But instead they had a really yucky taste. The girl thought, "I'll bet these pineapples have spoiled." She felt scared to eat them.

Do you think she should

A. protect herself,

or
B. try to get used to it?

391. A woman was a scientist. She had found out some very interesting things. She was about to give a talk to some other scientists. She noticed that her heart was pounding and she was breathing fast. Her hands were sweating. She thought, "Looks like I'm nervous before giving this speech. This usually happens. I guess I'm afraid I won't do a good job, even though I know what I'm going to say and I have practiced well."

Do you think she should

A. protect herself (by not giving the speech),
or
B. try to get used to it?

392. A writer was about to sit down to write. He felt a little bit scared. He thought, "I guess I'm worried that what I write won't be good and that people won't like it. But if it isn't good, I can always change it later. I often feel this way before I write, but I get over it once I get started."
Do you think he should

A. protect himself (by not writing),
or
B. try to get used to it?

393. A woman saw some very pretty paintings. She had the urge to buy lots

of them for her home. But then she felt a little scared. She thought, "I'm worried that if I spend all this money on these paintings, I won't have enough for things like doctor bills and paying my rent and buying food. I don't have money saved up. When I figure it up, I really don't have enough money to buy these paintings."

Do you think she should

A. protect herself (by not buying the paintings),
or
B. try to get used to the worry?

394. A child was a very picky eater. Her mother said, "Why don't you try some of that corn? I think you might like it." The girl felt scared that she wouldn't like the corn. She worried that it would be very unpleasant to have something that tastes bad in her mouth. She also worried that then she would be embarrassed by having to spit it out in front of her mother.

Do you think she should

A. protect herself (by not trying the food),
or
B. try to get used to it?

395. A man was outside in very cold weather. He noticed his hands getting colder and colder. They got so cold that they hurt badly. The man began to feel scared.

Do you think he should

A. protect himself (by warming his hands somehow),
or
B. try to get used to it?

396. A girl was running in a cross-country race. She twisted her ankle, and she hurt it badly. She thought to herself, "I could tough out the pain and keep running. But I think I've sprained my ankle. If I ignore the pain and keep running, I could hurt it worse. I could have a lot more problems with it in the future if I do that." She decided to stop the race and not put her weight on that ankle. She went to the doctor, and the doctor put a cast on her ankle. He said, "I'm glad you stayed off it."

Did she

A. protect herself,
or
B. try to get used to the pain?

397. There are two main ways of protecting yourself from danger. One is to avoid the scary situation. The other is to work on the skills you need for the situation and to prepare for the situation.

A musician had a concert to give. He felt scared whenever he thought about it. He protected himself by not thinking about music. He shoved it out of his mind and watched TV instead. On the day of the concert, he got so scared that he had to call it off.

Was he

A. protecting himself by avoiding a scary situation,

or

B. working on the skills he needed?

398. Another musician also had a concert to give. He felt scared whenever he thought about it. He protected himself by practicing. He practiced the music he would play, over and over. He played it very slowly. He played it faster. He practiced concentrating on playing it, even when there were distractions. He played a recording of different music and practiced playing his songs while ignoring this distraction. He imagined the audience. He imagined himself feeling relaxed while knowing the audience was listening to him play.

Was he

A. protecting himself by avoiding a scary situation,

or

B. working on the skills he needed?

399. A high-school girl had a test. When she thought about the test, she felt scared. She studied hard. She made up her own test. She practiced taking her own test. While she practiced, she imagined she was taking the real test. Then she graded her test. She went back and studied the questions that had been hard. She read her textbook and her notes and made up more questions. Then she practiced these, again

pretending she was taking the real test. She kept doing these things.

Was she

A. protecting herself by avoiding a scary situation,

or

B. working on the skills she needed?

400. A boy was very scared of throwing up at school. He was mainly worried that he would embarrass himself. He knew he could handle the physical pain of throwing up, even though it would not feel good.

He found some excuses not to go to school. He began to get more and more behind in his schoolwork. Then he also got scared of going to class when he was behind. He stayed away from school more and more. Finally he dropped out of school.

Was he

A. protecting himself by avoiding a scary situation,

or

B. working on the skills he needed?

401. A person was very scared of throwing up at school. He too was mainly worried that he would embarrass himself.

He decided that he would prepare, just in case he threw up. He decided he would take a plastic bag to school with him in his pocket. He also took some tissues. Before he went to school, he practiced getting the bag out quickly.

He practiced in his mind that, if he needed to throw up, he would just use the bag. He would wipe his mouth and nose with the tissues.

He practiced thinking that, if this happened, it would not be awful. He reminded himself that all his friends would still like him. Then he spent some time reminding himself that people would still like him even if he did not have a bag and he threw up on the floor. He got comfortable going to school, and after a while he stopped taking the bag with him.

Was he

A. protecting himself by avoiding a scary situation,
or
B. working on the skills he needed?

402. A teenaged boy thought, "It would be fun to climb Mount Everest." He began to read about Mount Everest. He found out that it is very cold and that there is not enough oxygen in the air. He read that very many very skilled climbers have died trying to climb this mountain. He realized that some bad weather could come and cause climbers to die. The boy realized that Mount Everest was a lot more dangerous than he had thought.

The boy realized that he was not a good mountain climber. He realized that it would take lots of time and practice to get to be skilled enough to climb Mount Everest. He decided that he could put that time and energy into other things

that would help people more. He decided to stay away from Mount Everest. He took up leading hikes through the woods near where he lived, with a hiking club. He enjoyed this a lot.

Did he end up protecting himself from the dangers of Mount Everest by

A. avoiding a scary situation,
or
B. working on the skills he needed?

403. A teenaged girl was shy. She realized she was scared of having chats with people. So she decided to get better at talking with people. She studied books on how to have good conversation. She thought of interesting things that she might say. She decided which things she would say to people she knew well and which things she would say to people she was just getting to know.

She practiced ways of listening well (such as reflections, facilitations and follow-up questions.) She practiced talking with people who did not make her feel shy. She practiced with her little brother and her mom. She practiced making up conversations by herself, playing both parts. She practiced every chance she got with anyone who wanted to talk. Finally she got really good at conversations and enjoyed them thoroughly.

Did she protect herself by

A. avoiding a scary situation,

or
B. working on the skills she needed?

404. Another teenaged girl was also very shy. She tried to stay away from situations where she would have to talk with people. She ate by herself at lunch. She never went to parties. If there were people standing around in a group, she would stay away from them.

Did she try to protect herself by

A. avoiding a scary situation,
or
B. working on the skills she needed?

405. A woman had a boyfriend who would get drunk and beat her up. One day her friend saw her practicing karate. The friend said, "What are you doing?"

The woman said, "My boyfriend gets drunk and beats me up. The next time this happens, I'm going to be prepared. I'm going to let him have it. I'll teach him not to beat me up."

Did she try to protect herself by

A. avoiding a scary situation,
or
B. working on skills?

406. Another woman had a boyfriend who got drunk and beat her up. She sent an email to her boyfriend and said, "You beat me up one time too many. I will never see you again. Good-bye." She stayed away from him from then on.

Did she try to protect herself by

A. avoiding a scary situation,
or
B. working on skills?

407. A man heard of someone who died from choking on some meat. He got scared of choking on food himself.

He read about choking. He found out that once you get older than about four years of age, the chance of choking goes way down. He found out that once you chew your food a few times, the chance that it will choke you goes way down further. He found out that if you don't run while you are eating or chew gum lying down, your chances of choking are even lower. He found out that many of the adults who choke on food are drunk on alcohol at the time.

After all his reading, he figured out that the danger of his choking was very, very small. But even so, he decided he would follow the guidelines he had read about, to make his chances even lower. He practiced chewing his food well and doing the other things.

Did he try to protect himself by

A. avoiding a scary situation,
or
B. working on skills?

408. Another man heard of someone who died from choking on some meat. He got scared of choking on food himself.

Whenever he started to eat, he would get scared. He found that if he just didn't eat, he felt less scared. But he got really hungry and felt weak.

Did he try to protect himself by

A. avoiding a scary situation,
or
B. working on skills?

409. A teenaged boy was planning to run on the cross-country running team. He felt scared that he might lose by a large distance and feel embarrassed. So he looked up the winning times in races. He started practicing running the same distance he would have to run in races. He ran this over and over, many times. He kept records of how fast he ran it and then made a graph. He saw that he had a good chance of reaching a winning time.

He got advice from a coach. He worked out with weights. He ran on a treadmill when it was bad weather. When the season started, he did not embarrass himself at all. He even won some races.

Did he try to protect himself by

A. avoiding a scary situation,
or
B. working on skills?

410. Another teenaged boy was planning to run on the track team. He wanted to run the 100-meter dash. He felt scared that he might lose by a large amount and feel embarrassed. He practiced running that distance many

times. He kept records of how fast he ran. He noticed that he got a little faster.

But he noticed that he was still not anywhere close to a winning time. He was not even close to the time for the runners who came in last. He read that some people have not inherited from their parents the types of muscle fibers they need to win short races. He thought, "I think I am one of those people."

He decided not to run the 100-meter dash on the track team, but to do something else. He took up tennis. He found out that this sport came much more easily to him. When he worked on it, he got better and better. He enjoyed playing tennis a lot.

The first scary situation for him was that of running the 100-meter dash in a race.

Did he finally decide to protect himself by

A. avoiding this scary situation,
or
B. continuing to work on 100-meter dash skills?

411. A man was scared of driving a car. He decided he wanted to learn to drive. He studied a driver's education book, over and over. He got a computer program that would make him seem to be driving. There were a steering wheel and pedals and a turn signal that came with it. He practiced with his computer program. He started on the computer with easy situations, like driving on a

country road with no traffic. Then he practiced with harder and harder situations.

Finally he felt ready to take driving lessons. He got a driving teacher and started with very easy driving situations. He gradually worked his way up. He finally became able to drive well.

Did he protect himself by

A. avoiding a scary situation,
or
B. working on skills?

412. Suppose there is a situation that is scary and you figure out that it is not dangerous. Sometimes you might want to use the phrase *unrealistic fear* when talking about this situation. This phrase signals you that you probably will want to get used to the situation rather than protect yourself from it.

A person is counting to himself. He finds himself for some reason feeling scared to stop counting on an odd number rather than an even number.

If he stops counting on an odd number, do you think that he is

A. in danger,
or
B. not in danger?

413. A person sees some things on his desk. They are lined up a little crooked. He has the feeling that something bad

will happen unless they are lined up perfectly straight.

Do you think this is

A. a realistic fear,
or
B. an unrealistic fear?

414. If someone has an unrealistic fear, one of the main ways to get used to it is by staying in the scary situation a long enough time, without stopping. That way, the person's mind has time to get used to the situation.

What does a long enough time mean? It takes different lengths of time to get over different fears. But when the fear has gone way down, you can figure that the person has been in the scary situation a long enough time.

Suppose someone is scared of being on elevators. The person decides that the danger is very small and that this is an unrealistic fear. He decides to try to get used to being on elevators.

He picks a time on a weekend when an elevator is not in use. He goes with a friend. He gets on the elevator, and he feels very scared. He rates his fear as nine on a scale of ten. He stays on and rides up and down for three minutes. He thinks, "This is the longest I've ever been on an elevator in my life!" His fear is still high, rated nine on a scale of ten.

Has he been in the scary situation long enough?

A. yes,
or

B. no?

415. Suppose that the man gets off the elevator after those three minutes. His fear level will go way down, quickly. And that will be a big relief. The big relief will come just after he gets off the elevator.

What lesson do you think his brain is learning from this experience?

A. It's a big relief to escape from an elevator,
or
B. it is OK to stay on an elevator?

416. If the lesson his brain has learned is something like, "Getting off elevators relieves that terrible feeling of being on them," has he learned to be less scared of elevators?

A. yes,
or
B. no?

417. Now suppose that, instead of getting off the elevator after three minutes, he stays on it. He finds that after fifteen minutes, his fear level has gone down to five on a scale of zero to ten. Then after twenty-five minutes, his fear level has gone down to a level of one. He is able to sit in a chair and read a book calmly. He stays on another ten minutes, and then gets off. He feels very proud of having stayed on a long time.

Do you think his brain has learned the lesson of

A. elevators are dangerous,
or
B. elevators are not dangerous?

418. The moral of this story is that if you want to get over an unrealistic fear, you have to stay in the scary situation long enough.

Suppose there is a girl who is afraid of going into the basement of her house if her mom is on the first floor. There is nothing dangerous in her basement – it is just another room like other rooms in her house.

Do you think that she has

A. a realistic fear,
or
B. an unrealistic fear?

419. Suppose the girl wants to get over the unrealistic fear. What is the scary situation that she has to stay in long enough?

A. being in the basement with her mother,
or
B. being in the basement while her mother is on a different floor?

420. Suppose that she goes down into the basement. At first she isn't very scared. But then, after a minute, she starts imagining bad people hiding. Her fear gets greater and greater. Finally, after two more minutes, the fear gets so great that she thinks she can't take it

any more. She runs out of the basement fast and joins her mother, who is working in the kitchen. The girl is greatly relieved.

Do you think she learned from this experience to be

A. less scared of being alone in the basement,
or
B. more scared of being alone in the basement?

421. Suppose that instead she goes to the basement. She feels really scared. But she does not let herself run away from the basement. She walks around and looks at all the things there. She sits down and practices relaxing her muscles. She imagines there is a powerful friend helping her. She reminds herself she is not in danger. She exercises some.

After about fifteen minutes she feels that her fear has gone down from ten on a scale of ten to five on a scale of ten. After forty-five minutes her fear has gone down to three on a scale of ten. She feels very proud that she has lowered her fear so much, and she comes upstairs and celebrates with her mom.

Do you think she learned from this experience to be

A. less scared of being alone in the basement,
or

B. more scared of being alone in the basement?

422. When you get used to a situation that is scary because of unrealistic fear, you have to stay in the situation not only long enough, but also often enough.

Remember our man who stayed on the elevator for half an hour or so? At the end of the session, his fear had gone down to one on a scale of ten. Suppose he then goes for two months without being on an elevator. His brain now has time to "forget" the lesson it learned about how safe elevators are. Suppose he then gets back on an elevator. He might be very disappointed if he expects his fear to start back at one on a scale of ten.

It is more likely that

A. his fear will be higher than one on a scale of ten,
or
B. his fear will have dropped to zero?

423. Remember that this man's fear dropped from ten to one during his first long time on the elevator. Suppose that he doesn't wait two months after this. Suppose he decides to go back on the elevator the very next day. Even then, his brain has forgotten some, but not all, of the lesson from the day before. Where do you think his fear will be when he gets back on the next day?

Which is more likely:

A. five on a scale of ten,

or

B. ten on a scale of ten?

424. The man finds out that his fear level the next day starts out at about five on a scale of ten. But now it only takes ten minutes to go down to one on a scale of ten. Within half an hour, it is down very close to zero.

The next day the man gets on the elevator again. Now his brain has forgotten a little of what it learned in the last couple of lessons, but not all of it.

What do you think his fear level is more likely to be now, when he first gets on the elevator?

A. two on a scale of ten,

or

B. ten on a scale of ten?

425. Let's think about the girl who spent forty-five minutes in the basement, whose fear went down from ten to three on a scale of ten. Suppose she thinks to herself, "I've succeeded! Three on a scale of ten is OK. I can live with that." And she stays out of the basement for another month. Her brain forgets a good bit of what she has learned in that lesson. Then she goes back to the basement by herself.

Do you think it's more likely her fear will be

A. eight on a scale of ten,

or

B. zero on a scale of ten?

426. Suppose she finds that her fear has risen to eight on a scale of ten. She decides that she wants to get rid of this fear totally. She takes a table, a chair and a lamp into the basement. She goes to the basement every day for a month and does schoolwork for at least two hours, by herself.

At the end of the month, do you think her fear is more likely to be

A. eight on a scale of ten,

or

B. zero on a scale of ten?

427. There are several ways you can make an unrealistic fear go down faster. You don't have to just put yourself in the scary situation and wait.

One of those things is to relax your muscles. You can practice relaxing your muscles when you are not scared. You can practice getting the muscles very loose and limp.

One of the ways you can practice relaxing muscles is to think about one group of muscles after another. You can first tense muscles just a little bit. Then you relax them. You ask yourself, "What did I do to tense them? What did I do to relax them?" You pay attention to how you go about relaxing muscles. Doing this a lot will help you to get to be more expert at relaxing your muscles.

When you are practicing relaxing, should you

A. never tense your muscles,

or

B. tense and relax your muscles, if you like, and pay attention to what each of these feels like?

428. When you get really good at relaxing your muscles, you can use this skill to calm yourself. You can do this when you feel an unrealistic fear.

When people are scared, they naturally tense up. If your brain notices that your muscles are loose and relaxed, the brain is more likely to get the idea that things are OK. The brain will get the idea that you are not in danger.

The idea of this is that

A. loose muscles tell the brain, "It's OK,"

or

B. loose muscles tell the brain, "It's time to eat."

429. There's another way of making unrealistic fears get smaller. Do you remember one of the sixteen skill groups called positive fantasy rehearsal? Let's talk about how this works with unrealistic fears.

Sue had a fear of germs. She got a very scared feeling if she touched things in the house and did not wash her hands right afterward. She noticed that other family members did not do this. They washed their hands before they ate and after they went to the bathroom, but not at many other times. They did not seem to get sick often. Sue decided that the danger from touching things and not washing her hands right away was very small.

She decided that the fear she felt was

A. a realistic fear,

or

B. an unrealistic fear?

430. Sue found out you can get used to scary situations by staying in them long enough in real life. But she also found out you can get used to them by imagining that you are staying in them, or staying in them in your fantasy.

So she decided how she would like to feel after touching things in the house but not washing her hands. She decided she would like to feel OK, in a good mood, maybe playful, maybe hard-working.

She started out by imagining her sister touching things around the house, not washing her hands and feeling in a good mood, playing and having fun.

Then Sue imagined herself doing the same thing. She pretended she saw a movie of herself touching things in the house, not washing her hands and going around in a good mood.

Then Sue did some more imagining. This time she did not pretend to see a movie. She imagined the same scene as though she were seeing it happen out of her own eyes. She imagined herself feeling good.

She is using

A. positive fantasy rehearsal,

or

B. compliance?

431. Fantasy rehearsal works better if you use it along with real-life rehearsal. In other words, Sue should not just use her imagination.

   She should

A. touch things and wash her hands right away in real life,

or

B. touch things and not wash her hands for a while in real life?

432. The next few stories tell about some people making their unrealistic fears smaller. Your job will be to tell what method they used when they did this.

   Bob had a fear that he had left the stove on when he left the house. He checked to make sure the stove was off when he left. But he would often feel scared unless he checked another time, or a few times. He knew that the stove was off. But he still felt scared. He decided that there was no danger.

   He decided that the fear was

A. a realistic fear,

or

B. an unrealistic fear?

433. Bob imagined himself checking one time, then walking out the door feeling confident. He imagined reminding himself, "I checked once,

and that is enough. The house is safe." He imagined letting the thoughts about the stove run their course and eventually go away as he went on about his business outside the house.

   Is he using

A. positive fantasy rehearsal,

or

B. muscle relaxation?

434. Jean did not like going to the dentist's office to get her teeth cleaned and examined. She knew this did not even hurt, but she still felt very scared.

   Jean practiced relaxing. She lay on her bed and tensed and relaxed her muscles. She took about ten minutes a day to practice. She got so skilled that she could make herself very relaxed, very quickly. When she went to the dentist's office, she lay back in the chair and relaxed her muscles thoroughly.

   Is she using

A. positive fantasy rehearsal,

or

B. muscle relaxation?

435. John was afraid of thunderstorms. He knew his house was safe from lightning. He decided his fear was unrealistic. He read about how to reduce fears. But he found there was a problem. Sometimes the thunderstorm ended before his fear went down much.

   John decided to videotape what he saw and heard from his window during the thunderstorm. He got several good shots of lightning. He recorded a lot of thunder. Then he played the videotape over and over for a long time. As he watched the videotape, he imagined he was really in the thunderstorm. He imagined himself feeling safe and secure.

Did John use

A. staying in the scary situation long enough, and positive fantasy rehearsal, or
B. conservation, and muscle relaxation?

436. Here's another thing that makes it easier to get over unrealistic fears. You can take it gradually. This means that you first try to get over being scared in a situation that isn't too scary. Then you work on a situation that's a little harder. Then you move up to a little harder situation. Each time you succeed at one situation, you prepare yourself for taking on the next one.

Marie was scared of being in high places. She didn't ever want to be able to stand on the edge of cliffs or climb steep rocks. But she wanted to be able to get onto the high floors of buildings without being scared. She knew that her fear of being in tall buildings was not realistic.

Marie had a good friend. She decided it wouldn't be very hard to be on the second floor of a building with her friend with her. It would be a little harder to be there alone. She decided that the higher she went, the scarier it would be.

So Marie took it gradually. She started out spending some time with her friend on the second floor of the building. She stood right by the windows and looked out them. Her fear started at four on a scale of ten. It went down to zero before very long.

The next day she did the same thing, only without her friend with her. She started out at three on a scale of ten and went down to zero fairly quickly.

She kept going higher and higher in this building. Finally she felt fine being on the eightieth floor without her friend.

Which techniques did Marie use:

A. positive fantasy rehearsal and self-talk, or
B. staying in the scary situations long enough and taking it gradually?

437. Mary had a fear of driving a car. She started out practicing driving in a deserted parking lot at six o'clock in the morning, when no one was around. She had the whole parking lot to herself. She drove very slowly. Then she practiced driving in a friend's long driveway. The friend blocked it off to make sure that no one else would be on it. Then she practiced driving on small dead-end streets.

She worked her way up to where she was able to drive in city traffic and on freeways. She said, "If I had started out on the city streets, or on the freeways, I couldn't have done it. I just wouldn't have tried it."

Mary was glad that she had

A. taken it gradually,
or
B. used muscle relaxation?

438. There's another method that is very useful in making unrealistic fears lower. This is paying attention to what you say to yourself. What you say to yourself is also called your self-talk. If you want to lower fear, you choose to say things to yourself that make yourself less scared.

Judy was scared of getting stuck by needles. She hated getting shots at doctors' offices or getting blood drawn.

She practiced getting blood drawn in her fantasy. She noticed that she got the urge to say things to herself such as, "Oh no! I can't stand this! This is terrible! Let me out of here!"

Would you expect that this self-talk would make her

A. more scared,
or
B. less scared?

439. After paying attention to this self-talk, Judy decided to say different things to herself as she practiced in her fantasy. She practiced thinking, "OK, it will hurt some. But I can take it. A second or two of pain won't kill me. My body is not in any danger from this. I don't need to escape. I don't need to protect myself. All I need to do is relax and wait till it's over." She imagined

herself getting the blood drawn and saying to herself, "Hooray for me! I am handling this well! I'm doing a good job!"

Would you expect this self-talk would make her

A. more scared,
or
B. less scared?

440. Jared had a fear of work. When he got a lot of math problems for homework, he felt very bad. Often he did not even start the work. When his parents assigned him chores to do, he thought, "That's too much. It's too unpleasant. I can't do it." Usually he did not do them.

He could play video games for a long time. And he could read comic books for a long time. He decided that, if he could use his mind on these things for a long time, he could use his mind for a long time on things that are more boring to him. He saw that other people could work for a very long time, and the work did not seem to hurt them.

He decided that his fear of working was

A. a realistic fear,
or
B. an unrealistic fear?

441. Jared looked at what he said to himself. He noticed that, when he thought about doing work, he would say

things like "Oh, no! It will take me so long! How can I stand it?"

He decided to say different things to himself. He started saying things such as, "This is a good chance to practice working. I can use this chance to get used to it. It won't hurt me. I just need to get over my fear. I'm not in danger." Then after Jared had worked for a while, he would say things like, "Hooray for me! I'm on my way! I'm succeeding!"

What method did Jared use?

A. changing his self-talk,
or
B. muscle relaxation?

442. Jared decided he would work on math facts. He decided to do twenty during the first session, fifty during the second session, and one hundred during the next. He worked his way up, step by step, to the point where he was doing two thousand math facts without stopping.

What method was Jared using when he did this?

A. taking it gradually,
or
B. fantasy rehearsal?

443. Jared noticed that when he would start to work, he would clench his jaw and grind his teeth. So when he was not working, he practiced letting his jaw get loose and limp. When he started to

work, he reminded himself every once in a while to let his jaw get less tense.

What method was Jared using?

A. taking it gradually,
or
B. muscle relaxation?

444. Jared worked his way up to where he was able to work at the math facts for an hour and a half without stopping. He also practiced reading a science book for a couple of hours without stopping. On another day, he practiced cleaning up the house for a couple of hours without stopping.

What method was Jared using?

A. staying in the scary situation long enough,
or
B. muscle relaxation?

445. Each time Jared had a success in working, he tried to remember it. At other times, he recalled and imagined those successful times again. He went over and over them in his mind. He practiced his successes in this way so he would be more likely to have more successes.

What method was Jared using?

A. fantasy rehearsal,
or
B. taking it gradually?

446. Here's another thing for people to keep in mind when they are getting rid

of unrealistic fears. Judge success by how you act, not how you feel, especially at the start. In other words, if you are doing something that is best to do, even though you have lots of unrealistic fear, say to yourself, "Hooray for me! I'm doing this despite the fear." Don't say to yourself, "Oh no! I still feel scared! That's terrible!"

The advice is to judge success by

A. behavior

or

B. emotion?

447. The trouble with judging your success by your emotion is that you can get scared about being scared.

Liz was giving a speech. She noticed her heart pounding. She noticed her legs feeling wobbly. Her hands were sweating. She felt scared. She got up and started reading her speech. She noticed that her fear was still there.

Suppose she were to think, "Oh no! I'm still fearful! This is terrible! I have not been successful in getting myself calm!"

Would she be judging her success by

A. her emotion,

or

B. her behavior?

448. Suppose Liz were to say to herself, "OK, I still feel scared, that's tough! But I'm giving this speech, fear or no fear, because I'm tough!"

In this case, she would be judging her success by her behavior, not her emotion.

Do you think these thoughts would make her handle the situation

A. with more success,

or

B. with less success?

449. A person was trying to get over a fear of elevators. The person got on the elevator, and, after ten minutes, the person still felt fear close to ten on a scale of ten. Suppose he were to say to himself, "Oh no! In the story I read about, the person started to get less afraid by ten minutes! Maybe I'm not ever going to get less afraid! Maybe I'm different from everyone else!"

Would he be judging his success by

A. his emotion,

or

B. his behavior?

450. Imagine again that the same person was on the elevator for ten minutes, still feeling very scared. Suppose he were to say to himself, "Hooray for me! This is the longest I've ever been on an elevator. I'm showing that I have the self-discipline to stay on here, despite the fear! I'm tougher than I thought I was!"

In this case, he would be judging his success by his behavior instead of his emotion.

Do you think these thoughts would make him handle the situation

A. with more success,
or
B. less success?

451. A woman's boss often asked her to stay late at work in order to work overtime. He would often ask her to do this just at the moment she was about to go home. Even when she had something else planned, she was scared to say no to him. She was scared to suggest that he ask her further ahead of time so that she could arrange her plans.

After a while, she got up the courage to say to him, "Could I talk with you about the system for overtime? There are times when I have plans after work, and I've cancelled them to stay overtime. But I was wondering if we could work out a system where I could plan ahead more."

She noticed, while she was saying this, that her fear was eight on a scale of ten. Suppose she said to herself, "This is terrible that I feel so scared! I feel like I want to get out of here. Why can't I do stuff like this without feeling so bad!"

Do you think these thoughts would make her handle the situation

A. with more success,
or
B. less success?

452. Suppose that instead she were to say to herself, "Hooray for me! Even though I'm feeling really scared, I'm getting across the point that I wanted to make, in a nice way. I'm glad I'm not letting this fear get in the way of doing what is best!"

Would she be judging her success by

A. her emotion,
or
B. her behavior?

453. A girl had a fear of lying in bed in her dark room by herself when she wanted to go to sleep.

She decided to lie on her bed in the daytime and imagine that the room was dark. She practiced taking the safe feeling she had in the day and moving it to the night.

What method is she using?

A. positive fantasy rehearsal,
or
B. changing her self-talk?

454. In the daytime, she practiced lying on her bed and relaxing all her muscle groups. She practiced this until she could make her whole body very limp whenever she wanted to.

What method was she using?

A. judging success by behavior instead of emotion,
or
B. using muscle relaxation?

455. She decided she would start out going to sleep with a fairly bright night

light on. Every few days, she turned down the brightness, until it was quite dark.

Was she

A. taking it gradually,
or
B. staying in the scary situation long enough?

456. As she lay in bed, she noticed herself feeling scared. She said to herself, "I'm feeling scared, but I'm lying here by myself. That's good! I am not getting up and running out; I am succeeding!"

Was she

A. judging success by behavior instead of emotion,
or
B. using positive fantasy rehearsal?

457. She found herself thinking, "What if a kidnapper should come in and get me?" When she noticed herself saying this, she decided on something different to say. She thought, "The chances that someone will try to kidnap me tonight are less than one in a million. I am safe."

Is she

A. taking it gradually,
or
B. changing her self-talk?

458. She didn't try to go to sleep quickly. She thought, "I want to get lots of practice in handling this situation. If I stay here a long time, I'll get a better chance to get used to it."

Was she

A. staying in the scary situation long enough,
or
B. using muscle relaxation?

459. Another way of making fear less is to change the pictures you make in your mind.

Let's think about the girl who was afraid of robbers and kidnappers. Suppose she changed what she said to herself and thought, "The chances that someone will do something bad to me are very small." But even so, suppose that she found herself imagining that someone was creeping around in the house or hiding in the closet. Even though the words going through her mind were comforting, the pictures were not.

Which things going through her mind were scaring her:

A. the words,
or
B. the pictures?

460. If there is a very scary picture in your mind, it is often hard to succeed if you just try not to think of it. In fact, trying not to think of anything is a hard task. For example: try not to think of a polar bear. If you are like most people,

the picture of a polar bear will come to mind when you try not to think of it.

Trying not to think of something is usually

A. hard,
or
B. easy?

461. In the same way, trying not to think of a robber or kidnapper may be hard. But it is easier to change around the picture than to get rid of it. You can control what you imagine. If you imagine a robber on purpose, you can control what he does. You can make pictures that are not scary.

Suppose the girl brings a pretend robber into her house. She talks to him about why he is a robber, and he tells her that he doesn't know what else to do to make money to eat. She feeds him, and he is very thankful. She teaches him to be a famous ballet dancer, and he no longer has to be a robber.

Do you think that having these pictures in her mind would make the girl

A. less scared,
or
B. more scared?

462. Suppose a boy wakes up from a bad dream. In the dream, a monster has been chasing him. As the boy lies in bed, he imagines a clear shield around him. This clear shield will keep the monster from getting to him. But it will let him talk to the monster. He imagines asking the monster what he is chasing him for. After talking with the monster a while, the boy does a magical thing that turns the monster into his devoted friend. The monster will always help the boy, but it can never be mean to anybody.

What way of reducing fear is this boy using?

A. changing the pictures in his mind,
or
B. using muscle relaxation?

463. Suppose that a boy was teased and picked on by lots of kids. Because of this, he got scared to try to make friends. Whenever he would meet new people, the picture of getting teased and picked on came back to his mind.

Then some people began to be nice to him when he met them. He decided that, just before he was to meet new people, he would recall those times when people had been nice. Getting these pictures in his mind helped him not to be so nervous.

Was he

A. taking it gradually,
or
B. changing the pictures in his mind?

464. A woman named June had a fear of doing math. She got a job where it would help her a lot if she could do math well.

When June was a child, a teacher had asked her math problems in front of the whole class. The teacher would say mean things if she could not get them right.

Do you think June's fear of math is a fear of

A. physical danger,

or

B. social danger?

465. She decided to start with very easy math work. She worked her way up, bit by bit, to the harder work. She also started by doing her work by herself. She worked her way up to doing math with a tutor and then with other people at work.

What way of getting over fear did she use?

A. taking it gradually,

or

B. changing the pictures in her mind?

466. June decided that getting over her fear of math meant a lot to her. She decided to spend a lot of time on math. She started working on it for an hour a day, every day, and sometimes longer.

What way of getting over fear was she using?

A. muscle relaxation,

or

B. staying in the scary situation long enough?

467. At the beginning, she found that when she worked on math, her heart pounded and her hands sweated. She felt scared. But she got the work done anyway. She said to herself, "Great! Even though I feel scared, I'm doing the work!"

What was she doing?

A. judging success by behavior and not emotion,

or

B. positive fantasy rehearsal?

468. When she felt scared, she also noticed that she clenched her jaw and tightened her face. She tried to make her face and jaw become loose and limp. This made her feel less scared.

What was she doing?

A. changing the pictures in her mind,

or

B. muscle relaxation?

469. She noticed that when she started getting to the harder work, she sometimes said to herself, "I can't do this. What's the use of trying? My brain isn't built for this."

So he started saying different things to herself. She said, "I've never done this before. It will really be great if I can do this. It will be a reason to feel really proud!"

What was she doing?

A. staying in the scary situation long enough,
or
B. changing her self-talk?

470. When she tried new and hard math, she sometimes did it well. She surprised herself with what she could do. When she had these successes, she tried to remember them. She recalled how she thought. She ran the memory through her mind over and over. She did this so that she could practice that good way of thinking and feeling.

   What was she doing?

A. positive fantasy rehearsal,
or
B. muscle relaxation?

471. When she started to do math with people at work, she found that the pictures of her school days came back to her. She remembered the times she felt embarrassed. These pictures made her more scared.

   She made some new pictures in her mind. She pictured what it would have been like in school if she had known all about lowering her fears. She imagined herself in class doing really well, surprising everyone and feeling great.

   What was she doing?

A. changing the pictures in her mind,
or
B. staying in the scary situation long enough?

472. When she did math with people at work, she started to say to herself, "It will be really awful if I make a mistake!" But when she noticed herself saying this, she changed it. She said, "Everyone makes mistakes. The people I work with have made mistakes too. We can help each other find them and correct them. If I do good work, it is really wonderful."

   Is she

A. working on skills,
or
B. changing self-talk?

473. She got to be very successful in her use of math at work. She felt good that she spent so many hours working on the math she would need to know.

   Was she feeling good about

A. working on skills,
or
B. muscle relaxation?

Dilemmas

474. When someone has a *dilemma*, he has a hard choice. There is a good reason to do a certain thing. But there's also a good reason not to do it.

Do you remember the sixteen skills and principles? Often we want to make a certain choice because it's a good example of one of these principles. But what if that choice is also a bad example of a different principle? What if the opposite choice is a good example of that different principle?

Here's an example. A man was very poor. His children were starving. He tried to find work. He tried to beg for money or food. But it didn't work. He saw some milk on someone's doorstep. He took it and ran. He gave it to his children.

He felt loyal to his children.

His taking the milk for them was an example of

A. loyalty,
or
B. respectful talk?

475. But when the man got the milk to give it to his starving children, he also took something that did not belong to him. He stole.

Thus, what he did is a bad example of

A. honesty,
or

B. friendship-building?

476. We say that this man found himself in a dilemma. It was as though loyalty and honesty were in a contest. The word *versus* means "in a contest with."

His dilemma was

A. loyalty versus honesty,
or
B. friendship-building versus respectful talk?

477. A man had a good job. He had a chance to do very important things for lots of people. He had a chance to be famous as someone who did good work. But he had two children. He wanted to spend lots of time with them. He wanted to teach them about how to live well. He felt that he owed them a lot of his time and attention. But he could not do all he wanted in his job and give his kids a lot of time too. There just was not enough time.

His dilemma was

A. productivity versus loyalty,
or
B. conservation versus positive fantasy rehearsal?

478. A woman was driving her car. She saw a man who had car trouble. He was waving for help. The woman thought, "I

144

would like to help him." But then she thought, "I need to take care of myself. I have heard of people getting hurt or kidnapped by people pretending to need help with their cars."

Her dilemma was

A. productivity versus joyousness,
or
B. kindness versus self-care?

479. A man was a student in a special outdoor school. Part of the goal was to help people learn to be brave. So the teachers asked people to climb down cliffs. The man looked at the cliff. He thought, "I want to get braver, all right. But I'm not so sure the teachers here know what they're doing. I'm not sure they know how to keep people safe in case they slip and fall."

His dilemma was

A. positive fantasy rehearsal versus loyalty,
or
B. courage versus self-care?

480. Jack's friend called him up. The friend said, "Could you go to this movie with me?" Jack knew he would have fun being with his friend. He had also heard that the movie was fun. But he knew the movie had lots of violence. The movie made the violence fun. It also had lots of mean talk.

Jack's dilemma was

A. joyousness versus positive fantasy rehearsal,
or
B. fortitude versus self-discipline?

481. Tom was in a race. People were trying to see who could get through the woods to a certain place fastest. Tom had worked very hard to learn the skills to win the race. He had learned to read a map well. He was working very hard to win.

On his way through the woods, Tom found a hurt baby deer. Tom knew he could help the deer not to suffer. He thought he could help it get well. Without Tom's help the deer would die a painful death. But helping the deer would make Tom lose his race. He would not get rewarded for all his work.

His dilemma is

A. fortitude versus friendship-building,
or
B. productivity versus kindness?

482. Jan was the head of a public health service. She worked in a land where lots of people were getting sick and dying. Jan figured out that mosquitoes were spreading the sickness. If she could kill the mosquitoes, she could stop the sickness. Jan had only one poison to use to kill the mosquitoes. This poison might harm other animals. It might have other bad effects on the environment.

Jan's dilemma was

A. conservation versus kindness,

or
B. compliance versus joyousness?

483. A man got married to a woman who seemed to be happy only if she bought many things that cost lots of money. They had enough money for her to get the things. The man wanted to get along well with his wife. But he thought the things she spent money on were wasteful. He thought their money could be spent in ways that helped people more.

His dilemma was

A. conservation versus friendship-building,
or
B. courage versus self-care?

484. A man was trying to lose weight. He took a trip. He knew he would enjoy his trip more if he would just forget about losing weight. He would enjoy eating the special food he could eat in the country he was in. But he also wanted to be tough and to keep on losing weight.

His dilemma was

A. joyousness versus self-discipline,
or
B. compliance versus positive fantasy rehearsal?

485. A boy's sister asked him, "Do you think I'm pretty?" The boy really did not think his sister was at all pretty. But

he did not want to say something that hurt her.

His dilemma was

A. fortitude versus self-discipline,
or
B. respectful talk versus honesty?

486. Kate had a mom who was old and sick. Kate's mom did not have much money. Kate wanted to ask her mom to come and live with her. Kate wanted to take care of her mom. But Kate's husband did not want Kate's mom to live with them. He thought it would stress their family too much. Kate wanted to do what her mom needed. She also wanted to have a happy marriage.

Her dilemma was

A. loyalty versus loyalty,
or
B. nonviolence versus conservation?

487. Ted was in a cross-country race. Ted was very tough. He thought he could win the race. He was ahead.

But then Ted twisted his ankle. It hurt really badly. Ted thought, "I can be tough. I can take the pain. I still might win the race." But then he thought, "If I keep running, I might do lots more harm to my ankle. Maybe it would not ever get well."

His dilemma was

A. joyousness versus kindness,
or

B. self-care versus fortitude?

488. Ralph was at home. He felt sleepy. He also felt cranky. He had not gotten much sleep the night before. He knew that, if he took a nap, he would feel more cheerful. He would be able to have a better time with his family for the rest of the afternoon. But he also had work to do. He could get the work done if he did not take the nap.

His dilemma was

A. compliance versus courage,
or
B. productivity versus joyousness?

489. A woman was trying to have a good diet. She was trying to lose weight. She wanted to take care of her health. Some neighbors invited her to an ice cream party. She did not know the neighbors well. She wanted to make friends with them. But she knew it would be very hard for her to go to the party without eating a lot of ice cream.

Her dilemma was

A. courage versus productivity,
or
B. friendship-building versus self-care?

490. A doctor lived in a town where many people made their living from letting people take baths in natural springs. The doctor found out that the springs were not healthy. It would cost a lot of money to clean them up. He wanted to keep the friends he had in the town. He knew if he told everybody that the baths were not healthy, people would be angry at him. But he also knew if he did not tell, many people who took baths in the springs would get sick. He wanted to help those people not to get sick.

His dilemma was

A. friendship-building versus kindness, or
B. positive fantasy rehearsal versus fortitude?

491. A guy was very interested in getting to know a certain girl better. The girl liked this. She liked him and wanted to get to know him better, too. He invited her to movies, concerts and parties. She felt these things were a waste of time and money. She would rather spend her time building houses for poor people or teaching kids. But she did not want to miss the chance to get to know him better.

Her dilemma was

A. conservation versus friendship-building,
or
B. nonviolence versus fortitude?

492. A teenaged girl worked for her dad. He sold used cars. He set back the odometer on some cars. This made the cars look like they had been driven fewer miles. Some people were looking at a car. They asked the girl, "Has this car really been driven only 20,000

miles?" She did not want to get her dad in trouble. But she did not want to lie.

Her dilemma was

A. productivity versus positive fantasy rehearsal,
or
B. loyalty versus honesty?

493. A teenaged girl was at a store with three of her friends. The friends were in a silly mood. They each stole a very small and cheap thing from the store. The girl refused to go along with this stunt. She wondered whether to turn them in to the store manager. She thought stealing was wrong. But she did not want to betray her friends.

Her dilemma was

A. loyalty versus honesty,
or
B. productivity versus self-discipline?

494. A woman had worked at a job for a long time. She still made just barely enough money to support her kids. Her kids went to a bad school. People picked on them all the time there.

One day while she was emptying the trash, she heard two people talking. She found out something about her company that not many people knew. She thought, "I just learned that this company is going to be worth a lot more money. I could borrow a lot of money and buy stock in this company. When the company becomes worth a lot more, I could get rich. I could send my kids to a school where other kids would be nice to them. I could do something that would help them a lot."

But she knew that making money by using "inside information" was against the law. She could get into a lot of trouble. She could even get put in jail.

Her dilemma was

A. positive fantasy rehearsal versus conservation,
or
B. kindness versus compliance?

495. Jean went to a new school. She made friends with three girls. One day she saw those three girls picking on another girl. They were being mean to this girl. They were teasing her because her family did not have the money to buy the types of clothes the other girls wore. Jean felt like getting angry at her three friends. But she did not want to find herself with no friends either.

Her dilemma was

A. respectful talk and courage versus friendship-building,
or
B. self-discipline versus fortitude?

496. A woman was running for mayor. She and the man she was running against had a debate. It was shown on TV. The woman had learned to be very polite when she made joint decisions with other people. But the man said very mean things to her. She felt that she would score more points with the

people watching the debate if she got angry at him and talked about the mistakes he had made, rather than by staying polite and cool.

Her dilemma was

A. good decisions and respectful talk versus self-care,
or
B. compliance versus loyalty?

497. A woman had a sickness. She was a doctor herself. She read a lot about how to treat her sickness. Her own doctor told her, "Don't waste your time on that. Just do what I say. It will work out best. Don't try to be your own doctor." She wanted to do what he said, but she wanted to take care of herself in the best possible way, too.

Her dilemma was

A. fortitude versus productivity,
or
B. compliance versus self-care?

498. A doctor found out that she could make lots of money taking care of rich people who did not really need much help. She thought that she could do more good by taking care of poor people who needed her much more. But she could not make nearly as much money that way. And she wanted enough money to take care of herself well.

Her dilemma was

A. kindness versus self-care,

or
B. honesty versus positive fantasy rehearsal?

499. A woman's husband started using an illegal drug. She knew the drug was bad for him. She tried many ways to get him to stop. Then she thought of one option she had not yet tried. She thought he might stop if he got into trouble with the police. She thought she might be able to tell the police in such a way that he would not know she had told them. She wanted not to do things behind his back and wanted to be on his side as long as she was married to him. But she was watching him destroy his life with the drug and wondered if turning him in would be the kindest thing.

Her dilemma was

A. loyalty versus kindness,
or
B. nonviolence versus fortitude?

500. A boy at school was teased and picked on by another kid, all day, every day. The boy tried many things to end this. Nothing worked. The boy thought, "Maybe if I hit this kid really hard one time, he might stop the teasing."

The boy's dilemma was

A. conservation versus productivity,
or
B. nonviolence versus self-care?

501. A man was trying to lose weight.
He noticed that when he ate less, he
would get angry more easily. He figured
he would be nicer to his family if he
gave up losing weight. But if he stayed
fat, he might not live as long.
   His
dilemma was

A. productivity versus conservation,
or
B. joyousness versus self-care?

The Journey Exercise

502. Do you remember the Guess the Feelings Stories? In almost all of them, people could feel very different emotions, depending on what they thought.

What people do in a certain situation also depends on their thoughts. Since thoughts are so important, it's great to learn to pick what types of thoughts you want to think. If you have names or labels for different types of thoughts, it's easier to pick among them. Many people have greatly improved their lives by learning to pick their thoughts in a way that helps them meet their goals.

What comes next is a story with several chapters. It gives you practice in thinking about thoughts.

The reason for learning names for different types of thoughts is

A. to make it easier to decide how you want to think,
or
B. to name the thoughts that nobody can really control?

Twelve Types of Thoughts

1. Awfulizing. Example: This is terrible. I can't stand this.
2. Getting Down on Yourself. Example: I did something stupid. I did something bad.
3. Blaming Someone Else. Example: You're a bad person. You did something bad. This is your fault.
4. Not Awfulizing. Example: It's not such a big deal. This isn't the end of the world.
5. Not Getting Down on Yourself. Example: I don't want to punish myself. I want to use my energy some other way.
6. Not Blaming Someone Else. Example: I don't want to keep thinking about how bad that person is. I want to use my energy some other way.
7. Goal-setting. Example: What do I want to happen now? I want to find the best way to make things turn out right. I want to protect myself. I want to make this other person happy.
8. Listing Options and Choosing. Example: How can I accomplish my goal? I could do this. Or I could do this other thing. Or maybe this would work.
9. Learning from the Experience. Example: Next time, I'll know how to keep this problem from coming up. Here's what I'll do.
10. Celebrating Luck. Example: I'm glad this thing happened, for this reason; that was good luck.
11. Celebrating Someone Else's Choice. Example: I'm glad this other person did this thing, because of this.
12. Celebrating Your Own Choice. Example: I'm glad I did this, for this reason.

Chapter 1: The Travel Box

503. Here are the types of thoughts we will go over in Chapter 1.

If somebody says, "I'm so stupid!" or "I'm no good!" then he is GETTING DOWN ON HIMSELF.

If he says, "I made a mistake, but I don't want to get down on myself about it," he's NOT GETTING DOWN ON HIMSELF.

If he says, "You're a terrible person," or "It's all your fault," then he is BLAMING SOMEONE ELSE.

If he thinks about what he can do and says something such as "Let's see, I could do this, or do that . . . or here's something else I could do," then he is LISTING OPTIONS AND CHOOSING.

And if he says, "I learned something from this," and then reminds himself what he learned, then he's LEARNING FROM THE EXPERIENCE.

One day Bo was sitting at the table eating breakfast, and, as he was passing the jelly to his sister, he knocked over a glass of milk. Bo said to his sister, "I wouldn't have knocked that over if it hadn't been for you! See what you made me do?!"

Was that

A. blaming someone else,
or
B. getting down on himself?

504. His sister, whose name was Lilly, reached over to put a napkin in the puddle of milk, and she knocked over a whole pitcher of orange juice! She felt really bad. She said to herself, "Oh, I'm such a nitwit! I've really done it now. I'm so clumsy. I can't do anything right!"

Is she

A. getting down on herself,
or
B. listing options and choosing?

505. When their father, whose name was Sam, saw all this, he said to himself, "Hmm. Those glasses and pitchers I bought seem to get knocked over easily. I bet that's because they're so tall and skinny. I learned something from this. The next time I buy glasses, I'm going to buy short, fat ones, so they won't knock over so easily.

Is he

A. blaming someone else,
or
B. learning from the experience?

506. There was a knock at the door. They opened the door to see a traveling salesman. He said, "I'm selling glasses that are specially made to be hard to knock over." The salesman kept on talking in a very loud voice and wouldn't stop.

Finally Sam got so tired of hearing him talk so loudly that he said to him, "When you talk so long and so loudly, it really gets on my nerves. So would you leave please, right now?" Sam closed the door, leaving the salesman standing outside.

The salesman stood for a second looking at the closed door. Then he walked away. He said to himself, "Hmm . . . the reason he kicked me out was that I talked too long and too loudly. I learned something that I can use next time. At the next house, I won't talk so long and so loudly. I'll stop talking and listen sooner."

Is he

A. blaming someone else,
or
B. learning from the experience?

507. As soon as the salesman had walked away, Sam said to himself, "I wish I hadn't done that. I needed some glasses that don't knock over so much. I just passed up the chance to get some at a good price. Oh well, I won't get down on myself about it. Nobody's perfect, including me."

Is he

A. getting down on himself,
or
B. not getting down on himself?

508. Sam said to himself, "Now let's see . . . what can I do about this? I can just forget it. Or I can go out to the store and get some more glasses while I'm still thinking about it. Or I can run after the man and buy the glasses from him

anyway. I think I'll run after him right now before he gets too far away."

Is he

A. getting down on himself,
or
B. listing options and choosing?

509. Sam ran and caught up with the man, and he bought the glasses.

The man then said, "I have something else for sale. It's an amazing travel box. It will let you go anywhere you want in just an instant. All you have to do is to stand inside the box and set a dial. You will disappear in one place and find yourself in the next place. Also, after you get there, you can fold the box into a very small space. You can carry it in a little backpack. It's the perfect way to travel! It's very cheap – only five dollars."

And then the salesman thought, "I could keep on telling him more, or show it to him, or just keep quiet. I think I'll just keep quiet now."

Is he

A. listing options and choosing,
or
B. blaming someone else?

510. The man stopped talking before he could tell Sam why the travel box was so cheap. There was a problem with how it worked. Most of the time it took you where you didn't want to go. But Sam thought it sounded fun, so he just bought it.

When he got back home, he said to Lilly and Bo, "Let's take a trip!"

Bo set the dial for a nice tropical beach. Sure enough, they disappeared! But when they appeared again, they wound up in the middle of a city where there was a war going on! Several bullets whizzed past them.

Lilly pointed her finger at Bo. She said, "You must not have set the dial on the box right!"

Was she

A. getting down on herself,

or

B. blaming someone else?

511. Bo said to himself, "Oh, I did something stupid! I don't deserve to ever feel good after making such a horrible mistake!"

Was he

A. getting down on himself,

or

B. not getting down on himself?

512. Sam said, "We have some options. We can stand here and maybe get hit by a passing bullet. Or we can run for cover. Or we can get back into our box and go somewhere else – anywhere but where we are now. I like the last one best. Let's go!"

Was he

A. blaming someone else,

or

B. listing options and choosing?

513. They all got back into the box and set the dial again to go to a different tropical beach. This time they wound up just outside of a bus station. They went in and figured out that they were in a very little town in Canada.

"What are our options?" said Lilly.

"Well, we could try the box again and see if we get any closer to home," said Bo.

"Or we could fold up the travel box, carry it in the back pack, and take the bus home," said Sam.

"Let's do that last option, taking the bus home," said Lilly and Bo, and so they started out.

Were they

A. listing options and choosing,

or

B. getting down on themselves?

514. As they were riding the bus, Sam said to himself, "I learned something from that. The next time I buy something like a travel box from a salesman, I'm going to have the salesman show me that it works before I buy it!"

Was he

A. not getting down on himself,

or

B. learning from the experience?

They sat on the bus and watched the countryside go past them, thinking that their journey was almost over. Soon,

however, they would find out that it had
only just begun.

Chapter 2: A Bus Trip

515. Chapter 2 adds another thought to our list of possible answers. Suppose something goes wrong. If someone says to himself, "Oh, this is terrible. I just can't take it. This is the end of the world!" then he's AWFULIZING. Now back to the story.

As they were getting back onto the bus after a rest stop, the bus driver had his foot out in the aisle of the bus. Lilly was not looking, and she stepped on it. "Oh, this is horrible!" said the bus driver. "You stepped on my foot. I'm in agony. I don't know if I'll ever walk again!" Actually, he was hardly hurt at all.

Was he

A. not getting down on himself,
or
B. awfulizing?

516. Lilly wasn't sure whether the bus driver was kidding or not. She said, "Sorry." But she thought, "Well, it's your fault. If you hadn't had your foot out in the aisle, it never would have happened."

Was she

A. getting down on herself,
or
B. blaming someone else?

517. The bus driver and Lilly both thought some more. The bus driver

thought, "Well, next time I'll keep my feet out of the way when I let people onto the bus. At least I learned that."

Was he

A. awfulizing,
or
B. learning from the experience?

518. Lilly thought to herself, "Next time I walk in the aisle of a bus, I'll watch out for people's feet in the aisle. That way I won't step on anybody's foot again."

Was she

A. getting down on herself,
or
B. learning from the experience?

519. The bus started up again, and Sam, Lilly and Bo settled back into their seats for a nap.

When they woke up, they found that they and the driver were the only ones left on the bus. They were off the main highway, on a dirt road. Woods were all around them. "I got us lost," said the bus driver. "I tried to take a short cut, but I didn't know the way well enough. Oh, I'm so stupid. I can't do anything right."

Was he

A. blaming someone else,
or
B. getting down on himself?

520. "Well," said Sam, "there are several things we can do. We can turn around and go back the way we came. Or we can look for someone to ask directions from. We can look for a house. Or we can look at the sun and figure out which way north and south are and keep following the back roads in one direction until we find a main road. Which do you think would be the best?"

Was he

A. awfulizing,
or
B. listing options?

521. Just at that moment, though, there was a loud bang! Then there was a flopping sound. "Oh, no," said Bo to himself. "We have a flat tire, and here we are out in the middle of nowhere. This is just awful; it's terrible."

Was he

A. awfulizing,
or
B. listing options?

522. "Oh, no," said the bus driver. "I forgot to bring along a spare tire. Oh, I'm so stupid. I just can't do anything right!"

Was he

A. learning from the experience,
or
B. getting down on himself?

523. When Sam saw this, he thought, "Hmm . . . I learned something from this. When I get home, if I ever get home, I'm going to make sure I always have a spare tire in my car."

Was he

A. learning from the experience,
or
B. getting down on himself?

524. "Well, what can we do about this?" said Lilly. "We can try to drive the bus even with the flat tire. Or we can try to go somewhere in our magic box. Or we can start walking and see whether we can find somebody who has a phone. We can call up the bus company or a service station to fix the tire."

"Let's start walking," said the bus driver. "I think I saw a house back down the road."

Were they

A. getting down on themselves,
or
B. listing options and choosing?

525. They walked along. In the middle of the woods, along a very small dirt road, they saw what they had least expected. It was a huge mansion. It had big columns at the front. There were "keep out" signs everywhere.

"The signs say 'keep out,'" said Lilly. "I guess we could turn around and go back, or we could go on, and explain to the owner that we are in trouble and need help, and hope the person will understand. Or we could wait here until the person comes out."

"Let's go ahead and walk to the front door," said Sam.

Were they

A. not getting down on themselves, or
B. listing options and choosing?

526. They walked up to the door of the house. They had not even knocked when they heard a deep voice coming from a loudspeaker, saying, "What are your names, please?"

They looked at one another for a few seconds. Sam said, "I'm Sam Fortwick, and these are my children Lilly and Bo."

And the bus driver said, "My name is Fred Rawls."

After what seemed to be a long time of silence, the front doors opened automatically. The voice over the loudspeaker said, "Dr. Fortwick and children, please walk inside." Bo and Lilly moved inside, partly because they were curious to see what was inside this mysterious house. Sam came in behind them. The bus driver stayed outside.

As soon as they had come in, the doors closed behind them, leaving them standing in total darkness. All of them immediately tried to open the doors again, but they were locked. "Oh, I apologize for this," said the voice over the loudspeaker. "I messed up something. I did something stupid."

Was the person

A. getting down on himself or herself, or
B. blaming someone else?

527. "Oh, I'm such a bad person for suggesting that we come to this mansion," Sam thought to himself. "I blew it."

Was he

A. listing options, or
B. getting down on himself?

528. "It's all that bus driver's fault," thought Lilly to herself. "If he had had a spare tire as he should have, we wouldn't have ended up in this mess."

Was she

A. blaming someone else, or
B. listing options?

529. "Oh, this is terrible," said Bo to himself. "Something awful will happen, I know."

Was he

A. getting down on himself, or
B. awfulizing?

530. "Well," said Lilly, "at least we learned that next time we'll want to think before we come through a door or at least prop the door open with something."

Was she

A. getting down on herself,
or
B. learning from the experience?

531. At that moment a light came on,
and they found themselves at the foot of
a staircase. The same voice came out
from somewhere, saying "Mr. Rawls,
the bus driver, please return to your bus.
I have asked a service person to meet
you and repair your tire. You who have
entered my mansion, welcome. Please
come up to my study."

   "I should feel brave now, but I
don't," thought Bo. "But I guess I won't
get too down on myself about that."

   Was he

A. getting down on himself,
or
B. not getting down on himself?

Chapter 3: A Conversation in the Chamber

532. In this chapter, we add to our list of types of thoughts one that is the opposite of awfulizing, called NOT AWFULIZING. Suppose something goes wrong, but the person thinks something like "I don't like that, but I can take it. It's not the end of the world." That person is NOT AWFULIZING.

"Let's see," said Lilly. "Here we are in this huge, strange house, invited to come up and talk. I think the doors are still locked. We could try to break down the doors and run out, or we could run through this mansion and try to escape that way, or we could try to fight this guy, or I guess we could just go up and see what he wants."
 Was she

A. listing options,
or
B. not getting down on herself?

533. "I would highly recommend that you not run through the mansion," the voice replied. "There are wild animals in this mansion, and I would not like you to disturb them. Plus, you might be frightened if one were to jump out at you. I'm sorry the doors locked. That was a mistake. Don't worry; you aren't captives. But please come up the stairs into my chamber."

"I think I want to go up there and see what's up," said Sam, and he started up the stairs, and Lilly and Bo came behind him.

This time, when they entered the door to the chamber, Lilly took a book that was lying around and propped it between the door so the doors wouldn't close behind them again. However, as soon as they entered, the doors closed behind them and sliced the book in half. Lilly thought to herself, "Next time I'll have to use something even stronger to prop between the doors."
 Was she

A. awfulizing,
or
B. learning from the experience?

534. Bo saw how the book had been sliced in two by the doors. He said to himself, "Oh, this is just terrible. I can't stand this. I don't think I can take it."
 Was he

A. awfulizing,
or
B. not awfulizing?

535. When they looked around in the room, they saw a curtain opening, as if by itself. As the curtain opened, they saw the image of a very muscular man in a cape, who looked like Superman or Batman or some such superhero. There was fire all around him, and when he spoke, fire came out of his mouth.

"Welcome," he said. "Do not be afraid. You will not be harmed. I investigated your background by computer while you were standing at the front door, and I think you may be able to help me. I assure you what I am doing is only for good."

When he heard this, Bo thought, "I still don't like doors that slice books in two, or men who breathe fire. But I guess this isn't so terrible. At least this fire-breathing fellow wants us to do something for him. That means that surely he won't kill us. So maybe it's not so terrible after all."

Was he

A. getting down on himself,
or
B. not awfulizing?

536. "I invited you here," continued the fire-breathing fellow, "because I understand that you, Sam, are a veterinarian and a very good one. In this mansion I have a new breed of animal. I have bred them for a special, top-secret mission. These animals are called squoos. My problem is that the squoos are sick, and I need you to figure out how to save them."

Sam thought, "Let's see: I can refuse, or I can say OK, or I can say "OK, I'll do it for you if you'll do something for me in return!"

Was he

A. awfulizing,
or

B. listing options?

537. Sam said, "I'll try to help them, but, in return, I'd like you to promise that you won't hurt me and that you will let my children go home right now."

"I have no reason to want to hurt you, Sam," said the fire-breather. "And you are all free to go whenever you choose. However, your children Bo and Lilly should stay with you. I would imagine they could be very helpful to you. And it could be that you may be invited to help me further in the all-important mission."

Sam just stood there and couldn't think of anything to say. At first he said to himself, "Oh, I'm so stupid for not being able to think of what to say or do."

Was he

A. blaming someone else,
or
B. getting down on himself?

538. But then he thought, "Well, I'll just take my time and think. I've got a lot to think about, and it won't help anything to punish myself."

Was he

A. getting down on himself,
or
B. not getting down on himself?

539. While Sam was thinking, Bo asked, "What is this all-important

mission that you're planning? And what's your name, anyway?"

The voice replied, "The mission is none other than an end to violence. My name is Dr. Kuolo. Of course you aren't seeing me right now; you're seeing a video screen projection that doesn't look the least bit like me. I'm sorry if the image looks a bit aggressive; it was the only one available at the moment. I had to be out of the mansion for a while. I'm on my way back. I'm speaking to you through a remote phone."

They all took a closer look. They saw that the fire-breathing person was only an image on a giant screen.

When he saw this, Bo said to himself, "Hey, he tricked us! He shouldn't have done that! He's a bad person."

Was he

A. not awfulizing,
or
B. blaming someone else?

540. When Lilly saw this, she thought, "Hey, maybe this situation isn't so dangerous and terrible after all. I sure can handle a fire-breathing person who is just a fake image better than I could a real fire-breathing person. This situation is still scary, but I can handle it."

Was she

A. listing options,
or
B. not awfulizing?

541. Sam thought, "Well, I guess I've got some choices. I can ask him to tell me more about this, or I can refuse to help the squoos, or I can accept, or I can bargain with him more."

Was he

A. listing options,
or
B. not awfulizing?

542. Sam thought, "I suppose I could get angry at this strange person for having these doors close behind us and all, but somehow I just don't want to come down on him too much."

Was he

A. not blaming someone else,
or
B. learning from the experience?

543. Sam said, "I'll help you with the squoos, if you'll assure me that you won't harm us and that you don't hope to end violence by harming someone else."

"I can promise you both of those things," said the image on the screen. "Come now, for the squoos need your help, and we have no time to waste."

At this, the doors to the chamber automatically opened. "Look at the floor," said the voice. When they looked at the floor, they saw a line of light leading out the door.

"Just follow that line of light," said the voice, "and you will come to the amazing squoos."

As they walked out of the room, Bo looked behind him. He saw a little robot come out of the closet, pick up the two pieces of the book and shine a light on them; as if by magic, the book was mended into one piece! Bo thought he saw the robot wink at him, just as the doors once again closed behind them.

Bo thought, "Hey, this isn't so bad. I can handle this."

Was he

A. listing options,
or
B. not awfulizing?

Chapter 4: Treating the Squoos

544. This chapter adds to our list of possible answers a type of thought called GOAL SETTING. When someone thinks, "What do I want to do? Here is my goal . . . ," then that person is GOAL SETTING.

The beam of light they saw on the floor took them down long halls, through huge rooms and up and down many stairs. The mansion was even bigger than it had looked from the outside because very much of it was underground. As they walked through the mansion, they saw all sorts of things—lots of scientific equipment, mountains of books and charts, and maps showing what countries were fighting wars.

Finally they approached an area where they heard all sorts of screeching and growling, and still the light led right toward this area. "I want to help the squoos, but it's even more important to protect myself if they are dangerous animals," thought Lilly.

Was she

A. awfulizing,

or

B. goal-setting?

545. The light led them to walk through a huge room where they saw all sorts of creatures. There were powerful gorillas who seemed to be talking to one another in sign language. There were two animals who looked like lions but were shaped more like cheetahs; one was running at incredible speed on a large treadmill.

There were other animals they had never seen before, and they looked very scary. The animals were running loose in this huge room. The room had trees and bushes and dirt.

"Hey, he led us into this. He never told us this was going to happen. He's such a bad person," said Sam.

Was he

A. awfulizing,

or

B. blaming someone else?

546. When the animals saw them, some of the animals began slowly to come toward them. "What can we do?" Sam thought quickly. "We can run, or we can grab one of those weapons and try to fight, or we can try to make friends with these animals."

Was he

A. awfulizing,

or

B. listing options?

547. But at that moment some iron bars came down from the ceiling to form a hallway for Sam, Lilly and Bo to walk down, where they would be separated from the animals.

"Hey," said Bo, "this isn't so bad after all. I guess that fellow, wherever he is, must be looking after us. These animals still look scary, but I can handle that just fine."

Was he

A. getting down on himself,
or
B. not awfulizing?

548. The next big room they came to had hundreds of little animals about the size of a dog hopping and waddling around in it.

"Aw, look at them," said Lilly, Sam and Bo all at the same time. "They're so cute; they must be the squoos." They found they were attracted to these little animals in a way that was hard to resist. Bo started running up to them.

But when the squoos saw him coming toward them, they were startled, and they ran to get away. And then they coughed horrible-sounding coughs. The whole room was filled with groaning and hacking and retching noises.

At this, Lilly thought, "Now you've done it, Bo; you've made them worse, and you've probably gotten us in trouble with Dr. Kuolo."

Was she

A. blaming someone else,
or
B. listing options?

549. At first Bo said to himself, "Oh, I'm just a bad person. I disturbed them; I'm so untrustworthy. I don't deserve to have any fun ever again."

Was he

A. listing options,
or
B. getting down on himself?

550. But then he thought, "Well, next time I'll remember not to make sudden moves around animals, especially sick ones. Next time I get the urge to do something in this mansion, I'll think about it a little longer first."

Was he

A. getting down on himself,
or
B. learning from the experience?

551. "Let's see," said Sam to himself. "I can fuss at Bo, or I can apologize to whoever is listening and watching. Or, because it looks as if Bo feels bad enough already, I can just try to go on about the business of curing the squoos."

Was he

A. awfulizing,
or
B. listing options?

552. Sam said, "I wonder whether there are any medical supplies nearby for treating the sick squoos?" Just as he said that, he saw a cabinet with lots of medical supplies inside it. So he helped himself to the things he needed.

While Sam was examining the squoos, Lilly said to herself, "I'm feeling scared of what might happen. These squoos look awfully sick. What if we don't succeed, and the squoos all die? How do we know whether the person who lives here will do anything bad to us? Well, what can we do about this problem? We could try to get out of here before the person who lives here gets back. Or we could try to talk with that person about the fact that we might not succeed. Or we could just concentrate on getting them better and try to deal with it later on if we fail. I guess the last one is best."

Was she

A. getting down on herself,
or
B. listing options?

553. So Lilly went to help with the squoos. "Lilly, you're just in time," said Sam and Bo. "We need you to help us do a blood test on one of the squoos. You hold his arm still, and Bo will hold the rest of him still while I draw some blood."

Bo looked at the needle and the syringe and got kind of a creepy feeling. "I'm afraid that drawing blood will make me feel yucky," he thought to himself. "But I do want us to succeed at helping the squoos. I want to do my part to help in that goal!"

Was he

A. learning from the experience,
or
B. goal-setting?

554. Then he said to himself, "Well, I've had blood tests myself. They don't hurt so bad. It will be over quickly. I guess it's not such a big deal." When he thought this, he felt better.

Was he

A. awfulizing,
or
B. not awfulizing?

555. The blood test was only the first of many tests. They worked for hours. Equipment broke down, and they had to fix it. Tests would get messed up somehow, and they would have to do them over.

But they kept on. Sam kept saying to himself, "I want to stay cool. I want to put up with the things that go wrong so I can get these cute animals better."

Was he

A. blaming someone else,
or
B. goal-setting?

556. After a while, they found a box sitting in the room. "Where did that come from?" said Bo. "I don't remember it being there before."

They went to look. It had sandwiches and fruit juice inside. There was a note saying, "Keep up the good work."

"Does this mean the person who lives here is back?" said Lilly.

"It's likely," said Sam. "But let's just keep going. I think we're making progress."

After many hours of hard work, Sam said, "This is a very rare disease that they have. It's called the Nooky-bong-blat disease. We should be able to treat it with a drug called Thingamycincillin. That drug happens to be here in this refrigerator. Let's see . . . what should I do? I can give all the squoos the medicine and see if it works. Or I can try it out on one of them. I would then use it for the rest if it does work for that one. I think I'll try it out for one first. This medicine works very quickly. I'll be able to tell how it works with one squoo."

Was he

A. listing options and choosing,
or
B. awfulizing?

557. So they gave the Thingamycincillin to one of the squoos who was lying on the floor groaning. As they watched, the squoo spun around three times, jumped up in the air and then fell over as if dead!

When Bo saw this, he said to himself, "Oh, this is the end of the world! We did a terrible job. We just can't do anything right!"

Was he

A. awfulizing and getting down on himself,
or

B. listing options and learning from the experience?

558. Lilly said to herself, "This is pretty bad, all right, but it won't help for us to punish ourselves. I guess we'll just have to go back to the lab and start over, and we've at least learned that the Thingamycincillin doesn't seem to work; and at least it's good we only tried it with one squoo."

Was she

A. awfulizing, and blaming someone else,
or
B. learning from the experience and not getting down on themselves?

559. Sam saw that they both looked sad. He said, "Don't worry about the squoo falling over like that. That is just something the medicine does. He will sleep for five minutes. Then, if the medicine works right, he will wake up well!"

In five minutes, the squoo did wake up! He started making well noises, including the delightful sound called the squoo coo.

"Hooray," said Sam, Lilly and Bo, and soon they gave the medicine to all the rest of the squoos, and they all got well!

A voice came from a speaker somewhere: "Congratulations! You have done the job well!"

When they heard the voice, Lilly said, "Are you home now, Dr. Kuolo? If so, come and talk with us. I can't wait to see what you really look like."

There was a pause for a moment. "OK," said the voice. "But the first me that you see won't be the real one either." Within a second, a trap door opened from the ceiling, a rope dropped down, and someone swung down from the rope. For a few moments they just stood there and stared at one another.

Sam thought, "I want to find out more about this interesting person."

Was he

A. awfulizing,

or

B. goal-setting?

Chapter 5: Kuolo and the Squoos in Action

560. Dr. Kuolo looked like a man in his fifties. "When I go out in public, I often go in disguise, for reasons I'll tell you later," said Dr. Kuolo. "But I'm very grateful to you. You certainly deserve to see me as I really look, after all these images and disguises. I will start by removing my voice transformer."

"There," she said, "from now on you will hear my true voice." It was the voice of a woman. Next she removed a mask from her face and hands, as well as a wig and all sorts of disguise material.

She looked not at all as she had looked before. She had long dark hair that she wore in braids, and she was very beautiful.

"I am Madame Kuolo, at your service, with much gratitude for what you have done," she said, smiling. She thought, "I want to treat these guests with the honor they deserve."

Was she

A. goal-setting,
or
B. getting down on herself?

561. Dr. Kuolo said, "I hope you'll forgive the way the doors locked behind you and the way the lights went out and the image of the fire-breathing person. It wasn't a very nice way to greet such honored guests. But being a host for honored guests is not my strong suit here, I'm afraid."

She thought, "But I don't want to punish myself for that. I'll forgive myself because I am not harming them and I am giving them the opportunity to take part in a great mission."

Was she

A. blaming someone else,
or
B. not getting down on herself?

562. Lilly had felt angry before. But when she saw Dr. Kuolo standing there looking so kind and gentle, Lilly said to herself, "Well, I don't like everything about this mansion. But I don't want to come down on her or yell at her."

Was she

A. not blaming someone else,
or
B. awfulizing?

563. "Tell us more about yourself and this mission, Dr. Kuolo," said Lilly.

"Come into the next room, and I'll tell you my story," she said. They walked toward the wall. When Dr. Kuolo stepped on a certain spot on the floor, the wall opened up. The opening led into a room where they could sit on a carpet and in comfortable chairs. Dr. Kuolo offered them all apple cider and roasted nuts, and she began to tell her story.

"When I was eighteen-years old," she said, "war broke out, and friends and relatives of mine were killed by the other side. Never mind who the sides were—it's unimportant at this time. When this happened, I was filled with hatred for the people of the country we were at war with. 'They're horrible people; they're monsters,' I would say to myself. 'They're the only cause of all this grief and misery that I feel.'"

Was she

A. blaming someone else,
or
B. not awfulizing?

564. Dr. Kuolo continued, "So I vowed revenge. I had quite some ability at science and invention, so I went to work at discovering new weapons to use against the other side. I kept telling myself, "My goal is to help my country get revenge on all the people of this other country."

Was she

A. awfulizing,
or
B. goal-setting?

565. Dr. Kuolo went on, "I did my job very well. I worked on all sorts of other weapons that were used immediately by our side in the war. For years I did this, and people praised me for my ability. It made me feel good to get back at the enemy.

"But then I noticed I was getting a bad feeling of some sort, an uneasy feeling. 'Maybe I'm just bored,' I said

to myself. 'What can I do about it? I can take some time off and go to the beach, or go read in the library, or maybe it would be exciting to go directly to the country we're fighting and see our war in action.'"

Was she

A. blaming someone else,
or
B. listing options?

566. "So I went," Dr. Kuolo continued, "expecting to feel very excited and uplifted. But what I saw sickened me. I saw people just like my friends and relatives hurt and in the hospital, hurt by the very weapons I had invented. These were people who had not done anything wrong, who were just minding their own business.

"When I saw these things with my own eyes, it was as if the terrible truth hit me all at once. 'I am a horrible person,' I said to myself. 'I am a monster, every bit as evil and bad as the people who killed my friends and relatives.'"

Was she

A. goal-setting,
or
B. getting down on herself?

567. "I quit my job," Dr. Kuolo said. "For several long months I wandered around in despair. I constantly thought of the terrible deeds I had done. I thought, 'How awful it is that people

must fight and kill each other! How can I stand to live in such a world! I just can't take it!'"

Was she

A. awfulizing,
or
B. goal-setting?

568. Dr. Kuolo continued, "But then I landed on an idea that gave me peace. I would try to stop violence. I would devote the rest of my life to helping people not need to fight. I would work for peace. I thought, 'This is a worthy reason to stay alive. If I can carry out this goal, I can make up for some of the harm I have done.'"

Was she

A. goal-setting,
or
B. blaming someone else?

569. "Next," Dr. Kuolo said, "I asked myself, 'How can I help people to live in peace? Maybe I can work for groups that try to end wars. Maybe I can try to figure out what causes people to fight in the first place.' I thought of lots of ideas."

Was she

A. listing options,
or
B. not awfulizing?

570. "And I carried out lots of those ideas, too," Dr. Kuolo said. "I've had

to disguise myself and keep myself hidden. There are people from the country we fought against who want to get revenge on me. There are people from my country who would like to get more knowledge from me about how to kill and destroy, even though my country's war is now over. It's hard to switch from a war-maker to a peacemaker. That's why I live out in these woods. That's why I have disguises and why I have these strange television images to hold conferences with people. I keep telling myself, 'I need to take care of myself, so that I can do something that will really stop violence.'"

Was she

A. goal-setting,
or
B. not blaming someone else?

571. "But despite several years of my work as a peacemaker," Dr. Kuolo continued, "there are some forty wars going on in the world at this moment. At times I have said to myself, 'Nothing that I have done has worked. I guess that means I'm not worth anything. I'm a failure.'"

Was she

A. goal-setting,
or
B. getting down on herself?

572. "But then I thought of one more option," she said. "Most people in the

world would think it's just crazy. I'm not so sure that it isn't crazy. But I became an expert in breeding new animals. The very smart gorillas and the other animals you saw were the results of some of my early experiments. Finally I bred a new animal, called the squoo, and I did it to try to help put an end to war."

"That sounds crazy to me, all right," said Lilly. "It makes me afraid you're off your rocker. These animals are cute, all right. But how do you expect them to put an end to war?"

When Dr. Kuolo heard Lilly say, "You're off your rocker," she said to herself, "I certainly can understand the way that girl could think that way. But I don't want to try to get back at her or get down on her because that wouldn't do any good."

Was she

A. not getting down on herself,
or
B. not blaming someone else?

573. Dr. Kuolo said, "I'm not sure whether my plan with the squoos will work. It does seem crazy, I'll admit. But now that you've gotten the squoos well, we can try it.

"Anyway, when my squoos got sick, with what you found out was the Nooky-bong-blat disease, I needed a veterinarian. Just by chance you showed up at my door. While you were standing there, I used my computer to look up who you are. I was overjoyed to find

that you're one of the world's best veterinarians, Dr. Fortwick. So I said to myself, 'Let's see, I could just tell these people to leave, or I could invite them in and seek their help.'"

Was she

A. not getting down on herself,
or
B. listing options?

574. "Dr. Kuolo, I truly admire how much you want this fine goal," said Sam. "But I'm curious too. How in the world can the squoos end wars?"

"If you don't participate in the mission, will you keep it a secret?" asked Dr. Kuolo.

Sam, Lilly and Bo agreed that they would keep the secret, even if they didn't help out on the mission.

"These squoos are irresistibly cute," said Dr. Kuolo. "They just look you right in the eye and make you have a warm feeling all over. But that's not how they are supposed to end wars.

"The squoos are amazing creatures. They are very sensitive to what people are thinking and feeling, almost as though they have extrasensory perception. They can look at two people and tell whether they are getting ready to have a bad argument or get violent with each other, or whether the two people are working on a problem in a way that's likely to work. They automatically sniff out people with conflicts and go to them, and they instinctively think, 'My goal is to help these people work things out well.'"

When they do that, they are

A. goal-setting,
or
B. awfulizing?

575. "But how do they do that?" asked Lilly.

"Come on," said Dr. Kuolo. "Let's go out, and I'll show you what I'm talking about."

The four people and one squoo left the big mansion and headed over the fields and roads toward the city. Soon the squoo began to look very excited. "I think he's on the trail of two people who are struggling with each other," said Dr. Kuolo.

Sure enough, in a little while they came upon two men standing on the sidewalk of the city. "Let's hide here, around this corner, and watch and listen to what goes on," said Dr. Kuolo.

The two men were standing beside their two cars; one had run into another. "It's all your fault, you dummy," said one of the men. "You were going way too fast."

Was he

A. blaming someone else,
or
B. goal-setting?

576. "Nobody calls me a dummy and gets away with it," said the other, drawing a knife. "I'll see whether you

still think I'm a dummy with this knife at your throat."

At this, the squoo gave out with a sound: "Squeak! Squeak!" And when the men heard it, they forgot what they were doing and just stood in a daze.

"That's the squoo squeak," explained Dr. Kuolo. "The squoo makes it when people are about to get violent with each other. It makes them forget what's going on for a few seconds."

A few seconds later the two men looked around them and saw the squoo. They played with it for a while, because it was so cute. Then they said to each other, "Oh, yeah, what were we talking about? It was what are we going to do about our cars, right?" said one.

"That's right," said the other. "I guess we could split the cost of the damage. Or we could go to court about whose fault it is."

"Or," said the other one, "I could try to straighten out our fenders myself, if you'd help me."

Were they

A. listing options,
or
B. blaming someone else?

577. When they said these words, the squoo made another noise. "That's called the squoo chuckle," said Dr. Kuolo. "The squoo makes it when people are working out things well and peacefully, really talking it out. The squoo chuckle goes straight to the pleasure centers of people's brains.

When people hear the squoo chuckle, they feel just great. They want to do more of whatever they're doing. That way the squoo rewards them for working things out peacefully. They do it more and more."

As the squoo chuckled, one of the men was saying, "I want to have this work out in a way that we can both feel OK about."

Was he

A. blaming someone else,
or
B. goal-setting?

578. Within a few minutes the two men had come up with an agreement. They were shaking hands.

"That was wonderful!" said Lilly to Dr. Kuolo. "They might have killed each other otherwise. You and the squoo are a big success!"

At this, the squoo returned to the four people, and they all congratulated the squoo for his fine work, and everyone hugged one another, and a big celebration was held.

"We shouldn't get our hopes up too high," said Dr. Kuolo. "But if it can work for two people, it just might work for two countries. And that," she said, "is what we may call the mission."

"Let's give it a try," said Sam, Lilly and Bo. "Let's go for it!"

Were they

A. goal-setting,
or

B. not awfulizing?

Chapter 6: The Next Trip in the Travel Box

579. In this chapter we add three more types of thoughts. These are thoughts that make us glad about good things that happen.

If you think, "I'm glad that person did that. I feel grateful to that person," then you are CELEBRATING SOMEONE ELSE'S CHOICE.

If you think, "I'm glad I did that! I made a good decision!" then you are CELEBRATING YOUR OWN CHOICE.

The difference is in who chose to do the thing. If I'm glad someone gave me a present, I am celebrating someone else's choice. If I'm glad that I gave someone else a present, then I'm

A. celebrating my own choice,
or
B. celebrating someone else's choice?

580. Some good things happen just by chance. Nobody chooses them. They are what people call "luck." If someone thinks happy thoughts about these things, the person is CELEBRATING LUCK. If I think to myself, "I'm glad it turned out to be snowy weather today!" then I'm not celebrating something I did. I'm

A. celebrating someone else's choice,
or
B. celebrating luck?

581. On the way back to the mansion, Lilly said, "Hooray for you, Dr. Kuolo; your plan kept those two men from hurting each other. And congratulations to you, little squoo; you did a fantastic job!"

Was she

A. celebrating luck,
or
B. celebrating someone else's choice?

582. "That makes me feel good to hear that, Lilly," said Dr. Kuolo. And Dr. Kuolo said to herself, "I am glad I decided to breed the squoos. And I'm glad I decided to stop inventing weapons."

Was she

A. celebrating her own choice,
or
B. blaming someone else?

583. When they got back to the mansion, they looked at a map showing all the places in the world where wars were going on. "Let's see," said Sam. "Next we want to try to end a war somewhere. We've got lots of choices. This one really needs help. This other one has been going on a very long time. Another option is these two countries here."

"Here is another option," said Bo. "This will cut down on travel time. We can just get into our travel box. We can go wherever it takes us. We can keep going till we come to some place where there's a war going on. It didn't take us long last time."

Were they

A. blaming someone else,
or
B. listing options?

584. "That option sounds good, except for two things," said Lilly. "First, what if we don't know the language in the place where we wind up? And, second, shouldn't we know a little bit about the people we're trying to help before we do it? For example, maybe we should find out who the two sides are and what they're trying to get from each other."

Dr. Kuolo said, "Good. You are really thinking." She thought, "I'm glad my friends think about what they do."

Was she

A. celebrating someone else's choice,
or
B. not awfulizing?

585. Then Dr. Kuolo said, "I think I can solve both of the problems you raised, Lilly. First, I have already found out all I can about every place in the world where fighting is going on. Now as to the problem of speaking the language, let me show you something I invented."

Dr. Kuolo took out two little things. They looked like hearing aids. "Do you understand this?" said Dr. Kuolo. "I'm going to say something in Spanish. "No

es bueno estornudar sin algo sobre la boca."

"No," said Sam, "I don't understand Spanish."

"Well, put these into your ears, and listen to me now," said Dr. Kuolo. "OK, right now I'm talking in Spanish still. It sounds like English to you, doesn't it? You understand it, because the things in your ears translate it to your language. They will also translate what you say into whatever language the people around you are speaking. That was the hardest part to build into these little machines. Only one person needs to wear these, and both can understand each other."

"Hooray," said Sam. "Dr. Kuolo, you think of everything!"

Was he

A. blaming someone else,
or
B. celebrating someone else's choice?

586. They loaded up all the squoos. They all crammed themselves into the travel box. They had to pile all over each other. Each of the four people had squoos hanging all over them. They didn't mind, because the squoos were so cute and cuddly. The squoos were especially lovable because they were so happy. They were all thinking, "Hooray, I'm so glad that Dr. Kuolo is finally taking us on the mission! We've been waiting so long!"

Were they

A. awfulizing,

or

B. celebrating someone else's choice?

587. Bo was thinking, "What if we land right in the middle of a fight as we did before? That'll be scary, but I can handle it. What should I do? One option is to turn on the travel box again, very quickly, so we can escape."

Was he

A. listing options and not awfulizing,

or

B. blaming someone else and getting down on himself?

588. They set the dial at the first setting, hoping to end up again in the country that was at war. When they turned on the travel box, they disappeared with a "Whoosh" sound. They appeared somewhere else as quick as you could blink your eye.

The place where they landed did not look like the country they had gone to before. In fact, it didn't look like anything they'd ever seen. The first unusual thing was that the ground was not made of dirt. It was covered with cloth, and there was something like foam rubber under the cloth, like the cushion of a couch.

The squoos all said to themselves, "Hooray, what a fantastic thing to play on," and just bounced around all over everywhere, having a great time. "I'm so glad we landed on whatever this is," they thought.

Were they

A. celebrating luck,

or

B. goal-setting?

589. When they looked up into the sky, there was a big green sun. They could also see a purple moon and a moon with red with white dots. "I don't know where on Earth we are," said Sam, "but I guess I can handle it; at least it's warm enough and no one is shooting at us."

Was he

A. goal-setting.

or

B. not awfulizing?

590. "That's just it; I don't think we're anywhere on Earth," said Dr. Kuolo. "The only place I know of that has a green sun and a purple moon and a red-and-white moon is a planet about two galaxies away from Earth called Cuckoo-Baffab."

"Oh, no," said Lilly, "This is terrible! Do you realize what this means? If our travel box is going to start jumping from planet to planet, we might never get home to Earth. There must be billions of planets, and who knows, we might end up inside a star and get burned up the next time we turn it on!"

Was she

A. awfulizing,

or

B. not getting down on herself?

591. Bo said, "I think we should try to fix the travel box before we use it the next time. We can put that on our list of things to do!"
Was he

A. goal-setting,
or
B. celebrating his own choice?

592. "I wish I had thought to do that before we left the mansion where I had my materials and tools," said Dr. Kuolo. But then she thought, "There's no use in getting down on myself about that now."
Was she

A. celebrating luck,
or
B. not getting down on herself?

593. Dr. Kuolo continued, "It's an important goal to get back home. But that can wait a while. I'd like also to find out all I can about Cuckoo-Baffab, or at least explore it a bit. As long as we are here, I want to make the most of it."
Was she

A. goal-setting,
or
B. blaming someone else?

594. At that moment, huge flocks of birds seemed to come out of nowhere. As they flew across the sky, they all cuckooed together, twelve times. Each time they would cuckoo, they would do a flip in mid-air.
"Hey," said Bo, "maybe that's why it's called 'Cuckoo-Baffab!' I wonder whether their twelve cuckoos means it's twelve o'clock here."
"Hooray," said Sam. "We know there's life on this planet! I'm glad we ended up on such an interesting planet! We lucked out!"
Was he

A. celebrating his own choice,
or
B. celebrating luck?

595. "Let's go over and see what that big wall is," said Lilly. "I think I see a cave going into it." She saw in the distance a huge wall going up as high as they could see. It was made out of the same sort of couch-like material as everything else.
"Oh, I don't want to go there," said Bo. "I want to go see what that noise is." From the opposite direction from the cave and the wall there came a noise like a vacuum cleaner. They could also hear a sound like voices—like people chanting or singing music to go with a war dance.
"Well," Sam said, "we could go to one place or the other. Or we could go to first one and then the other. Or we could go somewhere else here. Or we could try to go home."
Was he

A. listing options,

or

B. celebrating luck?

596. "Or, we can split up and meet back here," said Dr. Kuolo. So they finally decided to split up. Dr. Kuolo and Lilly would look at the cave and the wall, while Sam and Bo would see what the noises were.

"I can't let myself forget about my mission," thought Dr. Kuolo. "That's my highest goal. But I am so curious. I also want to find out about this place."

Was she

A. goal-setting,

or

B. blaming someone else?

Chapter 7: Exploration Begins

597. Dr. Kuolo shouted, "Here's a little valley! This will be a sheltered place to leave the travel box!" All of them, in their excitement, had forgotten that the travel box folded into a very small space.

"Let's see," she said. "What could we do with the squoos? We could leave them here with the travel box, or take them with one pair of us, or each pair of us could take some of them. We won't be gone long. I think they'll be OK if I ask them to stay here."

Was she

A. celebrating her own choice,
or
B. listing options and choosing?

598. Dr. Kuolo told the squoos to stay, and they all had a good time jumping on the bouncy surface of this planet.

Lilly thought, "How great it is that Dr. Kuolo trained those squoos so well. I really believe they'll stay here until we get back."

Was she

A. celebrating luck,
or
B. celebrating someone else's choice?

599. "Let's meet back here in an hour," said Bo.

Sam and Bo started out in one direction, and Lilly and Dr. Kuolo started out in the other.

Bo said, "Wow, we sure are lucky that we landed some place where we can breathe the air! Just think, we could have happened to land someplace with gases that are poison to us!"

Was he

A. celebrating luck,
or
B. not blaming someone else?

600. They walked on. They saw all sorts of curious things. Before long they came across a huge metal can many times taller than they were. "I wonder what they keep in that can," said Bo.

"It looks like there's a faucet coming out of the can about fifty yards over in that direction," said his father. "Let's go over and take a look at it. I want to explore as many things as we can!"

Was he

A. goal-setting,
or
B. not awfulizing?

601. By this time the chanting of voices they had heard before had gone away, and everything was very quiet.

Suddenly a big ugly face popped up on one side of them, and with it came a bloodcurdling scream. "Yipes!" they both said, and before you could list an option, they were racing in the other direction, away from this horrible face.

The next thing they knew, the cloth beneath their feet had nothing under it. They were falling into an underground trap. They landed on some foam rubber and stood up unhurt in a little room. Many spears pointed at them from all sides except one. In this direction there was a big hole. They could hear footsteps and voices through the hole.

"Hey," said one voice, "our trap worked. That sign with the scary face on it and the recording of the scream must have made them run right into the trap. I'll bet we've caught a couple of Bafs! Hooray for our plan!"

Was he

A. not awfulizing,

or

B. celebrating their own choice?

602. "I'll bet we have, too," said the other voice. "If we have, my goal is to make quick work of them!"

Was he

A. celebrating luck,

or

B. goal-setting?

603. "Oh, I can't stand this," said Bo to himself.

Was he

A. celebrating his own choice,

or

B. awfulizing?

604. "I'm glad they left foam rubber for us to land on rather than on those spears," thought Sam.

Was he

A. celebrating his own choice,

or

B. celebrating someone else's choice?

605. Sam thought, "Let's see. When they come out of the hole, we can try to jump them, or we can try to talk with them. Or maybe we can get one of these spears out of the wall to defend ourselves."

Was he

A. listing options,

or

B. learning from the experience?

606. At that moment two little men carrying spears popped out of the hole in the foam rubber wall. When they saw Sam and Bo, they just stood there looking amazed, and Sam and Bo just stared back at them. The two men were short, about half as high as Sam, and had purple skin and noses about a foot long that curled up round and round in a spiral.

They had lots of little pockets built right into their skin and lots of things stuck into their pockets, like books and a coffee cup and pictures of other people who looked like them.

"Oh, shoot," said one of them. "These aren't Bafs we've caught. Oh, how crummy. I had my hopes set on a Baf. This is just a real drag."

Was he

A. celebrating luck,
or
B. awfulizing?

607. "They aren't Bafs, that's for sure," said the other little man. "But then again, they aren't Fabs like us. I wonder what they are!"

One of the little purple men said, "I don't suppose there's any chance that you strange-looking creatures speak the Fabese language, is there?"

At this Sam said to himself, "I can't speak a word of Fabese. I wish I'd known better than to come to a place where I didn't know the language. But I don't want to come down on myself for it, because that wouldn't do any good."

Was he

A. not getting down on himself,
or
B. blaming someone else?

608. But Sam had forgotten something. He remembered it when Bo said to him, "Hooray, I am glad that Dr. Kuolo gave us these little things to wear in our ears!"

Was he

A. celebrating luck,
or
B. celebrating someone else's choice?

Bo continued, "I wonder if it'll let these Fabs understand us when we talk. Does it, Mr. Fab? Can you understand us?"

Chapter 8: Exploration Continues

609. Lilly and Dr. Kuolo meanwhile had gone exploring in the other direction. They found tunnels that went down into the foam rubber and branched into more tunnels, like a network of caves. Then the tunnels led back out to the surface of the planet. "Hooray," said Lilly. "I'm glad this planet turned out to be such fun to explore!"
  Was she

A. celebrating luck,
or
B. getting down on herself?

610. Soon they heard the buzz of voices. They also heard the buzz that sounded like a vacuum cleaner. Far in front of them, where a big wall went up, they saw all sorts of tunnels in and out of the wall. They saw several people scurrying around outside the tunnel. Some of them were riding around on carts that looked like vacuum cleaners. The people were purple. They had long noses that were about a foot long – like the Fabs that Sam and Bo had met. There was just one difference – their noses curled in a downward spiral, not upward.

  Beside all these people there was another huge metal can with a faucet on it. "Hooray!" said Dr. Kuolo. "I think we've found a little city! I can't wait to meet the people on this planet! Do you realize we will probably be the first human beings to be able to talk to people on another planet? I'm so glad we decided to stay here and explore!
  Was she

A. celebrating luck,
or
B. celebrating their own choice?

611. Lilly and Dr. Kuolo saw two of the purple people hiding behind a big mound of foam rubber, holding spears in their hands. They were watching something that was going on ahead of them. "I don't like this," said Lilly to herself, "because those spears make me feel scared. But I can take it, and it isn't so awful that I can't handle it."
  Was she

A. not getting down on herself,
or
B. not awfulizing?

612. When Dr. Kuolo saw the two people with spears, she thought to herself, "What do I want to do now? My main goal is to stop violence."
  Was she

A. goal-setting,
or
B. not getting down on herself?

613. Suddenly another purple person, one with a nose that curled upward, ran out from behind a mound of foam

rubber. "There he is! Get him," someone yelled. The two people with spears ran out, looking for a good spear-throwing position. At the same time, Dr. Kuolo ran toward them. Just as the first one threw his spear, Dr. Kuolo seemed to stumble into his throwing arm, pushing it to the side. An instant later the other one threw his spear, just as Dr. Kuolo stumbled into him. Both spears fell harmlessly into the foam rubber. The purple person with the turned-up nose scampered off to safety.

"Hooray," said Lilly to herself. "I did not want to see anybody killed or hurt. So I'm glad Dr. Kuolo did what she did!"

Was she

A. listing options,

or

B. celebrating someone else's choice?

614. Lilly thought, "I wish I had been able to help Dr. Kuolo instead of just standing by. But I don't want to get down on myself about that."

Was she

A. not blaming someone else,

or

B. not getting down on herself?

615. Then Lilly said to herself, "Next time I'll try to think ahead of time what to do, so I can act more quickly when something like this happens."

Was she

A. celebrating luck,

or

B. learning from the experience?

616. The two purple people whose arms Dr. Kuolo had knocked were angry. "Oh, you blew it. You messed things up royally, you clumsy stumbler," one shouted.

Was he

A. awfulizing,

or

B. blaming someone else?

617. The other said, "That was a spy from the Fabs. We Bafs were just trying to protect our families and friends. If the Fabs know all the secrets about us, they'll come and kill us all. Now they might kill us! This is just terrible!"

Was he

A. awfulizing,

or

B. getting down on himself?

618. Dr. Kuolo thought, "They're really coming down on me. I don't want to come down on myself, because I feel sure I did the right thing."

Was she

A. not getting down on herself,

or

B. awfulizing?

619. Dr. Kuolo said to them, "I'm sorry I bumped you. But maybe it's good that

you didn't kill him. Maybe there are some other ways to keep the Fabs from killing you."

"Oh, there's no way, other than killing them," said one of the Bafs in disgust.

The other Baf looked at Dr. Kuolo and Lilly very curiously. "Who are you anyway?" said the Baf. "You don't look like us, and you don't look like Fabs either. Your noses don't curl up OR down."

"We're from the planet Earth, and we're visitors to Cuckoo-Baffab," said Dr. Kuolo. "My name is Madame Kuolo, and this is Lilly."

"Earth, Kuolo . . . That sounds awfully familiar," said one of the Bafs to the other. "Where have I heard of those? I want to try to remember it. Let's try to recall it, OK?"

Was he

A. goal-setting,
or
B. blaming someone else?

620. "I'll try hard to reach that goal," said the other Baf. He thought so hard that his head seemed to glow a different shade of purple. Then he said, "Oh! I remember! Earth is where one of our scientists sent our ultrafast signals exploring. We were looking for new and devastating weapons to use against the Fabs. Boy, did we find them on Earth! That's who Dr. Kuolo was; she was a scientist who had invented all sorts of weapons! We all thought that, if

we could just make the weapons she had invented, we could wipe out every one of the Fabs. But we couldn't figure out how to make them. They were too complicated."

"I'm glad they couldn't figure them out," said Dr. Kuolo to herself.

Was she

A. celebrating luck,
or
B. goal-setting?

621. Dr. Kuolo thought, "I wish I'd never made those things, and I feel bad every time I think of them. But I don't want to get down on myself, because that wouldn't do any good now."

Was she

A. not awfulizing,
or
B. not getting down on herself?

622. The Bafs got excited. One of them asked, "Are you the same Dr. Kuolo who is so good at inventing weapons? Oh, I'm so glad we asked you who you are!"

Was he

A. celebrating their own choice,
or
B. celebrating someone else's choice?

623. The Baf continued, "You just have to help us fight the Fabs. When you hear about how they've been killing us

and making us live in fear all the time,
I'm sure you'll want to help us."

"What do you and the Fabs want
from each other? What are you fighting
to try to get?" asked Lilly.

By now the Bafs were very friendly,
because they wanted Dr. Kuolo to help
them. "Come join us for a cup of
looboola," said one of them, "and we'll
tell you all about it. Allow us to
introduce ourselves. My name is Boffo,
and this is Biffoo. Looboola, in case
you aren't familiar with it, is the stuff
we drink here. It's what we keep in that
huge metal can with a faucet on it.
Come meet our people, and we'll tell
you all about what's been going on here
on Cuckoo-Baffab. When you hear it,
I'm sure you'll decide to help us fight
the Fabs."

"I can't wait to hear what has been
happening," said Lilly. "I'm so glad
they decided to tell me about it!"

Was she

A. celebrating luck,
or
B. celebrating someone else's choice?

Chapter 9: Some Cuckoo-Baffabian History

624. Biffoo and Boffo led Lilly and Dr. Kuolo into the city of the Bafs. Lots of purple people with curled-down noses greeted them warmly. Biffoo and Boffo explained that Dr. Kuolo was a famous inventor of weapons. More people introduced themselves.

Soon they came to some tables and chairs in a little cave that was hollowed out from the foam rubber. The people gave them each a big cup of looboola. "Wow, this is fantastic stuff," said Lilly. "I'm glad you gave me this! This is the best stuff I've had to drink in my life!"

Was she

A. celebrating luck,
or
B. celebrating someone else's choice?

625. The looboola tasted like a milk shake, only much better.

"That huge can of looboola is one of the things that wasn't shrunk," said Biffoo.

"Shrunk?" said Dr. Kuolo. "Are you saying that some of the things on this planet of Cuckoo-Baffab were shrunk?"

"I'll tell you about it," said Boffo.

"Hooray," said Lilly to herself. "I'm glad he decided to tell us about this planet."

Was she

A. celebrating someone else's choice,

or
B. awfulizing?

626. Boffo said, "Long ago, in the pre-shrunk days, when most of us were just children, there was a population explosion here on Cuckoo-Baffab. There were just too many people. There wasn't enough land to live on and not enough food to eat. It was all the fault of those Fabs. If they had just kept to themselves, we would have been all right. But they kept on wanting land and food that really belonged to us, those bad villains."

Was he

A. goal-setting,
or
B. blaming someone else?

627. "So the Bafs and the Fabs constantly fought each other," Boffo continued. "They killed many of our people, and we of theirs, but still the population grew, and people started saying, "The food and the land will soon run out. We must figure out a way to solve this problem!"

Were they

A. goal-setting,
or
B. celebrating luck?

628. "One day a scientist named Raimondi made the great discovery. He made a plan to shrink every living thing on Cuckoo-Baffab. He would leave the

food supplies, like these huge cans of looboola, and all the land on the planet the same size. That way there would be space and food enough for everybody. We all said to ourselves, 'Thank goodness that Raimondi made this discovery!' And it worked! We all said, 'Wow, are we glad we went along with his plan and got shrunk!'"

Were they

A. celebrating their own choice,
or
B. awfulizing?

629. "Do you know how this planet looks like a couch?" Boffo continued. "Well, that's because the part that we're on IS a couch. There was a couch sitting outside in the Raimondis' back yard. He did make one mistake, though. He had wanted to make the Bafs and Fabs wind up far enough away from each other that they wouldn't fight. But it turned out that we all ended up on the couch. We've liked it here, except that the Fabs are also here.

"The caves in the wall are really dug into the back cushion of the couch, and the tunnels that go underground go into the seat cushion. We ride around on little vacuum cleaners. They clean up the planet while they take us from one place to another. We feel so proud of the way we made our city."

Was he

A. celebrating luck,
or

B. celebrating their own choice?

630. "You've made some wise choices," Dr. Kuolo agreed. "But why are you and the Fabs still fighting each other, now that you have enough food and land?"

"The Fabs are a bunch of ruthless killers, that's why," said Boffo. "You should hear about all the innocent people of ours that they've hurt and killed. They've attacked us many times. We all know that we can't be safe until we wipe them out. You should hear all the horrible things they've done. This war is all their fault."

Was he

A. celebrating luck,
or
B. blaming someone else?

631. "Why don't you move farther away from each other, now that you have so much space?" asked Dr. Kuolo.

"If anybody should move, it should be the Fabs! This is our home!" said Boffo.

"I imagine the Fabs would say exactly the same thing," Dr. Kuolo thought, but she did not say it. Then Boffo and Biffoo told all sorts of gory stories about the horrible things the Fabs had done to the Bafs. They were so gory that Lilly quickly lost her appetite. She wasn't even able to finish her looboola. "I wish he wouldn't go into such detail," she thought. "This is making me a little sick. But, I can take it. I'll get over it quickly, and I don't feel too awful."

Was she

A. celebrating her own choice,
or
B. not awfulizing?

632. "Do you ever talk to the Fabs?" Dr. Kuolo asked.

"I don't imagine they'd have anything good to say," said Boffo. "But no, we don't talk to them because they speak Fabese and we speak Baffese. We can't understand each other's language. No, the only way to deal with the Fabs is to wipe them out. This is where you come in, Dr. Kuolo. Raimondi, the Baf who invented the shrinking device, is a genius who could do anything with machines and inventions. He could invent something that would wipe them out in no time. But he has refused to help his people kill the Fabs. He is known as a traitor. No one respects him any more. He's an outcast among Bafs and Fabs. Perhaps you can do what he wouldn't do, Dr. Kuolo. Show us how to build weapons that will help us in our battle! But you must act quickly, because we will be attacking the Fabs in the biggest of battles this very afternoon! We have one goal in mind: to wipe them out in the big battle today!"

Was he

A. goal-setting,
or

B. getting down on himself?

633. Dr. Kuolo stood up. She had such a wild-eyed fanatic look that Lilly was a little frightened. "We must keep the Fabs from killing you any more!" shouted Dr. Kuolo. "Quickly, get me a bunch of materials. Let me write them down. Make room for me in a factory. Get as many workers as you can who can put things together! There's not a minute to lose!"

"Hooray," said Boffo and Biffoo, "I'm so glad you decided to help us make weapons!"

Were they

A. goal-setting,
or
B. celebrating someone else's choice?

634. Lilly thought, "What's going on? Is she really going to help them make weapons? What should I do? Should I join in and help make weapons, or should I try to get Dr. Kuolo to change her mind? Or maybe I should ask Dr. Kuolo what's going on."

Was she

A. blaming someone else,
or
B. listing options?

635. At that moment, however, they looked outside, and Lilly saw the cuckoos again cuckooing and turning flips in mid-air. "Hey," said Lilly to Dr. Kuolo. "The cuckoos do seem to be

telling the time! That reminds me, this is the time when we are supposed to meet Sam and Bo back where the squoos are. I'm so glad I noticed that!"

Was she

A. celebrating someone else's choice, or
B. celebrating her own choice?

636. By this time Dr. Kuolo was busy giving directions on how to put things together in the factory. She said, "Good. Run back, please, Lilly, and bring them back here. Meanwhile, I'll stay and show them how to build these things."

So Lilly made her way back toward the place where the squoos were. She was delayed by all the friendly and nice Bafs, who wanted to talk to her and find out all about her.

"Boy," she said to herself, noticing the time passing, "I'm going too slowly. But I don't want to get down on myself about it. I'll just learn from this and speed up and not stop to talk to these nice people so much."

Was she

A. not getting down on herself, and learning from the experience, or
B. not awfulizing, and celebrating luck?

637. Finally she made it back to the place where they had started. She saw Sam and Bo and the squoos all there, safe. "Hooray," she said to herself. "I'm so glad they've taken care of

themselves and nobody has done them any harm."

Was she

A. celebrating someone else's choice, or
B. awfulizing?

638. They all gave each other big hugs. The squoos came up, and she petted them. They told one another about what they had seen.

"Oh, Sam and Bo, you should meet these nice people called the Bafs," said Lilly. "They've been terrorized by these bad people called the Fabs. They are fighting a war with them. They asked Dr. Kuolo to help them."

Sam and Bo looked upset. Bo cried out, "Oh, no, she can't do that! The Fabs are very nice people! They caught us in a trap, thinking we were Bafs. When they found out we weren't, they talked with us, and we had a great time. They told us how they would leave the Bafs alone if the Bafs would just leave them alone. They're scared the Bafs will kill them all. That's the only reason they're trying to wipe out the Bafs. They told us all sorts of horrible things the Bafs have done."

Sam said to himself, "I wish these people weren't in this mess. And I wish Dr. Kuolo were here so that we could talk to her. I want to do my best to make things better for these misguided people."

Was he

A. getting down on himself,
or
B. goal-setting?

    Bo yelled, "Hey, where is the travel
box? Didn't we leave it here?"
They all looked around. The travel box
was gone.

Chapter 10: An Angry Mother Speaks Her Mind

639. No matter where they looked, they could not find the travel box anywhere. Lilly thought, "I guess this means we're stuck here on the planet Cuckoo-Baffab until we find it. Maybe we'll be here for the rest of our lives. I sure would like to be able to go home. But if I have to, I could live here for the rest of my life. At least I have my dad and my brother and Dr. Kuolo with me. And the people here are nice. I guess I could handle that."

Was she

A. not awfulizing,
or
B. blaming someone else?

640. When Sam saw that the travel box was gone, he thought, "It would have been a lot smarter of me to fold it up and take it with me. Nobody could have taken it. I wish I'd done that. Next time I'll try to think more before I act. But I don't want to punish myself too much, because that wouldn't do any good."

Was he

A. learning from the experience, and not getting down on himself,
or
B. celebrating luck, and blaming someone else?

641. Bo said to himself, "I wish whoever took the travel box had just left it there. But I guess I would have taken it myself if I had found it in the middle of nowhere. Anyway, it won't do any good for me to blame that person, whoever he is."

Was he

A. not getting down on himself,
or
B. not blaming someone else?

642. Suddenly they heard the noise of a whirring machine. Someone was riding toward them on one of the vacuum cleaners. It was Dr. Kuolo! It was funny to see her on this thing.

The squoos jumped up and down with great glee when they saw their trainer and friend, and Dr. Kuolo said to them, "Oh, you great, noble animals! You have stayed just where I wanted you to stay!" The squoos looked proud, as if they were saying to themselves, "Hooray for us! We did something good!"

Were they

A. celebrating their own choice,
or
B. celebrating luck?

643. Dr. Kuolo said, "I notice that the travel box is missing. That's a shame. But come on, we don't have a minute to spare. The great battle is to take place when the cuckoos cuckoo four times, which is just a while from now! I came

back because I've already taught the Bafs how to make the machines. They're turning them out like hotcakes. I need to get the squoos. Come on. Let's go back through the land of the Bafs, toward the battleground. We need to focus on getting there quickly!"

Was she

A. goal-setting,
or
B. blaming someone else?

644. "Hold on, Dr. Kuolo," said Sam, "not so fast. We've gotten to know the Fabs really well, and we think they're nice people. We don't want you teaching the Bafs how to build a weapon that will wipe them out. What's going on, anyway? I think we deserve an explanation."

"Well, let's see," said Dr. Kuolo. "I could explain here, or you could all come back with me and bring the squoos too, and I can explain on the way back. I think the second one would save time, because there isn't a moment to lose."

Was she

A. blaming someone else,
or
B. listing options and choosing?

645. They all ran back to the land of the Bafs. Dr. Kuolo explained as fast as she could. Still, she had that wild-eyed fanatic look in her eye, a look that scared Bo. But after listening to her for

a while, he thought, "She seems to be talking sense. I don't think she's crazy. I guess that wild-eyed fanatic look isn't something to be so afraid of. It just means she's excited. I guess it isn't so awful."

Was he

A. goal-setting,
or
B. not awfulizing?

646. They were riding under the caves that had been dug into the foam rubber wall. People lived in the caves above them. A window opened, and an instant later they found themselves splattered with something that smelled terrible. "Hey, where did that come from?" said Sam.

"It came from up here," said a woman's voice from the window above. "My name is Bafa. I dumped rotten looboola on you. If I had anything more to dump on you I'd dump that too! I've heard how you have some sort of new-fangled weapon that will allow us to wipe out the Fabs. Well, that's what they say every time there's going to be a big battle. But the Fabs have their weapons too, and all that happens is that more of my sons get killed. I've had five sons, and four of them have been killed in these wars with the Fabs. Now you're stirring up another big battle, and my last son is going to be in it. If he gets killed, that will be the end of the world, and it's your fault. You terrible people, you just don't know when to stay out of other people's business!"

Was she

A. blaming someone else and awfulizing,

or

B. getting down on herself and goal-setting?

647. "Boy," Lilly thought, "she's really coming down on us. But I don't want to come down on myself, because that wouldn't do any good. Besides, I think I'm doing the right thing."

Was she

A. blaming someone else,

or

B. not getting down on herself?

648. Dr. Kuolo thought, "She's really calling us bad people. I wish she hadn't thrown this rotten stuff on us. But there's no use getting down on her for it. I can understand how she'd be bitter. The poor woman has suffered so much."

Was she

A. not awfulizing,

or

B. not blaming someone else?

649. So Dr. Kuolo just yelled out to her, "Wait and see! This will be the battle that will end all battles!"

"That's what they always say," yelled back Bafa. "You war-makers are all alike."

But by then Dr. Kuolo and the squoos and the rest of our friends were speeding on. Bo said, "We don't have a minute to lose! The cuckoos just cuckooed three times! We need to get there on time!"

Was he

A. blaming someone else,

or

B. goal-setting?

Chapter 11: The Battlefield Scene

650. Our four friends and the squoos hurried on. But the squoos began to drag behind. They had started out running with great energy, but they now were tired and wanted to rest.

"They usually have more energy than this," said Dr. Kuolo. "What can the problem be? I know! They're hungry! They haven't had anything to eat or drink in a long time! Oh, my poor squoos. In my excitement, I've been forgetting about you! I don't want to get down on myself, but I do want to do something about it!"

Was she

A. awfulizing and blaming someone else,

or

B. not getting down on herself, and goal-setting?

651. Dr. Kuolo said, "I have to get you something to eat before you can go on. Sam, Lilly and Bo, run on ahead. The battlefield is just ahead of us. Whatever you do, don't let them start fighting until the squoos and I get there!"

Sam, Lilly and Bo ran ahead. Soon they came to a huge field where there were thousands of Bafs with all their spears and weapons, and far across the field they could see thousands of Fabs lining up to fight them back. Sam called out to Lilly, "You stay here and persuade the Bafs to wait, and Bo and I will try to persuade the Fabs to wait. We must stall them!"

Was he

A. celebrating luck,

or

B. goal-setting?

652. The Bafs were busy handing out something to all the men. One of them said, "Can you believe a secret weapon that you put into your ears? It's supposed to give us powers we didn't have before."

Another said, "Sounds strange, but I'll take whatever powers I can get!"

"Oh my!" thought Lilly. "What if they start fighting before the squoos get here. Then they'll just kill each other. That will be terrible."

Was she

A. awfulizing,

or

B. getting down on herself?

653. The Bafs all put into their ears the devices, which they thought were a secret weapon, but which were really the language translation devices Dr. Kuolo had invented. The Bafs and the Fabs lined up facing each other across the field. Despite anything that Sam or Lilly or Bo could say to them, they were getting ready to charge. "Oh, those fools," said Bo to himself. "Why won't they listen to me? They're so foolish!"

Was he

A. goal-setting,

or

B. blaming someone else?

654. "Get ready, men, this will be the battle of the century," said the general of the Bafs. "We'll charge when the cuckoos cuckoo four times. That will be in just a moment!"

On the other side, the general of the Fabs was saying, "Men, let them run across the field and get tired. Then throw your spears as soon as they get in range."

"Oh, where are Dr. Kuolo and the squoos?" said Lilly. "Why don't they get here?"

Just at that moment, the cuckoos cuckooed four times, with no squoos in sight!

"Oh no," said Lilly. "This is terrible. They're going to start fighting now!"

Was she

A. awfulizing,

or

B. learning from the experience?

655. "Men, get ready," said the leader of the Bafs. But just before he could say "Charge!" something happened that amazed them. Out in the field, in front of the Bafs, the travel box appeared, as if out of nowhere. A Baf who looked very old and wise was in it.

"It's Raimondi," said the Bafs to each other. "What's that he has?" The Bafs were so surprised to see the scientist appearing out of nowhere that for a moment they forgot about the battle.

Raimondi moved the travel box all around, appearing first in one place, then another, to the amazement of all the soldiers.

"He must have been the one who found the travel box," said Sam, "and he must have figured out how to fix it, too. Hooray! At least he's giving us a few more seconds."

Was he

A. celebrating someone else's choice,

or

B. celebrating their own choice?

656. Sam thought, "But I'm afraid they're going to charge anyway."

"Oh Bafs, don't start fighting yet," called out Raimondi. "I have found this amazing travel box. It was broken, and I have learned how to fix it. I am so very pleased to have gotten it working well."

Was he

A. celebrating his own choice,

or

B. not awfulizing?

657. Raimondi continued, "Perhaps this travel box can help the Bafs and Fabs solve their problems. We could move far away from each other very quickly and easily, using this travel box. Or there are lots of other options we could try. You can charge now, but lots of Bafs and Fabs will get hurt and killed.

But if we take our time and think of other solutions, no one needs to be hurt. I think you should choose the nonviolent plan."

Was he

A. blaming someone else,
or
B. listing options?

658. "Maybe we should listen to him," said one of the Bafs.

"No," said more of the Bafs. "We've heard this all before from him. We don't need better ways of traveling. We need to wipe out the Fabs!"

At this Lilly ran out and said to Raimondi, "Quick, Raimondi. I have to tell you something."

Then quietly, she whispered in his ear, "Raimondi, it's wonderful that you've been trying to keep them from killing one other. Here's something you didn't know: Dr. Kuolo doesn't want them to kill one another either. We must act quickly."

In a few seconds, after she'd explained a little more, Raimondi and Lilly got into the travel box and were gone.

"Where did they go?" said the Bafs to each other.

"It doesn't matter," said the general of the Bafs. Line up, men, and charge! Remember, our goal is not to give up until the Fabs surrender!"

Was he

A. goal-setting,

or
B. not getting down on himself?

659. The Bafs started running across the field with their spears raised. The Fabs waited for them. Suddenly the travel box landed just behind them. In it were Lilly, Dr. Kuolo and Raimondi, with all the hundreds of squoos! The squoos were in a high pitch of excitement. With great energy from their meal of looboola, they ran across the field just behind the Bafs. Just at the moment when the Fabs and the Bafs raised their spears to throw them at each other, a huge squeaking noise went up. It was all the squoos doing the squoo squeak at the same time.

At this, all the Bafs and Fabs dropped their spears and stood around looking very confused. "What's going on?" they said to themselves. For the squoo squeak dumbfounded anybody who was about to get violent.

A moment later, the Bafs and Fabs noticed that, for the first time ever, they could understand what the others were saying.

One of the Bafs looked at one of the Fabs and said, "I remember why we're out here fighting. It's because you are terrible people and you deserve to die!"

Was he

A. getting down on himself,
or
B. blaming someone else?

660. The Fab picked up his spear again and started to throw it. But one of the squoos squeaked again, and he was dumbfounded again.

Elsewhere, another one of the Bafs looked at one of the Fabs and said, "What's the reason we're out here? Oh, yeah, it's that I'm afraid you'll kill me if I don't kill you."

"That's just the problem I have," said the Fab.

"Well, what can we do about that?" said the Baf. "Maybe we could make an agreement not to kill each other. And maybe we could try to persuade the others to make the same agreement."

"Those are some good options," said the Fab. "And maybe now that we can talk to each other, we can try to get to know each other better, so that we can trust each other to keep our agreement."

Were they

A. blaming someone else,
or
B. listing options?

661. When a squoo heard these smart people working on their problem, he gave the squoo chuckle, that most pleasant of sounds. The two people felt just great. They felt like talking out their problems more with the other Bafs and Fabs.

The squoos delivered their squeaks and chuckles with precision for what seemed like a long time. Gradually all the people threw away their spears. They shook hands with one another and

found out all about one another. They met their former enemies and introduced them to their friends. They all decided not to fight any more! They decided that living in peace together was their foremost goal!

Were they

A. goal-setting,
or
B. blaming someone else?

662. After a while, they decided to have a huge party to celebrate that they and their former enemies would never again have to kill one another.

Were they

A. celebrating their own choice,
or
B. not getting down on themselves?

663. All the Bafs and all the Fabs came out and sang and danced together. They drank looboola together and cheered each other.

Sam and Lilly and Bo and Dr. Kuolo had a great time dancing and talking with the Bafs and the Fabs, and especially with Raimondi, the scientist.

"When I figured out how to shrink us all, I thought I had ended our fighting," explained Raimondi. "But I hadn't. I kept regretting that I hadn't succeeded in my plan to put these two tribes on opposite ends of our planet. They kept fighting. There were very few people who supported me in working for peace. But whenever the Bafs or Fabs invented a new weapon, I invented something to keep it from working. My friends and I managed to gum up the weapon works, over and over. That's why they are still using these primitive spears. Nobody respected me, but at least we could keep them from destroying each other. Now we have found peace, thanks to you."

"You did a very courageous thing, Raimondi," said Dr. Kuolo. "You sacrificed your own reputation to save your people."

Was she

A. listing options,
or
B. celebrating someone else's choice?

664. "I'm so pleased," said Dr. Kuolo, "that I could do what I did without ever telling the Bafs that the translating devices were weapons. I never lied to them. All I said was that the machines would help. They just guessed that they were weapons, not knowing that I'd gotten out of the weapons business and into the job of making peace." Then she thought, "I'm so glad I invented that translating device."

Was she

A. celebrating her own choice,
or
B. blaming someone else?

665. "And hooray for the squoos!" said Sam. "You came through when everyone needed you!" The squoos

crawled all over them and hugged them, and they petted the squoos.

Lilly said, "Hooray for Raimondi, who fixed the travel box so that we can get back home!"

Were they

A. celebrating someone else's choice,
or
B. awfulizing?

666. After very long celebrations and lots of talks and plans for peace, it was time for our friends to go back to Earth. Dr. Kuolo asked some squoos to stay on Cuckoo-Baffab to help the Bafs and Fabs keep the peace. The squoos looked proud to do so. Our four friends got ready to leave with the rest of the squoos.

Suddenly they saw one of the Bafs running toward them. She cried tears of joy, and she gave Dr. Kuolo a big hug. "Oh, how can I ever thank you?" said the woman. "You have done a miracle!" They recognized her as Bafa, the one who had thrown the rotten looboola on them out of the window. "That is my fine son you see over there celebrating," she said. "Look at him. Isn't he wonderful? Now, thanks to you, I will never have to worry that he will be killed in battle!"

Was she

A. celebrating someone else's choice,
or
B. getting down on herself?

She hugged them all, and she gave them each a fine Cuckoo-Baffabian shirt to take with them, to make up for the ones with rotten looboola spilled on them.

"Good-by, Bafa," said Dr. Kuolo, "and peace be with you. And good-by to you, Raimondi. You are a man after my own heart. Good-by to you for now, my noble squoos. Perhaps we shall see you all again soon."

And when they had all said good-by, they got into the travel box. This time it took them exactly where they wanted to go, back to Earth.

The End

The Twelve-Thought Exercise

667. The twelve-thought exercise is something you can do to gain more control over how you think about situations. Here's how you do it. You think of any situation. You think of what you would say to yourself if you were to "awfulize" about that situation, and you put it into words. Then you think of what you would say if you were to "get down on yourself" about that same situation, and you put that into words. You keep going until you have thought of an example of each of the twelve types of thoughts. So in the twelve-thought exercise, you make up

A. twelve different thoughts about one situation,
or
B. twelve different situations about one thought?

668. When you do the twelve-thought exercise, sometimes you have to do hard things. For example, suppose the situation is that you have done something really great. One of the twelve thoughts is to get down on yourself. It takes a little thought to figure out how you could get down on yourself about doing something great. Or suppose the situation is that some really bad luck has happened. When you do the twelve-thought exercise, you have to celebrate luck. You have to use your mind to figure out some plausible way to think each of the twelve thoughts, no matter what the situation is.

When you get good at this, you will realize that the situation does not force you to think anything. You can think whatever you want about a situation.

One purpose of doing all twelve thoughts, even if some are far-fetched, is that

A. you learn that the situation forces you to think something,
or
B. you learn that you can choose what to think about any situation.

Here are the twelve thoughts, again:

1. Awfulizing
2. Getting Down on Yourself
3. Blaming Someone Else
4. Not Awfulizing
5. Not Getting Down on Yourself
6. Not Blaming Someone Else
7. Goal-setting
8. Listing Options and Choosing
9. Learning from the Experience
10. Celebrating Luck
11. Celebrating Someone Else's Choice
12. Celebrating Your Own Choice

Let's first review what these mean. I will describe the type of thought, and you guess which one I'm describing.

669. This one can sound like this: "What do I want to try to do in this situation? Here is my first priority. This is my second priority. This other thing isn't important at all for me." This type of thought helps you figure out what you are trying to do.

Is it

A. awfulizing,

or

B. goal-setting?

670. The next one sounds like this: "Next time a situation like this comes up, I will know what to do. I learned this from what happened this time." This type of thought helps you to be ready for the next time you run into a situation like the one you were in. It helps you to get something good out of a bad decision. It helps you to know to repeat a good decision.

Is it

A. celebrating luck,

or

B. learning from the experience?

671. The next one can sound like this: "Even if the other person did something bad, I don't want to keep going over in my mind how bad it was. I have better things to do with my energy." This type of thought tends to make you less angry.

Is it

A. not blaming someone else,

or

B. getting down on yourself?

672. The next one sounds like this: "Hooray, I'm glad I did this!" This thought tends to make you feel proud about what you have done. It helps you to be more likely to repeat what was good about what you did. Often there is some good part even in your mistakes.

Is it

A. getting down on yourself,

or

B. celebrating your own choice?

673. The next one sounds like this: "It's not such a big deal. It only takes this much time or work or money to correct this situation. I can handle it. It's not the end of the world." When you think in this way, often you don't feel so bad about the situation.

Is it

A. not awfulizing,

or

B. blaming someone else?

674. This thought can sound like this: "This is terrible. I can't stand this. What a horrible thing." This thought tends to make you feel bad about the situation. Sometimes this is a good thing. Sometimes people don't feel bad enough about very bad things that are going on. But many people do this thought too much.

Is it

A. celebrating someone else's choice,
or
B. awfulizing?

675. This thought may sound like this:
"I could do this thing, or this other
thing, or maybe this. Here are the pros
and cons. I think this is the best thing to
do." This type of thinking helps you
figure out what to do.
  Is it

A. listing options and choosing,
or
B. not blaming someone else?

676. This is a thought such as "I made a
bad mistake. How could I have been so
stupid? Oh, I really blew it." This tends
to make you feel guilty or ashamed or
regretful. It is useful at times, because
these bad feelings can help us not make
the same mistake in the future. But too
much of this can just get people
depressed. It can make people not want
to do anything.
  Is it

A. goal-setting,
or
B. getting down on yourself?

677. This thought sounds like this:
"Hooray, there is something lucky
about this situation, and it's this . . ."
This type of thinking can make you feel
good. When you do it, you "look on the
bright side."

Is it

A. celebrating luck,
or
B. not blaming someone else?

678. This one sounds like this: "It's that
person's fault. What bad things he is
doing! He shouldn't be acting like that."
This type of thought tends to make you
feel angry. Anger is sometimes very
useful to feel, because it can help you
get the energy to work against someone
who is doing something bad. Too much
anger can be very destructive.
  Is it

A. not awfulizing,
or
B. blaming someone else?

679. This thought can sound like this:
"Even if I made a mistake, I don't want
to punish myself too much. I choose to
forgive myself. I don't want to beat
myself up over this." This thought
makes people feel less guilty or
ashamed.
  Is it

A. goal-setting,
or
B. not getting down on yourself?

680. This thought sounds like this:
"Hooray, I'm glad this other person did
what he did." This thought makes you
feel grateful. It makes you feel like
saying, "Thank you." Even when

someone has done something very bad, often there is someone else you can think of who has done something good.

Is it

A. celebrating someone else's choice,
or
B. goal-setting?

681. Now we'll see some examples of people doing the twelve-thought exercise. I'll put the thoughts out of order, so you'll have to think a little to say which is which.

Here's the first situation:

A man has gone to the doctor to get checked because of dizziness. The doctor says, "All the tests came back normal. I think maybe your illness is all in your head."

Which is each of the following thoughts?

Great! Those words are music to my ears! I don't have a brain tumor!

Is this

A. awfulizing,
or
B. celebrating luck?

682. This doctor sounds like he thinks he knows everything! How could he possibly know that this is all in my head? It could be an illness that his tests couldn't pick up. He has no business saying that to me!

Is this

A. blaming someone else,

or
B. goal-setting?

683. I did something stupid. I threw away my time and money, only to be told that there is nothing wrong.

Is this

A. listing options and choosing,
or
B. getting down on himself?

684. I'm so glad I got this checked out. Now I can feel more confident about my health, because I made that choice.

Is this

A. celebrating his own choice,
or
B. celebrating luck?

685. I still think this dizziness may have come from a virus or something. But at least I know I don't have something horrible, or it would have shown up on the tests.

Is this

A. not getting down on himself,
or
B. not awfulizing?

686. I'm not too thrilled with the way this doctor spoke to me. I didn't like the way he said "all in your head." But I don't want to come down on him about that. I don't want to get all bothered about it. Nobody's perfect, and I don't need him to be.

Is this

A. not blaming someone else,
or
B. not getting down on himself?

687. I can just go and not give this another thought, or I can do some reading about dizziness. Or I can look into ways that people have worked with illness caused by stress. Or I can ask this doctor more, to learn more while I'm here. After that I can get another doctor's thoughts on it.
   Is this

A. celebrating his own choice,
or
B. listing options?

688. I spent a lot of time worrying that I might have a brain tumor. Next time I get some sort of symptom, I'll try not to worry about really bad illnesses until I find out that I have one.
   Is this

A. learning from the experience,
or
B. celebrating someone else's choice?

689. I'm very glad this doctor chose to get all these tests done. They cost a lot of money. The "managed care" people would have liked him not to get those tests. I'm grateful to him for that.
   Is this

A. learning from the experience,

or
B. celebrating someone else's choice?

690. Oh, no. Now my mind is doing strange things to my body in ways I don't even understand! Probably no one else understands it either! Now what's going to happen next? It's terrible not having any answer!
   Is this

A. blaming someone else,
or
B. awfulizing?

691. Well, if it is true that I have dizziness because of reasons that are in my mind, I don't want to punish myself for that. It's not a disgrace in any way.
   Is this

A. not awfulizing,
or
B. not getting down on himself?

692. What are my priorities? I want not to wreck my relationship with this doctor. I want to get as much useful information as I can from him. I want to take care of my health – that's the first priority. I want to stay in a mood that will help me make calm and good decisions.
   Is this

A. goal-setting,
or
B. celebrating his own choice?

Situation #2:

A woman has just found out that she has won the lottery and will get seven million dollars.

693. I could move to a rich neighborhood. I could start a foundation to help poor people. I could get my parents a new house. I could read some books on how to invest it.
   Is this

A. blaming someone else,
or
B. listing options?

694. Now I'll never be able to trust anybody again, for the rest of my life, because they'll all be trying to get money out of me. I've lost my chance at true friendship. This is terrible.
   Is this

A. celebrating luck,
or
B. awfulizing?

695. Even though I just know this will wreck my life, I'm too weak just to give it all away and live a normal life. I have no backbone on this, or anything else.
   Is this

A. getting down on herself,
or
B. blaming someone else?

696. Hooray, what good luck I had!

Is this

A. celebrating luck,
or
B. celebrating her own choice?

697. I guess this teaches me that sometimes when you act on a hunch and take a risk, it pays off.
   Is this

A. learning from the experience,
or
B. not awfulizing?

698. What, they're going to pay it off over years rather than give it to me in one lump sum now? Those cheats! They should give me all seven million now!
   Is this

A. getting down on herself,
or
B. blaming someone else?

699. I'm so glad I finally chose to buy a lottery ticket!
   Is this

A. celebrating her own choice,
or
B. not awfulizing?

700. Hey, if I find being rich changes my life in ways I don't like, it's easy to solve that problem. So there's no terrible problem that can't be solved.
   Is this

A. not blaming someone else,
or
B. not awfulizing?

701. My first priority is keeping a normal life going while I'm getting used to the changes in my life. I want to keep my friends. I want to take my time and carefully think about how to use this money.
    Is this

A. goal-setting,
or
B. not awfulizing?

702. I know this was just luck, and I didn't work for it or show any skill to get it. But I don't want to get down on myself about that.
    Is this

A. blaming someone else,
or
B. not getting down on herself?

703. I'll bet that soon all my long-lost friends and relatives who haven't cared about me in years will be calling me up. They'll be saying they've had me on their mind all the time. If that happens, I'm choosing not to blame them for being human. I'll just enjoy it and not rile myself up over it.
    Is this

A. not blaming someone else,
or
B. celebrating luck?

704. I'm glad the man at the store was pleasant and friendly. If he had been grumpy, I might not have bought a ticket.
    Is this

A. celebrating her own choice,
or
B. celebrating someone else's choice?

Situation #3:
    At a restaurant with outdoor seating a very large fly has landed in and drowned in someone's soup.

705. I'm so happy this happened while I happened to have been looking at the soup bowl. It's nice to find out about this by seeing it rather than tasting it.
    Is this

A. celebrating luck,
or
B. getting down on himself?

706. I just learned an advantage of eating inside. I never had thought of this before. I'll remember that for next time.
    Is this

A. celebrating his own choice,
or
B. learning from the experience?

707. I can show this to the waiter and ask for a new bowl of the same soup. I can use this chance to try a different

type of soup. Or I can just ask the waiter to take the bowl away and not have any more soup.

    Is this

A. listing options,

or

B. blaming someone else?

708. I can ask to go to a table inside. Or I can stay here. Or I can look around and see how many other flies are out here before making that decision.

    Is this

A. getting down on himself,

or

B. listing options?

(The previous two questions illustrate the fact that there can be several different ways of listing options, depending on what question you pose to yourself.)

709. I'm glad I'm able to remain cool and calm about this.

    Is this

A. celebrating his own choice,

or

B. goal-setting?

710. I'm glad about times in the past when folks in places like this have been willing to replace food. Their choices give me a nice feeling that the people here will come through this time.

    Is this

A. celebrating someone else's choice,

or

B. not blaming someone else?

711. If it hadn't been for my wife, I would have eaten inside. This never would have happened. Why did she have to want to eat outside?

    Is this

A. goal-setting,

or

B. blaming someone else?

712. I'm starting to feel angry at the fly. But I want to choose not to get worked up about what a bad thing it did. It had a very little brain. And the poor thing paid for it with his life.

    Is this

A. getting down on himself,

or

B. not blaming someone else?

713. I should just give up on socializing with people. I wanted to impress my friends, and then I get into this embarrassing situation. I probably look like an idiot.

    Is this

A. getting down on himself,

or

B. celebrating luck?

714. I just can't stand it! This seems like a little thing, but it just goes to

show how out of control everything really is. You never know when something really terrible is going to happen just by chance.

Is this

A. blaming someone else,

or

B. awfulizing?

715. My first priority is not to upset my friends or myself. My next priority is to get some food that I feel like eating.

Is this

A. blaming someone else,

or

B. goal-setting?

716. Well, this certainly isn't something I want to punish myself for. It wasn't my fault. Even if it were my fault, why should I punish myself for such a little thing?

Is this

A. celebrating someone else's choice,

or

B. not getting down on himself?

Situation #4:

A man is driving his car. He is going the speed limit. Another driver feels that he should be going faster. This driver honks and screams at the person. As the angry driver passes, he makes angry gestures with his hands.

717. I'll choose not to do the same sort of blaming that he's doing. I'm going to try not to run through my mind how bad he is, over and over. This is not because he doesn't deserve it, but because I've got better things to think about.

Is this

A. celebrating his own choice,

or

B. not blaming someone else?

718. He doesn't like the way I drive, but I don't agree. So I'm not going to punish myself for making him angry.

Is this

A. not getting down on himself,

or

B. awfulizing?

719. I'm glad I've chosen to drive carefully. I'm proud that I haven't had a wreck in all these years of driving.

Is this

A. celebrating luck,

or

B. celebrating his own choice?

720. I'm glad there happened to be a passing lane so this person could get past me. I'm glad it wasn't a curvy two-lane road instead. Who knows what he would have done then?

Is this

A. celebrating luck,

or

B. listing options and choosing?

721. I do prefer to go more slowly than most people on this highway go. What do I want to do about this? I could go on side streets. I could move my office so that it's closer to home. Or I could just keep going like I am and not worry about it when people like this get angry.
  Is this

A. awfulizing,
or
B. listing options?

722. It's so crazy that people make laws and post speed limits, and then nobody enforces them. If they would just enforce the law, I wouldn't have this problem!
  Is this

A. blaming someone else,
or
B. learning from the experience?

723. I have something to be glad about. Several hundred people have passed me today, and he was the only one who was rude. I'm glad all those others chose to act in a mature way.
  Is this

A. celebrating someone else's choice,
or
B. not getting down on himself?

724. This teaches me that you can't please everybody all the time. Pleasing

everyone is not a goal worth fretting about.
  Is this

A. learning from the experience,
or
B. not blaming someone else?

725. I just can't stand it. The way people act to each other is getting worse and worse every year. This world is the pits.
  Is this

A. not blaming someone else,
or
B. awfulizing?

726. My goal is not to teach that person a lesson. My goal is to drive safely and not to let behavior like this upset me.
  Is this

A. not awfulizing,
or
B. goal-setting?

727. He's right. I'm too careful. I'm a coward. I just make other drivers angry all the time. They shouldn't let me on the road.
  Is this

A. celebrating luck,
or
B. getting down on himself?

728. This isn't so bad. Somebody I'll probably never see again was angry at

me. I'm not in danger. Nobody was hurt or killed. It's no big deal. I can handle this just fine.
Is this

A. not awfulizing,
or
B. learning from the experience?

Situation #5:
At a party, someone teases me about my clothes. He says, "Hey, where did you get those clothes, the Salvation Army Thrift Shop?" In fact, I did get my clothes there.

729. This person knows I don't think clothes are important. So he's not really trying to hurt my feelings but just to horse around and have fun. I'm glad he's choosing to do that instead of trying to hurt my feelings.
Is this

A. awfulizing,
or
B. celebrating someone else's choice?

730. I'm glad I've gotten confident enough in myself that I don't get upset with this sort of teasing.
Is this

A. celebrating his own choice,
or
B. getting down on himself?

731. I'm glad I'm living at a time in history when clothes are not a big deal. A century ago it would have been a different story.

A. celebrating luck,
or
B. celebrating his own choice?

732. I could say, "How did you know? Have I left the sales tag on for the last five years?" Or I could say, "Just call me the last of the big spenders," or I could pretend to be angry and say in a real deep voice, "Hey, buddy, you got a problem with that or something?" or I could look at my clothes and whisper in his ear, "You're right!"
Is this

A. celebrating luck,
or
B. listing options?

733. He noticed what I'm wearing, right away. This teaches me or reminds me that not everyone cares as little about clothes as I do.
Is this

A. celebrating his own choice,
or
B. learning from the experience?

734. Who does he think he is, making fun of me?
Is this

A. blaming someone else,

or
B. not awfulizing?

735. Oh gosh, it's true. Everyone else is dressed better than I am. What a fool I was for not thinking more about what to wear.
   Is this

A. getting down on himself,
or
B. goal-setting?

736. Well, no one will be hurt or killed or will even lose any sleep over what I wear. This is no big deal. Who cares?
   Is this

A. not awfulizing,
or
B. goal-setting?

737. Even though I'm not as dressed up as most other people here, I don't want to punish myself for it. People have done much worse things in history. This doesn't even compare to the really bad things people have done.
   Is this

A. not getting down on himself,
or
B. not blaming someone else?

738. I want to look good enough that I don't make people reject me. But I also have a goal of making a statement by what I wear. I want to let people know that I'm not going along with wasting

resources on buying expensive junk when other people don't have enough to eat.
   Is this

A. not awfulizing,
or
B. goal-setting?

739. Maybe this person wants me to feel bad. But many other people here have been very nice to me. I'm very glad they chose to act that way.
   Is this

A. celebrating someone else's choice,
or
B. getting down on himself?

740. Oh no! It's true! Everyone else is dressed nicer than I am! I stick out like a sore thumb! People are all rejecting me in their minds!
   Is this

A. awfulizing,
or
B. not blaming someone else?

741. Even if he is trying to make me feel bad, I don't want to get angry about it. I'll just let him say what he wants and not worry about it. I'll enjoy the party more if I don't spend my energy condemning him.
   Is this

A. celebrating luck,
or

B. not blaming someone else?

Situation #6:

A woman has just finished a painting. She likes the painting and is very pleased with it. She shows the painting to a man who knows a lot about art. He studies the painting, and then he says, "This section here is a little too dark. You should have used some brighter colors here."

742. I think he is trying to help me. Even if he isn't, his advice may turn out to be helpful anyway. So I don't want to waste energy condemning him for criticizing my painting.
    Is this

A. awfulizing,
or
B. not blaming someone else?

743. I could do some thinking and decide whether I agree with him or not. I could get some reactions from other experts. If I decide he's right, I could paint over that part. Or I could do the whole painting over. Or I could just enjoy the painting the way it is now.
    Is this

A. getting down on herself,
or
B. listing options?

744. I hate it when people are so picky. They can't enjoy anything; they have to build themselves up by tearing something else down.
    Is this

A. blaming someone else,
or
B. listing options?

745. I think he has a good point. Next time I'll think more about the brightness and darkness when I'm planning the painting.
    Is this

A. celebrating luck,
or
B. learning from the experience?

746. It's great that he's willing to be honest about what he thinks. It helps me improve. I'm glad he isn't just lying to make me feel good.
    Is this

A. getting down on herself,
or
B. celebrating someone else's choice?

747. I'm very lucky that I can even spend time in this hobby of painting. Some other people have to be working at a job all the time if they want to eat.
    Is this

A. celebrating luck,
or
B. getting down on herself?

748. It's not terrible that he is criticizing my painting. My paintings don't have to be perfect.
    Is this

A. celebrating her own choice,
or
B. not awfulizing?

749. My goal is to become the best artist I can and to enjoy doing it. My goal is not to prove to this man that I'm already a great artist.
    Is this

A. goal-setting,
or
B. awfulizing?

750. If he is right that I should have used some brighter colors, I don't want to punish myself about that. I'm still learning about painting.
    Is this

A. listing options,
or
B. not getting down on herself?

751. Oh, no! I spent so much time on this painting, but I ruined it. This is so bad!
    Is this

A. not getting down on herself,
or
B. awfulizing?

752. Why didn't I notice that? I'm a bad painter not to have seen it.
    Is this

A. getting down on herself,
or
B. blaming someone else?

753. Wow, I must have drawn this well, if this man, who is usually a hard critic, doesn't criticize any worse than this! Hooray for me!
    Is this

A. goal-setting,
or
B. celebrating her own choice?

754. I'm glad I decided to paint this picture in the first place, because I like the way it looks.
    Is this

A. celebrating her own choice,
or
B. not blaming someone else?

    Situation #7:
    Someone is about to take a plane trip. She is planning to go for a business meeting. She has already boarded the plane. Just before takeoff, the pilot says, "We have just found out that there may be something wrong with this plane. It will take at least an hour to check it out. We're asking everyone to get off the plane. We'll let you know when you

can get back on this plane, or maybe a different plane."

755. I can call up the people I was planning to meet with and explain what has happened. I can ask them to rig up a speaker phone at the meeting, so I can meet with everyone by phone if I'm late. I can check out the phones on the plane and see if they will work. I can charge up my own cell phone while I'm still on the ground so that it will be ready if I need it.
    Is this

A. listing options,
or
B. not awfulizing?

756. Now I'm going to arrive late at my meeting! This is terrible; everybody is going to be angry at me.
    Is this

A. learning from the experience,
or
B. awfulizing?

757. I should have booked an earlier plane, to have more time to spare. Why do I keep doing stupid things?
    Is this

A. getting down on herself,
or
B. celebrating luck?

758. It's so lucky that whatever was wrong with this plane was found. Just think, it could have been some hidden thing instead.
    Is this

A. celebrating luck,
or
B. learning from the experience?

759. Thank you, whoever checked the plane and found this problem. I may owe my life to you.
    Is this

A. celebrating luck,
or
B. celebrating someone else's choice?

760. This should have been checked out long before now. What sort of lazy people are running this airline, anyway?
    Is this

A. not awfulizing,
or
B. blaming someone else?

761. I guess these delays happen. This isn't such a bad thing, when you compare it to being in a plane crash!
    Is this

A. not awfulizing,
or
B. blaming someone else?

762. I guess this time it would have been better for me to book an earlier flight. But I don't want to punish myself for cutting it close. Lots of other

times I've not left much time to spare, and it's worked out just fine.

Is this

A. not blaming someone else,
or
B. not getting down on herself?

763. My main goal is to be safe. I want to be in on the meeting if I can figure out a way to do it. And since life is short, I want to keep from getting upset over things like this.

Is this

A. not getting down on herself,
or
B. goal-setting?

764. I've got lots of things to do right now. I don't want to waste my energy blaming the airline people.

Is this

A. not awfulizing,
or
B. not blaming someone else?

765. Maybe next time when I have a very important meeting, I'll build in some extra time to get there. I can keep on cutting it close for the less important meetings.

Is this

A. not blaming someone else,
or
B. learning from the experience?

766. I think I've made a pretty good plan about what to do. I'm glad I used my energy in this way.

Is this

A. celebrating luck,
or
B. celebrating her own choice?

Situation #8:

A father has built a tree house for his son. One of the son's friends comes to play. This friend is very active and fearless. The friend runs around on the tree house, falls off and hurts his arm. The friend's family takes him to the hospital. The father learns later that he broke his arm.

767. How can I make it safe from now on? I can take the tree house down. I can put up guard rails. I can make a rule that no one outside the family uses it. I could have people use ropes like mountain climbers use.

Is this

A. listing options,
or
B. celebrating luck?

768. Why does that kid have to be so fearless and impulsive? He hurts himself every time he's given half a chance. Someone should teach him to be careful.

Is this

A. blaming someone else,
or
B. celebrating his own choice?

769. I guess it's not as bad as it could be. At least he didn't get killed, and his brain wasn't hurt, and he wasn't paralyzed. His arm will heal.
    Is this

A. blaming someone else,
or
B. not awfulizing?

770. I wish I'd done things differently. But I don't want to punish myself about it too much now. That won't do any good.
    Is this

A. not getting down on himself,
or
B. celebrating his own choice?

771. How can we show our concern? We can send a get well card to the boy. We can go over to see him. We can bring a gift for him.
    Is this

A. not awfulizing,
or
B. listing options?

772. Whenever I plan anything having to do with children from now on, the first thing I'm going to think about is safety.
    Is this

A. learning from the experience,
or
B. not blaming someone else?

773. It's so lucky that he happened to land so that the arm took the impact, instead of his spinal cord or his head.
    Is this

A. celebrating his own choice,
or
B. celebrating luck?

774. Even though I wish he had been more careful, I don't want to spend my energy condemning him.
    Is this

A. not awfulizing,
or
B. not blaming someone else.

775. Oh, no. His family will sue us for everything we own. We'll probably lose all our money. Plus my reputation will be ruined.
    Is this

A. awfulizing,
or
B. getting down on himself?

776. My first priority is keeping anyone else from getting hurt. I also want to keep on good terms with his family. Another goal is to let the boy know we care about him.
    Is this

A. goal-setting,

or

B. not blaming someone else?

777. I should have known something like this would happen. Now I'm to blame that he got hurt.

Is this

A. goal-setting,

or

B. getting down on himself?

778. I'm glad that, so far, his family has been nice to us about this.

Is this

A. not getting down on himself,

or

B. celebrating someone else's choice?

779. I'm glad I've been able to stay cool about this. I'm glad I haven't let it bother me so much that it keeps me from doing other things.

Is this

A. celebrating his own choice,

or

B. celebrating luck?

Situation #9:

A business man has agreed to give up his lunch hour every day to tutor a child. As soon as he meets the child for the first time, the child looks at him with a really sullen look. The child says,

"I don't want to spend time with you. You can't do anything for me."

780. This ungrateful brat! When I'm giving up my lunch hour, he should at least talk respectfully. He should be punished.

Is this

A. getting down on himself,

or

B. blaming someone else?

781. Maybe he acts this way because other people have treated him badly. I don't want to come down on him for it.

Is this

A. not awfulizing,

or

B. not blaming someone else?

782. I'm so glad I chose to study the training materials. What I read talked about this sort of thing. I think I know more about how to handle this because I did that work.

Is this

A. not getting down on himself,

or

B. celebrating his own choice?

783. This isn't what I wanted to hear, but that doesn't mean the whole thing is ruined. It may take a lot of time for him to learn to trust me. I can handle that.

Is this

A. not awfulizing,

or

B. celebrating luck?

784. I mainly prepared for teaching the child how to do math. I learned something: next time I'll do more preparing in how to help the child get a good relationship started with me.
    Is this

A. learning from the experience,

or

B. not getting down on himself?

785. I'm glad I happened to learn about this program, because it looks like it's connected me to someone who needs a nice friend.
    Is he

A. celebrating luck,

or

B. awfulizing?

786. He's saying I can't help him, after taking one look at me, before I even do anything. This shows he's not really rejecting me; he's rejecting the person he thinks I am. I certainly don't want to punish myself when I haven't even done anything yet.
    Is this

A. not getting down on himself,

or

B. celebrating someone else's choice?

787. My goal is to help this child if I can. If I can help him learn to get along well with me, that will be great. But I don't want to let it spoil my day if he's too far gone to be able to get help from me.
    Is this

A. goal-setting,

or

B. blaming someone else?

788. Let's see, what should I say? I can find out more by saying, "Oh, did you not want to do this?" I can say, "I'm sorry you feel so discouraged." I can say, "Oh? Why do you say that?" I can not say anything, but just listen some more. I can say, "Sounds like you'd rather be doing something else right now?" I can say, "Well, at least you came. I'm glad for that." I can say, "Maybe I can't do anything for you, but maybe you can do something for yourself. So let's get going!"
    Is this

A. awfulizing,

or

B. listing options?

789. He's right; I can't help him; I don't have what it takes. I knew I was taking on something that was too hard for me.
    Is this

A. getting down on himself,

or

B. listing options?

790. I'm grateful to the person who wrote the training materials. I'm so glad this person told us this might happen.

A. celebrating someone else's choice,
or
B. not awfulizing?

791. Now I've given up my lunch hour to have a horrible time each day. I don't see how this can possibly turn out right.
   Is this

A. awfulizing,
or
B. not blaming someone else?

792. It must be because I'm so ugly. Even little kids can't stand to have me near them.
   Is this

A. not awfulizing,
or
B. getting down on himself?

793. After reading these examples, you are ready to do the twelve-thought exercise yourself. Think of a situation – it could be anything – and practice making up a way of thinking each of the twelve types of thoughts. I believe that almost everyone who does this exercise will find it helpful.
   In reading the last few pages and answering these questions you have been

A. doing the twelve-thought exercise,
or
B. reading examples of how to do the twelve-thought exercise?

Ways of Listening to Another Person

794. Some of the world's biggest problems come when people aren't able to listen to each other well enough. Every day millions of people focus on talking, without spending enough effort to listen. Hard feelings, lost friendships, failed marriages, and even wars can result when people don't listen to each other.

The stories in this section will show examples of three ways of listening to someone else. These are three types of things you can say. The first is called a facilitation. You pronounce this word fuh-sill-ih-TAY-shun. Examples of facilitations include:

Huh!
Is that right?
Oh! (or, Oh?)
Um hmm.
Yes.
Right.
Wow!
OK.
Really.
I see.

Facilitations give people the message, "I'm listening. I'm glad you're telling me this. Please keep going."

Suppose a person says, "I've been thinking about a problem the world has and how to solve it!"

A second person says, "Oh?"
Did the second person do a facilitation?

A. yes
or
B. no?

795. The second way of listening is called a reflection. To do a reflection, you say back what you understood the other person to be saying, to make sure you understood it right. Reflections often begin in one of these ways:

So you're saying _____?
What I hear you saying is

_____.
In other words, _____?
So if I understand you right,

_____?
It sounds like _____.
Are you saying that _____?
You're saying that _____?

Suppose the first person says, "I've been thinking about a problem the world has and how to solve it!"

The second person says, "It sounds like you've come up with an idea that you think could be useful to the world, huh?"

Is this a reflection?

A. yes

or
B. no?

796. The third way of listening is called a follow-up question. It asks for more information about something the other person just said. The other person can tell that you're tuning in to what she's saying. Good follow-up questions often prompt the other person to say what she was really getting ready to say next anyway.

Suppose the first person says, "I've been thinking about a problem the world has and how to solve it!"

The second person says, "Great! What is that problem, and how should we solve it?"

Is this a follow-up question?

A. yes
or
B. no?

797. Suppose the first person says, "Our family got a new dog from the animal shelter today."

The second person says, "What kind of dog was it?"

A. reflection
or
B. follow-up question?

798. Suppose the first person says, "Our family got a new dog from the animal shelter today."

The second person says, "Wow!"

A. reflection
or
B. facilitation?

799. Suppose the first person says, "Our family got a new dog from the animal shelter today."

The second person says, "So if I understand you right, this will be a new pet for your family to keep?"

A. reflection
or
B. facilitation?

800. The first speaker in the next few sections is a ten-year-old boy. Suppose he says to the second person, "Wait until you hear what happened to me while I was hiking through the woods the other day!"

The second person says, "It sounds like it was something pretty exciting!"

A. reflection
or
B. follow-up question?

801. First person: I was going for a walk. I was also running a little to get in shape. I was in the woods by myself. I decided I'd get off the trail and go through the woods. All of the sudden I saw a big hole in front of me. I jumped out of the way quickly so that I wouldn't fall into it.

Second person: Hmm!

A. reflection

or
B. facilitation?

802. First person: Then I looked down into the hole, and I saw there was a little shelf of rock down at the bottom of the hole. I jumped down onto it. And then I saw that a little cave opened at the side!
  Second person: Really!

A. facilitation
or
B. reflection?

803. First person: Yep. And I just happened to have taken a flashlight along with me, in case I stayed out after dark.
  Second person: Did you feel lucky to have taken the flashlight?

A. follow-up question,
or
B. facilitation?

804. First person: Yep. But I still didn't feel safe in going back into a cave by myself, without anyone's knowing where I was. It was a little cave. You would have to crawl through it. It was not big enough to walk in. I shined my light back into the cave. I heard something that sounded like a human cry!
  Second person: Is that right?

A. reflection
or
B. facilitation?

805. First person: So I yelled, "Who is that?"
  Two voices yelled back to me, "Help us! Help us!" It sounded like boys about my age, or maybe a little older.
  Second person: So you're saying you heard two boys back in the cave yelling for you to help them?

A. facilitation
or
B. reflection?

806. First person: Yes. I yelled back and forth to them. They shouted to me that one of them had gotten stuck in a narrow passageway in the cave. The other one was blocked behind him. They had been in there for several hours, and they couldn't get out!
  Second person: In other words, they had crawled in, but somehow they couldn't crawl back out again?

A. facilitation
or
B. reflection?

807. First person: That's right. They had crawled in, and they reached a little room where they could turn around. Then, when they tried to crawl back out, they just couldn't do it. I think the boy in front had panicked and had wedged himself in somehow.
  Second person: So what happened next?

A. follow-up question,

or

B. facilitation?

808. First person: I crawled back there. The first boy was stuck tight. He was really upset, but he was glad to see me. He said, "Go get help! Get an adult! Go get somebody with a bulldozer to get me out of here!"

Second person: So did you do what he asked?

A. facilitation

or

B. follow up question?

809. First person: I thought for a while. I said, "I can go get an adult. But what's an adult going to do? If we can hardly fit back here, how's some person twice as big as we are going to get back here? And messing around with a bulldozer would just crush you. Let's think some more." So I sat and thought. The boy just lay there and cried. He was crying, and I was trying to think, for what seemed like a very long time!

Second person: Was it hard to think in that sort of situation, with all that pressure on you?

A. follow-up question,

or

B. facilitation?

810. First person: It sure was. But then I got an idea. I looked closely at the boy who was stuck. I saw that he had on a fairly thick jacket. I said, "If we could just get that coat off you, there would be room for you to squeeze through."

He said, "I tried that. I'm in here too tight to be able to get it off."

Second person. Hmm . . .

A. facilitation

or

B. reflection?

811. First person: But then I got another idea. I happened to have a pocket knife with me. I said to him, "I'm going to take my pocket knife and start cutting out pieces from your coat. If we cut it into little pieces, we can get it out, piece by piece. It will take a while. But when we get all of it off you, you'll get out easily."

Second person: How did he react when you said that?

A. reflection

or

B. follow-up question?

812. First person: That seemed to give him some hope. I helped him cut, and we pulled out piece after piece of the coat. It took a long time. Then we pulled out the last piece that was wedging him against the cave wall. He could finally move! He inched forward, just a little at a time. Then he was able to crawl forward! It was such a thrill to see him start moving!

Second person: So you were really thrilled when that happened!

A. reflection

or

B. follow-up question?

813. Yes. It still took a few minutes longer for all of us to get out, but we finally did. Then I invited them over to where I live to get something to eat and drink. It turns out that they were two boys who went to my school, a couple of years older than I am. They were really grateful.

Second person: So if I understand you right, you have two people you can call on if you ever need anything, huh?

A. reflection

or

B. facilitation?

814. First person: I guess so. But I felt really good just to be able to help them out. It doesn't matter whether they will ever pay me back.

Second person: OK!

A. reflection

or

B. facilitation?

And that's the end of that story.

815. We've talked about three ways of listening: facilitations, reflections and follow-up questions.

Another way of listening is by giving "positive feedback." This means telling the other person that he or she did something good.

Here are some examples of positive feedback:

I'm glad you told me about that.

That's very interesting.

You did something courageous by saying that to her.

I think you just came up with a great idea.

Suppose Rex and June are two people who are thinking of getting married to each other.

June says, "I read an article the other day that I think has some ideas we might want to try out, Rex."

Rex says, "Tell me more, please."

Did Rex do a

A. positive feedback,

or

B. follow-up question?

816. June says, "The article said that when people think of getting married to each other, they usually do things with each other that are very different from what they will do once they get married. And so they don't really know whether they would enjoy being married to each other."

Rex says, "So in other words, if people want to make a good decision about marriage, they should do more of the types of things they will do when they get married?"

Did Rex do a

A. positive feedback,
or
B. reflection?

817. June says, "That's right. People go to movies and concerts together, and eat supper together, and go to parties. And from this, they're supposed to decide how they would be at sharing family chores, and deciding how to use money, and raising children, and that sort of thing."

Rex says, "I'm glad you're thinking about this. I'm glad you're thinking about how to make a good decision."

Did Rex do a

A. facilitation
or
B. positive feedback?

818. Rex says, "So what I hear you saying is, before they are married, people mainly play together. That might not tell them how they will get along when they try to work together."

Did Rex do a

A. reflection
or
B. follow-up question?

819. June says, "Yes, that's exactly right. And you put it in very simple words."

Did June do a

A. follow-up question,
or

B. positive feedback?

820. Rex says, "Thanks. You know something? I think I might enjoy getting some work done together more than going out and being entertained all the time anyway. We could do some babysitting together for my nephew. We could work together on cleaning up our places. We could work together on that project for building houses for poor people."

June says, "I like those ideas!"

Did June do a

A. facilitation
or
B. positive feedback?

821. Here's another conversation. Please look for the examples of facilitations, reflections, follow-up questions and positive feedback.

Paul and Gary are brothers. Paul says, "Hi Gary! How was your day today?"

Gary says, "It was pretty good, thanks! I did some tutoring. I taught my student how to do long division. It was the first time he had ever done it."

Paul says, "Hey! Congratulations!"

Did Paul do a

A. reflection
or
B. positive feedback?

822. Gary says, "Thanks! I felt good about it. How did your day go, Paul?"

Paul says, "It was frustrating, but I think I handled it pretty well. My car battery died today."

Gary says, "Oh my. Today of all days, when it didn't stop snowing hard, all day. What did you do?"

Did Gary do a

A. follow-up question,
or
B. positive feedback?

823. Paul says, "I called the road service and got a jump start and drove it straight over to the car parts place. I got a new battery."

Gary says, "Hey, it sounds like you solved that problem quickly."

Did Gary do a

A. reflection
or
B. facilitation?

824. Paul says, "Not exactly quickly, because I had to wait an hour and a half to get the battery put in. I hung out at the bookstore while I was waiting, though, so it was kind of fun."

Gary says, "So you had to wait an hour and a half. Now I see why you say it was frustrating."

Did Gary do a

A. reflection
or
B. positive feedback?

825. Paul says, "I would have put the battery in myself, except that so much snow was coming down and blowing so hard. And the people who sell car parts won't let you use their building to put parts into your car. But that's OK. I did some good reading, in the bookstore."

Gary says, "What did you read about?"

Did Gary do a

A. reflection
or
B. follow-up question?

826. Paul says, "Part of the time I was reading about tutoring. I found this really good book about how to do it well."

Gary says, "Hmm!"

Did Gary do a

A. facilitation
or
B. reflection?

827. Paul says, "And I got a copy, just for you. Here it is!"

Gary says, "Wow! Thanks, Paul! That is so nice of you!"

Did Gary do a

A. reflection
or
B. positive feedback?

Joint Decision-Making and Conflict-Resolution

828. When people don't agree with each other, sometimes they get angry. Sometimes they even hurt or kill each other. But at other times, they stay cool and work out the problem in a good way. The stories in this section are meant to teach ways of solving problems with other people well. I call it "joint decisions" when people decide what to do about something that will affect both of them.

When you have a joint decision to make, there are seven things you can do to increase the chances of coming to a good solution. Here they are:

1. Defining. Each person defines the problem from his or her point of view, without blaming, and without telling what the solution should be.
2. Reflecting. Each person reflects to let the other person know he understands the other person's point of view.
3. Listing. They list at least four options.
4. Waiting. They don't criticize the options until they've finished listing.
5. Advantages. They think and talk about the advantages and disadvantages of the best options.
6. Agreeing. They pick one to try.
7. Politeness. They don't raise their voices or put each other down or interrupt.
The mnemonic for these 7 guidelines is formed by the first letter of each

guideline. It's an imaginary person's name: "Dr. L.W. Aap."

Sometimes people work out problems well without doing all seven of these things. Sometimes they work out problems well without doing even one of them! But it's a good idea to practice doing each of these seven things, because each of them helps in good joint decisions. And doing joint decisions well is one of the great keys to happiness and peace.

The seven things that are listed are meant to help with

A. joint decisions,
or
B. compliance?

829. Let's think about the first thing on our list, defining the problem. To get "credit" for doing it well, you have to tell what the problem is. But you can't blame the other person. And you can't boss him by telling him what he should do. You want to tell what the problem is and let both of you think of possible solutions.

Here's a sample problem. The first person in a family likes to listen to a certain type of music. The second person does not like that music.

Suppose the second person says, "Why do you listen to that dumb music? Turn it off!"

Does the second person get credit for defining the problem well, or not?

A. yes
or
B. no?

830. When the second person said, "Why do you listen to that dumb music?" he was blaming the first person. When he said, "Turn it off," he was telling what the solution to the problem should be.

Suppose that instead the second person were to say, "Could I talk with you about a problem? When I hear that music, it bothers me, because I don't like that type of music. Could we think about what to do?"

Now does the second person get credit for defining the problem well?

A. yes
or
B. no?

831. Here's another problem. Two people are in a boat. The first of them is moving around a lot and rocking the boat. Suppose the second says, "What are you, a fool? Quit rocking this boat!" Did the second person both blame the other person and tell what the solution should be?

A. yes
or
B. no?

832. Suppose the second person had said, "It worries me when you rock the boat like that. I'm afraid the boat will sink. Can we talk about what to do about this, please?"

Did the second person either blame the other person or tell what the solution should be?

A. yes
or
B. no?

833. Here's another problem. The first person in a family wants to study, and the second person is playing his drum. The noise from the drum bothers the first person. Suppose the first person says, "I want to study for a test now. The noise from the drum is keeping me from being able to concentrate. Can we think about what to do about this, please?"

Does the person get credit for defining the problem as the guideline said he should?

A. yes,
or
B. no?

834. Suppose the first person had said, "Don't be so selfish. The way you are playing your drum is not nice to me at all."

Does this statement get credit for defining the problem well?

A. yes,

or
B. no?

835. Saying, "Don't be so selfish. The way you are playing your drum is not nice to me at all" does not tell what the solution to the problem should be, does it? Then why doesn't it get credit for defining the problem well?

A. Because it blames the other person, or
B. because it tells what the solution should be?

836. Jen wants to take a vacation to a place that costs a lot. Her husband, Jack, thinks they don't have enough money to be able to afford that.
Jack says, "When I think about taking a vacation there, I worry we won't have enough money for things we need more. Can we talk about this problem?"

Jen says, "You are just too cheap. You want us never to enjoy anything, because you're afraid to spend money."

Which of the two people gets credit for defining the problem well?

A. Jack
or
B. Jen?

837. Jim wants to go to see a movie. His wife, Beth, does not like to see movies. Jim says, "You've gotten to be like an old woman. You don't like to go out and do things. You're no fun any more."

Beth says, "When I go to movies, I get restless because I've been sitting still all day at work, and when I am at the movie I have to sit still some more. Can we talk about some different ways to solve this problem?"

Which of the two people gets credit for defining the problem well?

A. Jim
or
B. Beth?

838. Tom is Jane's brother. Tom and Jane have been taking turns caring for the dog. Tom says, "Jane, I think that lots of times our dog is getting fed late because it's hard for both of us to remember whose day it is to feed him. Could we talk about this problem?"

Jane says, "I agree that it's hard to remember whose day it is. Plus some days I get home late. And I feel bad when the dog doesn't get fed on time or when one of our parents has to remind us. Yes, let's think about what we could do."

Which of the two people gets credit for defining the problem well?

A. Jane,
or
B. both of them?

839. Sandra's father says to her, "When you talk with your friends on the phone for a long time, it ties up the line. I worry that my mom might need me and

not be able to get through. Could we talk about what to do about this?"

Does he get credit for defining the problem well?

A. yes,
or
B. no?

840. Sandra says to her father, "I want Grandmom to be able to call us if she needs us. And you deserve to be able to use the line for other things too. At the same time, I have a great time talking with my friends on the phone. I want to be able to do that a lot, if there's a way to do it without causing other problems."

Does Sandra get credit for defining the problem well?

A. yes,
or
B. no?

841. The second thing on the list is to do a reflection to make sure you understand the other person's point of view. Do you remember reflections from the section on listening? To do a reflection is to say back what the other person said in order to make sure you understood it right.

Mr. Brown said, "I have a problem I'd like us to talk about. I'm noticing that our son is doing a lot of whining these days. I think that when we go to him and listen to him right after he whines, we make him whine more.

Mrs. Brown said, "So if I understand you right, you think our son's getting into a bad habit of whining too much. You also think we might be making him whine more by looking at him and listening to him right after he whines."

Mr. Brown said, "That's right."

Who defined the problem from his or her point of view?

A. Mr. Brown,
or
B. Mrs. Brown?

842. To continue this conversation:

Mrs. Brown said, "My point of view is that I, too, think he's got a whining problem. It really gets on my nerves. I need to get away from him sometimes because of that. I never thought about what you said about our making him whine more. But any idea that can help is one I want to think about."

Mr. Brown said, "So, if I understand you right, you agree with me that his whining habit is a problem. You are interested in thinking about any idea that has a good chance of helping."

Mrs. Brown said, "You got it."

Who did a reflection?

A. Mr. Brown,
or
B. Mrs. Brown?

843. Mr. Green and Mrs. Green were talking about a different problem.

Mrs. Green said, "I'd like to talk with you about a problem. When our children go ice skating with you without wearing helmets, it scares me. I don't want them to fall and hurt their heads."

Mr. Green said, "In other words, you feel it's too dangerous to go ice skating without helmets, and you are worried that our children will fall and get hurt."

Who defined the problem from his or her point of view?

A. Mr. Green
or
B. Mrs. Green?

844. To continue this conversation:

Mr. Green said, "I guess it never seemed all that dangerous to me. I skated all the time without a helmet when I was a boy, and I never got badly hurt. It seems to me as if you are more likely to hit your hip or your elbow than your head when you fall while you're ice skating."

Mrs. Green said, "So you're saying ice skating without a helmet isn't something that worries you, because you have done it a lot in your life. You also think the hip or elbow is more likely to get hurt than the head."

Mr. Green said, "That's right."

This time who defined his or her point of view on the problem?

A. Mr. Green
or
B. Mrs. Green?

845. Jack said to his brother Tom, "I have a problem I want to talk with you about. There are lots of times when you sneak up on me and say, 'Boo!' It seems to be a lot of fun for you. But it startles me when you do that, in a way that has become very unpleasant."

Tom said, "So if I understand you right, when I sneak up on you and startle you, that doesn't feel good for you."

Jack said, "That's right."

Who defined the problem from his point of view?

A. Jack
or
B. Tom?

846. To continue this conversation:

Tom said, "I guess, as your older brother, I have always felt a duty to make sure you don't end up a wimp. I want to make sure you are tough and strong. So I figure if I can do things that will scare you enough, you will get used to them. You'll be better off for them. And on top of that, it's fun to startle you."

Jack said, "So you're saying you think it will make me tougher and stronger if I get used to being scared by you, and it's fun for you as well."

Tom said, "That's right."

Who did a reflection?

A. Tom
or
B. Jack?

847. To continue this conversation: Jack said, "You know, when you say you are interested in making me tougher and stronger, I think I believe you. And I think maybe I've gotten less scared to be startled over time. But now the problem is not so much that it's scary, but that it makes me angry. I want to know I can concentrate on something, especially school work, without your yelling really loudly all of the sudden."

Tom said, "So what I hear you saying is that my saying 'Boo' doesn't so much scare you, but it makes you so angry that your attention is pulled away from something else. Plus, I'm hearing you say that I yell too loudly."

Jack said, "You got it right."

This illustrates that:

A. You should be able to define the problem by saying just one thing,
or
B. Sometimes it takes several rounds of talking to get the problem defined well enough?

848. Mr. Smith teaches a Sunday school class. Mrs. Jones's son Biff is in the class.

Mr. Smith said, "Mrs. Jones, could I talk with you about Biff? I like Biff, and I'm glad he comes to Sunday school, but I have a problem because he won't do what I ask him to do. He keeps talking when I'm trying to have a lesson. He does things that take the other kids' attention away from the lesson. I'd like to talk with you about how to handle this."

Mrs. Jones said, "So what you're saying is that Biff is interfering with the class and making it hard to get things done. He does that by not listening to what you say. Do I have it right?"

Mr. Smith said, "That's right."

Who did a reflection?

A. Mr. Smith
or
B. Mrs. Jones?

849. To continue this conversation:

Mrs. Jones said, "I'm glad you told me about this. I have to tell you, I think Biff is spoiled rotten. He thinks he can do whatever he wants, whenever he wants it. His dad and I have split up. We both tried to get Biff on our side for a long time. And I think we turned him into a brat. I'd love to do whatever I can to help you with him."

Mr. Smith said, "So, if I hear you right, you think Biff has gotten into some bad habits of doing whatever he feels like. You'd like to help me in trying to make that better, at least in the Sunday school class."

Mrs. Jones said, "That's right."

Who defined his or her point of view about the problem?

A. Mr. Smith
or
B. Mrs. Jones?

850. When people have disagreements, it's often very hard for them to do "pure" reflections. When you do a pure reflection, you are just saying back what you understood from the other person. You are not putting in your own ideas. You are focusing on understanding the other person. You are willing to wait until later, to try to get the other person to understand you. You are not telling your own ideas, disguised as a reflection.

Mrs. Lancey said, "When our kids are signed up for so many things, it worries me. I think children should have some time just to relax and come up with their own ideas about what to do."

Mr. Lancey said, "So what I hear you saying is that you want them just to be able to goof off, without any duties at all, and that if they ever get busy on something useful that will somehow hurt their poor little souls."

Was Mr. Lancey doing

A. a pure reflection,
or
B. telling his own ideas, disguised as a reflection?

851. Suppose Mr. Lancey had said this instead: "So what I hear you saying is you are worried that our kids have too much they are committed to do. You feel they need more time to come up with their own things to do." In this case, it sounds like Mr. Lancey is really trying to understand Mrs. Lancey, rather than argue against her.

Is this

A. doing a pure reflection,
or
B. telling his own ideas, disguised as a reflection?

852. It's OK to argue against someone else. You just don't want to do it when you are trying to do a reflection. Reflections are supposed to help people understand each other. They are not supposed to be ways of arguing with each other.

Tom said to Jan, "It bothers me when I ask you to get together with me, and you say no, and then I see you with some of your friends."

Jan said, "So what you're saying is you think I should just drop any plans I have with my friends, including plans I might have made a week before. You're saying you have a right to have me say yes any time you feel like being with me, even if you've only decided at the last moment. Is that right?"

Is Jan

A. doing a pure reflection,
or
B. telling her own ideas?

853. Suppose Jan had said, "So, if I understand you right, there's something about it that bothers you when I can't get together with you and you see me with my friends?"

Now is Jan

A. doing a pure reflection,
or
B. telling her own ideas?

854. Suppose Frank says, "I'd like to talk about the problem of getting the dog fed and watered and walked. I feel bad when I see that the dog sometimes doesn't get what he needs, because you and I aren't organized enough about whose turn it is to take care of him."

Lisa says back to him, "So you're saying you think this is OUR problem, when I feed and water and walk the dog faithfully ninety-eight per cent of the time and you almost never do it unless I remind you, huh?"

Is Lisa

A. doing a pure reflection,
or
B. telling her own ideas?

855. Suppose Lisa had said, "So you're saying that you feel bad when the dog doesn't get what he needs, and you'd like to get things organized better so this doesn't happen so much. Is that right?"

In this case, is Lisa

A. trying to understand Frank,
or
B. arguing against him?

856. Suppose William says, "If you want to stay on the Internet very long, it will be a problem for me, because I need to make a phone call to invite someone to a party on Saturday night."

Suppose William's sister Pam says, "It sounds like you have an important call to make, and you want me not to tie up the phone for a long time, so you won't have to wait a long time to make your call, huh?"

Is Pam

A. doing a pure reflection,
or
B. telling her own ideas?

857. Suppose Pam had said, "So you're saying that after you spent the whole evening putting off making that phone call, now when I finally am able to get on the Internet and I'm in the middle of something, you want me to drop what I'm doing, huh?"

Is Pam now

A. doing a pure reflection,
or
B. telling her own ideas?

858. Now let's talk about the third and fourth things that make joint decisions go well: listing and waiting. Listing means that the two people list four or more options on what they could do about the problem. Waiting means that they wait until they are finished listing options before they start to say what's bad about any options.

Suppose the problem is that someone in a family likes a certain type of music, but the music bothers the second person because he doesn't like it.

The second person says, "You could listen with some headphones; that way, only you could hear the music."

The first person says, "I don't like having things on my head. It gives me an unfree feeling."

The second person says, "Well, you should care about the unfree feeling I get when I can't get away from that music of yours."

The first person says, "What do you mean you can't get away from it? Just go down to the basement."

The second person says, "Why should I be the one to have to move? You seem to think I should be the one to go out of my way for you."

Do they get credit for waiting until the listing is over before criticizing the options?

A. yes
or
B. no?

859. Now suppose they had said this instead.

The second person says, "You could listen with some headphones, so that only you could hear the music."

The first says, "That's an option. Or you could go to the basement when I play the music."

The second says, "Or you could move your music to the basement and play it there. Or you could just play it much more quietly."

The first says, "Or we could get some more sound insulation between our rooms."

The second says, "Sounds like we have several options on our list. Are you ready to start thinking about the pros and cons of them?"

The first says, "Yes."

Do they get credit for waiting until the listing is over before criticizing the options?

A. yes
or
B. no?

860. Suppose the problem is that one of two people in a boat is rocking it. This bothers the other one. Suppose they speak as follows:

First: One option is that I could just get out of the boat and let you take it by yourself.

Second: Or you could get out and maybe take the boat ride with someone else who doesn't move around as much as I do.

First: Or I could get a life preserver on.

Second: Or I could try to enjoy myself without rocking the boat so much.

First: Or I could try to get over being scared that you will sink the boat.

Second: Want to talk about pros and cons of these options, or keep listing?

First: Just one more: You could take the boat for twenty minutes, and then I could take it for twenty minutes, and we could keep taking turns.

Do they get credit for listing at least four options?

A. yes
or
B. no?

861. The problem is that the first person in the family wants to practice the drum while the second wants to study for a test. The noise from the drum bothers the person who wants to study. Suppose they talk like this:

First: I could move my drums down to the garage. And you could help me move them.

Second: You could drive me over to the library for the evening, and I could study there.

First: I could put mutes on the drums so that they would be a lot quieter.

Second: Or you could study in the basement. Or you could wear earplugs or head phones.

First: You could practice drumming on pillows or something that is quiet, instead of the drums themselves.

Second: I think we've got enough to think about. Do you?

First: Yes. Let's talk about their advantages and disadvantages.

Do they get credit for waiting until they are through listing before criticizing options?

A. yes
or

B. no?

862. What is the point of waiting until you are through listing before criticizing options? When someone criticizes an option, the other person usually needs to defend it. Then it's likely the two people will get into an argument over whether that option is good or not. Meanwhile, there might be several other options that would suit both of them. They are not thinking of these options because they are too busy arguing over the first one.

On the other hand, if you focus all your energy on just listing options, you can think of more and better options. It's almost always easier to do something if you're not trying to do something else at the same time.

What is it that lets you concentrate on listing options, and do a better job of listing?

A. criticizing each option right after someone names it,
or
B. waiting until you are through listing before criticizing?

863. The next step on our list is talking about the advantages and disadvantages of the options. The words *pros and cons* mean the same thing as advantages and disadvantages. The important thing is to talk about the good and bad points about the *options* and not the good and bad points about *the other person*.

Suppose two people are talking about the problem where one is bothered by the music that the other person plays. Suppose they talk like this:

First: The advantage of my listening to the music through headphones is that you wouldn't be bothered by it at all. The disadvantage is that we don't have headphones and they cost money. Plus, I don't like the feeling of having something on my head.

Second: The money isn't much of a disadvantage, because I would be willing to pay it all, if I had to, to solve this problem. I've heard people say that the sound quality is even better with headphones, so that's a possible advantage.

First: The advantage of my turning the music way down is that it would solve the problem quickly. The disadvantage is that I've gotten used to listening to it loud.

Second: Another advantage of that is that you could protect your hearing. I have heard that loud music really does bad things for your ears.

First: That sounds like a pretty important advantage.

Are they talking about

A. the pros and cons of options,
or
B. the good or bad points about the other person?

864. Suppose the people are talking about the problem where one person is rocking the boat and the rocking worries the other person.

First: I think you are too scared. You should get braver.

Second: The problem isn't that I'm not brave enough. The problem is that you are not careful enough.

First: Have I ever sunk a boat? Have I one time?

Second: That's because you hardly ever are in boats. Have you broken things? Yes. Have you had to go to the emergency room to get stitches? Yes.

First: And you don't have any fun because you're always playing it safe.

Second: Who are you to tell me whether I have fun or not? Do you live in my head?

Are they talking about

A. the pros and cons of options,
or
B. the good or bad points of the other person?

865. Suppose the same two people had spoken to each other in this way:

First: The advantage of our taking turns with the boat is that each of us gets to handle it the way we want. A disadvantage is that we can't go as far out on the lake, if we have to keep coming back to switch with the other person.

Second: The advantage of my switching into a boat with someone else is that this would probably solve the problem; one disadvantage is that it feels a little embarrassing.

First: Another disadvantage of that is that you could wind up with someone who rocks the boat even more than I do.

Are they talking about

A. the pros and cons of options,
or
B. the good or bad points of the other person?

866. The problem is that Mrs. Green wants her kids to wear helmets when they go ice skating with Mr. Green, and Mr. Green thinks it's safe enough without helmets. Suppose they talk with each other in this way.

Mr. Green: I suppose there's not a huge problem with just wearing the helmets. The main con is that most other kids there don't wear helmets, and our kids will want to be like the others.

Mrs. Green: The pro of their doing that is that they learn to be OK with not being like everyone else. But I like the option of looking up statistics on how often people get their heads hurt by skating accidents. That will tell us more about how much need there is.

Are they talking about

A. the pros and cons of options,
or
B. the good and bad points of the other person?

867. Suppose they had talked in this way.

Mr. Green: Why do you have to always try to boss me around? Let me do my own thing every now and then.

Mrs. Green: Why can't you see that this isn't just you? This is our kids' safety you're willing to give up so you can have your selfish wish to be free from anyone telling you what to do.

Are they talking about

A. the pros and cons of options,
or
B. the good or bad points of the other person?

868. Let's talk about the sixth thing on our list, agreeing on something.

Jim wants to see a movie. Beth doesn't like to see movies because she has to sit all day at work and doesn't want to sit more.

Suppose the conversation ends like this:

Beth: That option sounds worth trying. We will take a very long run together and then go to the movie after that.

Jim: Great! Let's see how you like it if we do that, and if you do, maybe we can try it again in the future.

Beth: OK.

Did they get credit for agreeing on something?

A. yes
or
B. no?

869. Suppose they had ended up their talk like this:

Beth: I suppose we could take a long run before the movie. It might work.

Jim: But don't say I got you to go to the movie if you don't like being there.

Beth: Well, I wouldn't go see it on my own. I just wouldn't.

Jim: OK, have your way then.

Beth: Don't be like that.

Jim: Don't be like what? Oh, just forget it.

Did they get credit for agreeing on something?

A. yes

or

B. no?

870. Suppose Mr. and Mrs. Brown have a problem with a child who whines too much. Suppose they end up their talk like this.

Mrs. Brown: It's an interesting theory – that he whines more because we pay more attention to him when he does.

Mr. Brown: It's interesting, but nothing usually comes of it if you don't stick to the rule.

Mrs. Brown: I'm still not sure that's the problem.

Mr. Brown: Maybe not, but I think so.

Did they get credit for agreeing upon an option?

A. yes

or

B. no?

871. Suppose Mr. and Mrs. Brown ended up their talk in this way instead:

Mrs. Brown: OK, so let's see if I can say the plan. We'll make a rule never to give him what he wants right after he whines, unless he really needs help to keep him from getting hurt or something like that. And we'll try not to even pay attention to him when he whines. We will remind each other of this when we are both around. We'll keep track of how much he whines each day and see if it gets less over time as we try not to reward it.

Mr. Brown: That's it, exactly.

Mrs. Brown: OK, let's see how it works for two or three weeks and then be sure to talk again with each other about it. I'll put it in my book for maybe three weeks from now?

Mr. Brown: Sounds good. I'll put it in my book too.

Did they get credit for agreeing on an option?

A. yes

or

B. no?

872. Let's talk about the last thing on the list: politeness. This means the two people do not yell at each other. They do not interrupt each other. And they don't insult the other person.

Suppose that one person uses the word *stupid* or *lazy* to talk about the other person.

Could that person get credit for politeness?

A. yes
or
B. no?

873. Suppose one person says to the other, "You don't know what you're talking about," or "What you did was really idiotic." Or suppose the person curses at the other, or calls the person names. Or suppose the person says, in a sarcastic voice, "Yeah, right. Tell me another one."

Could that person get credit for politeness?

A. yes
or
B. no?

874. In each of the following conversations, the people will do each of the seven things on the list except for one of them. Both people, or one person, will fail to do that thing. Please figure out which one of the seven things you can't give credit for to at least one of the people.

The situation is that Fran had agreed to babysit for Mr. and Mrs. Black. But five days before Mr. and Mrs. Black were planning to go out, Fran got an invitation to get together with a boy she is very interested in, on the same night. Fran talks to Mrs. Black.

Fran: I want to talk with you about a problem. I made a commitment to babysit for you next Saturday night. But I got an invitation after I did that, to get together with someone I'd really like to see more of.

Mrs. Black: So you have something that feels like an important opportunity, that is on next Saturday night.

Fran: Right.

Mrs. Black: I'm glad you mentioned this ahead of time. Mr. Black and I have a party to go to that we're looking forward to, on that night. And it's not the type of thing you can take kids to.

Fran: So you're going to something that will only happen that night, that you can't take the kids to.

Mrs. Black: Right.

Which two of the things have they done so far?

A. defining and reflecting,
or
B. listing and waiting?

875. To continue:

Mrs. Black: So shall we think of some options?

Fran: An option is that I have a friend, Sue Gray, who would be a very responsible babysitter. She has done a great job babysitting with other kids.

Mrs. Black: I know who she is. I've heard good things about her. I could call her up.

Fran: I've already asked her if she would be available that night, and she would be.

Mrs. Black: You get to go out, we do too, and we get to know one more person we can call at times like this. The only disadvantage is that our kids don't know her, but between now and then there is time for her to come over and get to know them while we're here.

Fran: I'm sure she'd be willing to do that.

Mrs. Black: Sounds great to me. Thanks for thinking about this, Fran.

Fran: I wanted to figure out something rather than just back out on my job.

Which of the seven things did they not do?

A. Politeness
or
B. listing at least four options?

876. Jon works on a construction crew, where Tim is the boss.

Jon: Tim, I wanted to talk with you about a problem. A lot of the guys and I have been talking about how hot it is this summer. Some people have gotten sick, and I don't think we're working as fast as we usually do.

Tim: So you're pointing out that the summer sun is making some people sick and slowing down the work.

Jon: Right.

Tim: It's unpleasant, too. It's as unpleasant for me as anyone else. One option is giving everyone lots of water and salt.

Jon: Another option is wetting our clothes with water to cool ourselves off. But another option we've been thinking

of is starting really early in the morning, before daylight even.

If at this point, Tim were to say, "That would not work because people will be too sleepy early in the morning," then he would not get credit for

A. politeness
or
B. waiting?

877. To continue:

But Tim did not say that. Instead he said,

Tim: That's an interesting one. I suppose we could also start in the evening. Or, we could just tough it out. I'm ready to think about pros and cons if you are.

Jon: The advantage of the early morning is that it's cooler in the early morning light than it is in the evening light.

Tim: That's true, because it has cooled off during the night. Another advantage of the early morning is that people could still be with their families in the evening.

Jon: The disadvantage of starting, say, at three in the morning is that everybody would have to go to bed really early, but I think most people would do that as long as this heat keeps up.

Tim: We have a small crew. Let's see if anybody has any problems with starting earlier. I can also talk to my boss too. If all of us can do it, and it's OK with my boss, it's OK with me.

Jon: Sounds great.

Which one of the seven things did they not do?

A. Jon did not do a reflection,

or

B. Tim did not do a reflection?

878. Frank is thinking of renting an office in a building that Bob owns.

Frank: Bob, I have just one problem with this office. I don't like windows that you can't open. I like to get fresh air from outside sometimes, or at least to know that I can. I want to know I can do something if it feels like the air is not clean enough.

Bob: So if I understand you right, Frank, you want to be sure that if the indoor air is not clean, you can get fresh air from outside.

Frank: That's right.

Bob: I want to make it so that you'll be happy renting this office, if we can work it out somehow.

Frank: So you want to solve this problem with me if it's possible.

Bob: Right.

What Frank just did was a

A. reflection

or

B. talking about advantages and disadvantages?

879. To continue:

Frank: The option I've been thinking about is replacing these windows with windows that you can open or close.

Bob: Another option is that I could go over with you the tests we've had done on the indoor air, and show you the system we have, and see if you still feel you need windows after that.

Frank: If the cost of replacing the windows is a problem, an option is that I could pay what's necessary to have them replaced.

Bob: One possibility might be to replace one or two of the windows instead of all of them, and get a powerful fan to move the air in and out.

Frank: Are you ready to think about the pros and cons of these options?

Bob: Yes. The advantage of my showing you the air system and the tests we've done is that you might feel OK without windows after that.

Frank: The disadvantage of that is I am sure I will still want windows you can open, if I can get them.

Bob: The disadvantage of replacing the windows is that I think our insurance company charges us less if the windows don't open. To change one or two of the windows would cost us a lot more in insurance, I think.

Frank: Are you sure about that?

Bob: No.

Frank: How about if you check on that, and we talk again after you know for sure?

Bob: Excuse me for a minute please, Frank.

Bob picks up the phone and listens. It's an urgent call. Bob rushes out of the room, saying, "Please excuse me."

Which one of the seven things did
they not do?

A. waiting
or
B. agreeing?

880. Some kids are playing baseball.
Paul and Ron are on different sides. A
ball is hit. It rolls out of bounds after
landing near the third base line.

Paul: I think that was a good hit. It
landed in bounds.

Ron: You think it landed in bounds,
and then rolled out?

Paul: Yes.

Ron: The way I saw it, it landed out
of bounds.

Paul: So you think it was a foul,
huh?

Ron: Yes.

Paul: One option is that we could
take it over, without counting the foul
as a strike.

Ron: Or we could let the third
baseman call it, since he was closest to
it.

Paul: Or we could let that man over
there who was watching call it, since
he's not on either team.

Ron: We could also just count it as a
fair ball since we're behind anyway and
it's not likely that we'll catch up.

Paul: Or another option is just to
finish up the game now anyway, since
it's getting late.

Ron: Let's just take it over.

Paul: I agree. (Paul yells to the other
boys) We're just going to take it over!

Which one of the seven things did
they not do?

A. advantages and disadvantages,
or
B. reflecting?

881. Ruth and Rita sit next to each other
in class in school.

Ruth: Rita, I have a problem I want
to talk with you about. When we're in
class . . .

Rita: I know what you're going to
say. I always talk with you, and, when
you talk back, we get in trouble with the
teacher, right?

Ruth: That's it. And I think I'm
getting a bad reputation with the
teacher, and I think she's starting not to
like me as much.

Rita: So you think that all this
talking is getting the teacher down on
you, huh?

Ruth: Right.

Rita: Well, the way I see it, life is too
short to worry about stuff like that, and
what fun is it to go to school if you
can't have a conversation with someone
every now and then?

Ruth: So it doesn't bother you too
much whether the teacher likes it or not,
and talking makes school more fun for .
. .

Rita: Right, it makes me look
forward to going to school more. It's
something fun to do.

They have now each done two of the
seven things on the list. The next thing
on the list is

A. listing options,

or

B. agreeing on something?

882. To continue:

Ruth: Well, let's think of some things we could do. I could …

Rita: I know what you're going to say. You could see if you can move your desk to another part of the room, away from me.

Ruth: Well, that's an option, but what I was going to say was that I could just not talk back to you when you talk to me.

Rita: Or maybe we could write notes back and forth instead of talking.

Ruth: Or another option is . . .

Rita: That I could just stop talking and pay attention to the teacher, right?

Ruth: That's another option. What I was going to say this time is that maybe we could talk more with each other at times other than when we're in class.

Rita: Hmm. I can't think of any more, can you?

Ruth: No. The disadvantage of my not talking back to you is that it might make you angry.

Rita: The advantage of my paying attention to the teacher is that I'd get better grades.

Ruth: You might even find that it is fun, when you put yourself into . . .

Rita: Fun? No way, Jose. That's really a stupid idea.

Ruth: If we get my desk moved and plan to spend more time talking outside

class, it would solve the problem and we could stay friends.

Rita: Let's do that.

Ruth: I agree. I'll ask the teacher about the move.

Rita: OK.

Which of the seven things did one of them not get full credit for?

A. waiting until all options were listed before criticizing them,

or

B. politeness?

883. Mr. Land is the father of Nicole, who is fifteen years old.

Mr. Land: Nicole, I have a problem I'd like us to talk about, please. It's that you like to get on the Internet in the evening. But that ties up the phone lines for everyone else in the family.

Nicole: So you're saying my being on the Internet and tying up the phone line prevents you and other people in the family from being able to use the phone.

Mr. Land: Right.

Nicole: My point of view is that I try to do it later in the evening, when there are fewer phone calls being made. And it's such a reward for me to do it when I've finished my homework. It's like my payoff that I give myself when I'm all done.

Mr. Land: In other words, you use it as a reward to help you celebrate finishing your homework, and because it's late, other people don't need to use the phone as much then.

Nicole: That's right.

Mr. Land: I appreciate that you are doing it when there are not a lot of calls. And I'm glad you use it as a reward for getting your work done. But there are still times when other people want to call us, and when we want to call out. And there are times when we want to use the Internet, too.

Nicole: So the fact remains that it still ties up the line.

Mr. Land: Right.

Nicole: Well, one option is that you could just ask me to get off whenever you need to use the phone.

Suppose Mr. Land were to say, "We've already tried that, Nicole, but often you're in the middle of things that you don't want to interrupt right away, and we don't like waiting for fifteen or twenty minutes."

If he did this, he would not get credit for

A. advantages and disadvantages,
or
B. waiting?

884. To continue:

Mr. Land did not say this. Instead he said:

Mr. Land: That's an option. Or we could set a limit on how many minutes you could stay on each night, like half an hour.

Nicole: Or I could use the money I make babysitting to buy another phone line or a high-speed Internet connection.

Mr. Land: Or you could make some more money to pay for it by doing some work for me. I have some recordings that need to be typed.

Nicole: I want to do the typing and use the money to pay for a high-speed connection.

Mr. Land: Well, let's give it a try, then!

Which one of the seven did they fail to do?

A. advantages and disadvantages,
or
B. defining?

885. In the next few stories, please tell which of the seven things the person did do.

Jane hears her husband Rudy say, "One option is that you could just put up with how I get loud and say embarrassing things at parties when I get drunk, and learn to enjoy it."

Jane gets the urge to reply, "But I've already tried that, Rudy."

She stops herself before saying that, though, and she says, "That's an option. Another option is that you could stop drinking altogether. Another option is that we could not go to parties together any more."

Which of the seven things did Jane do?

A. waiting before criticizing an option,
or
B. defining the problem without blaming or telling the solution?

886. Frank sees a bill for his wife's health club. He gets the urge to say to her, "What? Two hundred dollars a month for this health club that you hardly ever go to? We've got to cancel this membership, now!"

He stops himself before saying that. Instead, he says to her, "Could I talk with you about a decision? I noticed that the bill for the health club is a couple of hundred dollars a month. We need to save some money, and I thought we might think about whether this or some other things might be good ways to save some money."

Which of the seven things did Frank do?

A. defining the problem without blaming or telling the solution,
or
B. listing at least four options?

887. Mary and John are talking about ways of playing chess with each other. Mary says, "Well, come on, let's give it a try."

John says, "Let's see. What you want us to try is, rather than playing the chess game to the end, whoever is ahead after twenty minutes will win. We're also going to have the rule that you have to move within half a minute. Is that it?"

Mary says, "Yes. That's it."

John says, "OK, I'll go along with that, for one game at least. Let's see how it works."

Mary says, "OK."

What did they do?

A. define the problem without blaming or telling the solution,
or
B. agree upon something?

888. Randy says, "Mom, I want to talk with you about something. It seems to me that my brother Lunk has so many problems that you and Dad are always dealing with him. But my sister and I sort of miss out on your attention, because we aren't always making trouble. I'm not so sure it's even good for Lunk to get so much attention from you for getting into trouble. He learns that getting into trouble gets him attention."

Randy's mom says, "So, Randy, if I understand you right, you're saying that your dad and I are always paying attention to Lunk because he's getting into trouble. You and your sister miss out. And, you think we might be rewarding the bad things he does by our attention. Is that right?"

What Randy did was

A. defining the problem,
or
B. waiting until finishing listing options before criticizing them?

889. Fred and his sister Tina are talking about options for dividing up housework. Fred has listed an option that they could take turns, with one

person doing all the chores every other month.

Tina gets the urge to say, "You're too untrustworthy for the option of taking turns every other month. You'd want me to go first, and you probably wouldn't do anything the second month."

But she stops herself. Then she says, "One of the cons for taking turns every month is that whoever goes first may not trust that the other person would take their turn. For that reason, a month might be too long."

Is she

A. talking about a disadvantage of an option,

or

B. doing a reflection?

890. Let's spend some time talking about the difference between polite and impolite talk. If you get the urge to say something in an impolite way, you can almost always translate it. You can make the same point in a more polite way.

Please read each of the following pairs of things that people might say. Then tell which of them is more polite: the first or the second.

The first situation is that someone wants to ask someone else in the family to help out more with the chores.

The first way of saying it: You never clean up anything in this house. You're always leaving it for someone else to do.

The second way of saying it: It would really make me feel good if you would put more effort into cleaning up the floors and the dishes and doing some laundry. I would appreciate that, a lot.

Which was more polite:

A. the first,

or

B. the second?

891. The situation is that a parent is giving a child some homework help in the parent's office at home. The parent asks the child to come in.

The first way of saying it: I'm ready for you to come in here now. Welcome.

The second way of saying it: OK, get in here.

Which was more polite:

A. the first,

or

B. the second?

892. The situation is that someone is playing music that another person in the family dislikes and thinks is too loud.

The first way of saying it: Why can't you understand that everybody in this family hates that music you play? Why can't you think of someone else other than yourself?

The second way of saying it: I believe it's a big problem, not only for me, but also for your mom and your sister, when the music you play is loud. Can we think of what to do about this?

Which was more polite:

A. the first,
or
B. the second?

893. The situation is that two people are talking about a decision. One of them asks, "How much will it cost to do this?" The other person has just said a minute ago how much the thing would cost.

The first: I already told you that. Can't you hear?

The second: It costs twenty-five dollars an hour. I'll write it down so it's easier to remember.

Which was more polite:

A. the first,
or
B. the second?

894. The situation is that someone in a family starts to walk away from the kitchen table, without putting away his dishes and cleaning off the table.

The first: Before you leave, could you please take your dishes to the sink, rinse them and wipe off the table?

The second: Where do you think you're going? Why are those dishes still on the table?

Which was more polite:

A. the first,
or
B. the second?

895. The situation is that someone in a family is trying to move a big box somewhere, and someone else is standing in the doorway.

The first: Excuse me, please. I need to get through this door before I drop this thing. Thank you.

The second: Get out of the way. Can't you see I'm trying to get through?

Which was more polite:

A. the first,
or
B. the second?

896. The first person has said, "I think welfare should be totally ended. It just keeps people from helping themselves. If someone does not want to work, then they don't deserve to have money."

The second person very much disagrees with this.

The first: I can't believe I'm hearing someone say such a thing. That's not only dumb. It's also very uncaring and unfeeling.

The second: I can't agree with you that it should be totally ended. Don't you feel that somewhere there are people who can't work? And if so, shouldn't we set up a fair way to keep those people from starving or freezing?

Which was more polite:

A. the first,
or
B. the second?

897. Five-year-old Maria is dancing around, singing the same song over and over again. This gets very annoying for her ten-year-old brother.

The first: Hey Maria, shut up!

The second: Maria, how about a different song? That one is starting to grate on me. How about singing "The More We Get Together?"

Which was more polite:

A. the first,

or

B. the second?

898. Seven-year-old Fred wants a box of cereal on a shelf that's too high for him to reach.

The first: Would you be willing to hand me that box of cereal on the top shelf, please?

The second: Get me that box of cereal on the top shelf right now, please.

Which was more polite:

A. the first,

or

B. the second?

899. Sarah has received an invitation to go and play with a friend. Sarah's mom says, "I'm sorry, Sarah. You can't go until your homework is finished and the chores are finished. I don't think you're going to have time at all." Sarah replies to her mom:

The first: What about the idea of my just playing for an hour? After that I would have time to get it all done.

The second: You NEVER let me do anything fun.

Which was more polite:

A. the first,

or

B. the second?

900. Someone says, "That doctor must not be any good. I went to him, and I was sick, and he didn't even give me any medicine! I think I should have gotten some antibiotics."

The other person disagrees with the idea that this means the doctor is not any good.

The first: I'll bet the doctor thought you had a sickness caused by a virus. It does not do any good to treat sicknesses like that with antibiotics.

The second: I don't think you know much about this topic.

Which was more polite:

A. the first,

or

B. the second?

901. Someone asks a teacher a question. The teacher thinks the student can figure out the answer.

The first: Don't ask me that. Figure it out for yourself.

The second: I could tell you, but wouldn't you get a kick out of figuring it out yourself? Please give it a try. What do you think?

Which was more polite:

A. the first,

or

B. the second?

902. A man says to his wife, "I don't get drunk very often. It's not often enough to be a problem." In fact, the man has gotten drunk about half the nights of the last month. His wife replies:

The first: Oh, yeah, right. Tell me another fairy story, please.

The second: I can't agree with that. I estimate you've been drunk about half the nights of this last month. I would call that a problem.

Which was more polite:

A. the first,

or

B. the second?

903. A man is handling an expensive musical instrument in a way that his wife feels is too rough. She speaks to him:

The first: Hey, watch it! What are you trying to do, break that thing? Didn't anybody ever teach you to be careful with things?

The second: I'll bet you didn't know, that thing breaks very easily. We have to put it down only on soft objects and be very gentle with it.

Which was more polite:

A. the first,

or

B. the second?

904. A woman asks her husband, "Please wash the dishes." He is feeling tired from working all afternoon on another household chore. He feels as if he has done his share of the work.

The first: No, I'm not going to wash the dishes. It won't hurt you to do some work. You wash them.

The second: I'm tired from working on the driveway, and I'm also feeling as if I've done my share for today. So I want to bow out of washing the dishes tonight.

Which was more polite:

A. the first,

or

B. the second?

905. A woman uses hair spray. Her husband doesn't like the smell and thinks that the fumes may be poisonous. He speaks to her.

The first: How could you use that stupid stuff? You're just messing up our air. It doesn't make you look any better anyway. Get rid of it, or you'll find that I've gotten rid of it.

The second: It's very important to me not to breathe the hair spray. I don't think it's good for you, either, or for anybody. I very much dislike the smell, too, but that's not as important. Can we talk about this problem, please?

Which was more polite:

A. the first,

or

B. the second?

906. A person is standing in line to buy something at a store. Someone else gets in front of her in the line.

    The first: Excuse me. Are you getting in this line? The line is forming back there, please.

    The second: Hey. What do you think you're doing, breaking in front of me?

    Which was more polite:

A. the first,
or
B. the second?

Deciding Whether to Get Help

907. The choice of whether to get help on something is often very important. Sometimes this choice even makes the difference between life and death.

Here's a thought pattern that people often use. Suppose a person really needs help on something, but admitting that he needs help feels bad. Maybe it feels bad because he feels ashamed of needing help. Maybe it feels bad because it's scary to think about the problem at all. So the person, instead of getting help, tells himself, "I don't have a problem," and doesn't do anything about it. The problem continues. It can be very unwise to deny that such problems exist.

On the other hand, sometimes people are able to do things themselves, even though they don't think they can. Sometimes they make a very good decision when they try to do it on their own.

This section is saying:

A. It's always wise to get help,
or
B. it's sometimes wise to get help?

908. The following stories will give you practice in deciding when it is a good decision to get help. Please decide two things about each story: 1. Did the person decide to accept help?, and 2. Was the person's decision smart?

A man heard a noise in his car. He thought, "Should I get somebody to help me see what it is and maybe fix it?" But he just did not have the energy to do that. He kept driving the car.

One day it broke down and would not run any more. He had to get it towed. The mechanic said to him, "If you had it fixed earlier, it would have cost you only fifty dollars. Now you'll need your whole engine replaced. It will cost a few thousand dollars."
When the man first heard the noise, was his decision not to get help

A. a smart decision,
or
B. a not smart decision?

909. A little girl was learning to tie her shoes. She thought, "Should I get my dad to tie my shoes, or should I try it myself?" She had plenty of time. She decided to try it herself. She was able to do it. She felt proud.

Was her decision not to get help

A. smart
or
B. not smart?

910. A person drank too much alcohol. People told him he had a problem with drinking too much. People said to him, "You should get some help with this problem."

The thought of being an alcoholic made him ashamed. He thought, "I don't drink too much. There are lots of other people who drink as much as I do."

One night when he drank too much he drove his car recklessly, ran into a tree and was hurt badly.

Was his decision not to get help

A. smart

or

B. not smart?

911. A woman saw a mole on her skin. She noticed it had started to grow. It was shaped in a way that was not symmetrical. It had borders that were not clear. It was not the same shade of color all the way through. She remembered reading that moles like this could be cancer. The thought of going to a doctor scared her. She was worried the doctor might say, "You have cancer."

But then she thought to herself, "If I don't go to the doctor, I don't solve the problem. I just pretend it isn't there." She went to the skin doctor.

The skin doctor said, "This mole should come off." Later when another doctor had looked at the mole with a microscope, her skin doctor said, "You have a skin cancer. But because you caught it early, you have a great chance of living. If you had waited longer, this probably would have killed you."
Was her decision to get help

A. smart

or

B. not smart?

912. A man was trying to move a big and heavy filing cabinet. Someone said, "Do you need some help?"

The man thought, "I should be tough enough to do this all by myself. Only wimps need help with things like this." The man said, "I can do it myself." The man carried it. People were impressed with how strong the man was. But the next morning the man's back hurt very badly. It turned out that the lifting had hurt his back. He had to miss work for several weeks while his back healed.

Was the man's decision not to get help

A. smart

or

B. not smart?

913. A woman was very pretty. She wanted to be even prettier. She hired someone to show her how to be beautiful. She gave the person lots of money for telling her what clothes to buy, for getting people to work on her hair, and for getting doctors to do operations that made her body look just a little better.

The woman still wasn't happy. Later, she saw a friend who had spent her time helping other people. The friend seemed to feel good about her life. The woman thought a long time. She finally decided, "I wasted my time and money trying to make myself beautiful. I should have been doing something that would make the world a better place, as my friend did."

Was the woman's decision to get lots of help in being a more beautiful person

A. smart
or
B. not smart?

914. A boy had a problem with his speech. This problem made it hard for people to understand him. His parents said to him, "You can go to a speech teacher, if you want."

He talked to a friend. The friend said, "I heard that only stupid people go to speech teachers."

But the boy knew that he wasn't stupid. He knew that going to a speech teacher would not make him stupid. He decided that going to the speech teacher might help him speak better. So he said to his parents, "I want to go."

The speech teacher taught him lots of good things. He worked hard on them. He worked so hard, in fact, that he learned to speak much better than most people do. He began to get lots of compliments on his way of speaking. He used this skill throughout his life.

Was the boy's decision to get help

A. smart
or
B. not smart?

Degrees of Gentleness In Assertion

915. Often we don't like what someone else does. Often we don't like what someone else wants to do. When we ask or tell someone not to do what he wants, we are using assertion. When someone asks you to do something, and you say no, you are also using assertion.

Sometimes problems come when people oppose other people in an "all-or-none" way. Some people either keep quiet or have a tantrum. They have to either let the other person have his way, or attack the other person with great anger. Sometimes someone will do or say nothing for a long time while someone is doing something he does not like. Then all of the sudden he gets very angry at the other person.

It's often much better if you can ask someone to change what they're doing, in a very gentle way. Sometimes you will have to use more forceful talk. It's good to pick and choose how gentle you sound. You want to make your gentleness fit the situation.

In assertion, you should

A. always be very gentle,
or
B. let the amount of gentleness be right for the situation?

916. Somebody buys a new shirt, and at home when he tries it on, he sees that two buttons are missing. He takes the shirt back and speaks to the person at the store.

Here is the first way of being assertive: Hi. I bought this shirt earlier today. But when I opened the package, I found it had two buttons missing.

Here is the second way of being assertive: I bought this shirt new here today, and it wasn't made right. It's missing two buttons. It makes me irritated to have to bring it back, because it is taking up lots of time. Please exchange it.

Which is the more gentle:

A. the first,
or
B. the second?

917. A girl has an agreement with her brother that they will take turns feeding the dog. But the brother tends to forget on his days. The usual time for feeding has passed again today, and the dog is hungry and whining.

The first: Excuse me, do you remember our agreement about your feeding the dog every other day? Are you planning to keep it or not? If you're not going to do it, please let me know, because you're neglecting the dog and it's cruel to him, and I'm not going to stand for this any more.

The second: I think we should talk about what to do about the dog-feeding. More often than not on your days you forget, and I think we need to think about a different arrangement.

Which is more gentle:

A. the first,

or

B. the second?

918. Someone is playing tennis with a partner who is goofing around and hitting the balls way up in the air and laughing and being silly rather than paying attention to the game.

The first: Could you please not goof around like that? I think you're distracting the other people who want to play on either side of us. And I'd like to play rather than goof off.

The second: It's fun to watch them go up and down, isn't it? But come on, let's play in the regular way, OK?

The third: You are a real embarrassment. The other people trying to play must think you're really immature. If you can't act your age and play right, then I'm getting out of here.

Which is most gentle?

A. the third,

or

B. the second?

919. Someone wants to practice the piano, but a little brother keeps playing with the keys while he is doing so.

The first: Will you do me a favor and wait until I'm done practicing? I'm trying to concentrate on my song for just a little while. It won't be long.

The second: When you do that, it is really irritating. Please get away from me now!

The third: Please don't do that. It distracts me from my song.

Which is most gentle?

A. the first,

or

B. the second?

920. A child is in an adult's office and is handling electronic equipment without getting permission.

The first: Those things are NOT TOYS. Plus, they are not yours. Don't ever touch them without asking me first. To handle other people's things without asking is very rude.

The second: The rule for these things is: Do not touch them without permission. Do you think you can follow that?

The third: I'm going to move some of these things that I don't want handled out of your reach. That way it won't be such a temptation for you to handle them. It's hard to resist them when they're out like this, isn't it?

Which is most gentle?

A. the first

or

B. the third?

921. Someone in a library is tapping his pencil on his desk, and it is annoying someone else who is trying to work at the next desk.

The first: Hi. Could I please ask you to try not to tap the pencil on the desk? I just can't concentrate well enough to tune it out. Thanks. I really appreciate it.

The second: Please stop tapping that pencil on the desk. You are interfering with my work when you do that. It's extremely annoying.

Which is more gentle?

A. the first,
or
B. the second?

922. Somebody takes his car to be fixed. He is told the car will be ready at a certain time. He shows up at that time. The person who works there says, "It'll just be a couple of more minutes." Fifteen minutes later, it still isn't ready. The person who works there says, "Just a minute more." Fifteen minutes later, it still isn't ready.

The first: Listen. I've been waiting here thirty minutes while you've been saying it will be ready in a couple of minutes. If it's not going to be ready, quit stringing me along. I've got other things I could be doing! So concentrate on this question, and tell me truthfully: When will it be ready?

The second: Hey, if you need more time, that's no problem. But I've got other things I could be doing, and I can leave and come back. If it won't be ready in five minutes, I'll just take off and be back in an hour or so.

Which is more gentle?

A. the first,
or
B. the second?

923. A child is looking forward to going on a hiking trip. The child keeps asking her parent, "Is it time to go yet?" "Now is it time to go?" "When will it be time to go?" The parent has already told the child that they will leave at a certain time.

The first: Please do not ask me that again. You are getting on my nerves. If you do ask me again, the trip is going to be put off by five minutes for every time you ask me.

The second: You're really excited about this, aren't you? I'm glad you are. But you're going to have to wait, and I'd appreciate it if you could keep from asking me when it will be.

Which is more gentle?

A. the first,
or
B. the second?

924. Someone is smacking his lips really loudly as he eats. This bothers his brother.

The first: Could you please do me a favor? Could you keep your lips together while you chew? I just have a thing about the sound of smacking lips.

The second: Please quit smacking your lips. I find that sound really irritating.

The third: I hate the sound of those lips smacking. It's really bad manners, and it drives me up the wall. Please eat in a civilized way, or else go off by yourself to do it.

Which is most gentle?

A. the first,
or
B. the second?

925. A boy in a classroom is in the habit of talking out and interrupting the teacher and other students. This bothers another student.

The first: Are you working on trying to talk out and interrupt less? If you are, that's great, because it sure will be more fun for the rest of us if you can master that.

The second: I hope it's going to happen soon that you can do less talking out and interrupting. It is irritating when you do that.

The third: I wish you could learn to keep quiet and let other people finish talking, instead of interrupting all the time. I resent it when you do that. And lots of other people do too.

Which is most gentle?

A. the first
or
B. the third?

Frustrations and Fortitude

926. Whenever you don't get what you want, the situation you're in is called a frustration. It is also a frustration when something happens that you don't want.

A man had been looking forward very much to taking a nice swim. When he got to the pool, he found it was closed. He could not swim there that day.

Would we call this situation a frustration?

A. yes
or
B. no?

927. A woman wrote an article she wanted to publish in a magazine. She sent the article in. Soon she got a reply. The editor of the magazine told her, "We would very much like to print your article in our magazine."

Would we call this situation a frustration for the writer?

A. yes
or
B. no?

928. A farmer planted some seeds. The crops started to grow. But then a cold spell came along and killed the crops. All the plants died.

Would we call this situation a frustration for the farmer?

A. yes
or
B. no?

929. Someone ran a business. He sold some stuff that you put around water pipes. This stuff kept the heat or cold in the pipes. One day he found out that the stuff that goes around the pipes makes a dust that gets in people's lungs and causes cancer. He found out he was going to get sued by many people who got cancer from using the stuff he sold.

For the man who ran the business, was this

A. a frustration,
or
B. not a frustration?

930. A man fell in love with a woman. He wanted to marry her. One day, he asked her, "Will you marry me?"

She said to him, "I'm sorry. I don't want to marry you. I don't think we should even see each other any more."

For this man, was this

A. a frustration,
or
B. not a frustration?

931. A girl went to a party. She was a little nervous because she didn't know the people there. Right away, she made a new friend who was very nice to her.

All the other kids at the party were very nice too. Some of her new friends planned to get together with her.

For this girl, was this

A. a frustration,

or

B. not a frustration?

932. A man was ready to give a big speech. Lots of people were set to listen to him. But as he walked by a table, his pants snagged on something sharp. The sharp thing made a big tear in his pants.

For this man, was this

A. a frustration,

or

B. not a frustration?

933. We call the skill of handling frustrations well fortitude. Fortitude usually means staying cool and figuring out what's best to do about the frustration.

Suppose a girl climbed up to the top of a slide. But when she got to the top, she didn't like the look of this slide. She was not sure whether it was safe. So she came back down the steps. A boy yelled at her, "Scaredy cat! Scaredy cat!"

She did not like it that he said this. But then she thought to herself, "Who cares what he thinks?" She ran over to play on something else. She had fun with it.

When the boy called her names, did she handle it

A. with fortitude,

or

B. not with fortitude?

934. A boy was trying to make a model airplane out of very light wood. He tried fitting two parts together. He could not get them to fit. Then he tried a different way. He still could not get them to fit. He got so angry that he smashed his hand down on all the airplane parts, breaking them into little pieces.

Did he handle the frustration

A. with fortitude,

or

B. not with fortitude?

935. A woman was trying to get a computer program to make a chart. The chart did not come out looking right. She tried a different way. Still it didn't work. She felt irritated. She thought, "This is a harder job than I thought it was. It might take some time to figure it out." She read in a book about how to do the job. Finally she figured it out. She was glad she had stayed cool and kept on working on the problem.

Did she handle the frustration

A. with fortitude,

or

B. not with fortitude?

936. A boy was playing baseball. The game was close. He was up at bat. The pitcher threw good pitches, and the boy swung at them. But he missed. He

struck out. His team lost. Another boy on his team said, "You lost the game for us."

The boy thought, "I tried as hard as I could. Everybody strikes out some of the time. I made some good plays in the game, too. I don't want to worry about this much. I'll keep practicing, and I'll get better at hitting the ball." The boy still felt bad, but he did not feel awful.

Do you think he handled this

A. with fortitude,
or
B. not with fortitude?

937. A woman was at a party. The woman wanted very much to look good. Someone at the party said to her, "You're not looking very well. Have you been sick or something?" The woman burst into tears. She rushed out of the party and did not come back. She thought, "I'm starting to look worse and worse! This is terrible!" She felt so bad that she did not want to speak with anybody for two days.

Did she handle the frustration

A. with fortitude,
or
B. not with fortitude?

938. A father came home. He said to his younger daughter, "I've been to the bookstore. I got a book for you."

His older daughter thought, "Maybe he got one for me, too." She asked, "Did you get any others?"

The father knew what she was curious about. He said, "I thought about getting one for you. But you already have a lot of books on your shelf that you haven't read yet. So I did not."

The older daughter felt a little bad. But she thought to herself, "This doesn't mean he doesn't love me. He's right. I don't need any more books for a while. It always feels good to get a surprise, but I can handle it when I don't." The older daughter said to her dad, "No problem. You're right; I have plenty of books for now." She said to her sister, "That book looks interesting. Maybe some time you would like me to read it to you."

Did the older daughter handle this

A. with fortitude,
or
B. not with fortitude?

939. A girl was walking in her house, looking at something that had caught her interest. A chair was in a different place than it usually was. The girl walked right into the back of the chair. The chair was made of hard wood. She hit her face on it. It hurt a lot. She could tell that her mom and dad were very worried. The first thing she said after she hurt herself was, "I'll be fine." She cried some, because it hurt so much.

Finally it stopped hurting so much. She thought to herself, "I want to learn from this. I'll try to remember to keep a lookout and watch where I'm going, so I won't walk into things any more."

Do you think she handled this

A. with fortitude,
or
B. not with fortitude?

940. A man got a new guitar. He did not
know how to play the guitar. He picked
it up and tried to make it sound good.
But it was not in tune. He started getting
angry. Then he tried to tune it. He could
not get it in tune. He started cursing and
swearing. His wife said to him, "Having
trouble?"

He said to her, in an angry voice,
"Well, what do you think?"

She said, "I was just trying to be
nice."

He said, "Well, you're not helping.
Just leave me alone."

Did he handle this

A. with fortitude,
or
B. not with fortitude?

941. A man got a new part for a
computer. He tried to get it to work. But
he kept reading strange messages on his
computer screen. The messages said
that a certain file was missing. The man
looked for the missing file. But he could
not find it.

His wife saw that the program wasn't
working. She said to him, "Having
trouble?"

He said to her, "Yes, this new thing
won't work without a certain file. But it
looks like I don't have it."

She said, "That must be
disappointing. I know you wanted this
to work."

He said, "I've still got some ideas
about how to solve this problem. But
you're right; it will take me longer than
I'd hoped. Thanks for your concern."

Did he handle this

A. with fortitude,
or
B. not with fortitude?

942. A girl and her sister were going to
a birthday party. They both had presents
to give. The girl looked at the wrapping
for both the presents. The girl thought,
"Humh, the wrapping on my sister's
present looks lots better than the
wrapping on my present." She started to
feel upset.

But then she thought to herself,
"Wait a minute; this is really no big
deal. By the end of the party the
wrapping paper will all be thrown away
anyway. This is not worth worrying
about." So she said to her sister, "Wow,
what a pretty wrapping you have." Her
sister felt good.

Did the girl handle this

A. with fortitude,
or
B. not with fortitude?

943. A doctor was doing an operation.
Someone was helping him. Part of the
helper's job was to put the doctor's
tools into his hand, when the doctor

asked for them. That way the doctor could keep working without having to look away from the person's body.

The doctor said, "Scissors." The helper put something called forceps in his hand, not scissors. The doctor felt irritated. But he just said, "Scissors, not forceps, please."

Later, the doctor asked for the knife he was using in the operation. This time the helper gave him scissors.

The doctor had the urge to throw the scissors onto the floor and scream at the helper. He had seen other doctors do this sometimes. But he took a deep breath instead. He thought for a while. He said to himself, "What is the best thing to do?"

He said to his helper, "I'll bet you've been working for a long time. Are you very tired?"

The helper said, "I'm so sorry. You're right; I'm so tired I can't think straight. Do you mind if I try to find someone to take my place?"

The doctor said, "That's a good idea. But do it quickly, please."

In a minute another helper came in. They finished the job well.

Did the doctor handle the frustration

A. with fortitude,
or
B. not with fortitude?

944. A mother sent her son to the market to buy food for his family. He put the money into his pocket. He also had a list of things to buy. He put this into his pocket too.

On his way to the market, he pulled out the list several times to look at it. Just as he was about to walk into the market, he realized the money was no longer in his pocket. He thought, "Oh, no. It must have fallen out when I pulled the list out of my pocket!"

He quickly walked back along the way that he had come, looking for the money on the ground. But lots of other people were walking along too. He could not find the money. He thought, "I'm sure someone else has picked it up."

His family did not have much money. He knew his mother would be upset. He thought about staying away from home for a few days. He thought about trying to steal food from the market. But then he said to himself, "She'll be upset, but I'll just have to get tough and take it." So he walked home and told her what happened.

She was very upset. She sat down and cried. She said, "We don't have any more money to get food with."

The boy thought, "Maybe I can do some work to make the money back." He went back out and asked people if he could work for some money. Everyone said no.

But finally one man said, "Yes, I need to unload a bunch of cabbages from a wagon. The man who was going to help me did not show up."

The boy worked hard. The man gave him some money and some cabbages.

The boy went home and showed his mother. Even though the money was not as much as he had lost, she felt much better.

Did he handle his frustration

A. with fortitude,
or
B. not with fortitude?

945. Once there was a boy at school. The teacher asked the boy and his classmates to write something. The boy wrote a little story. He was very proud of what he had written. Another boy looked at it. The other boy said, "You sure can't write very well, can you?"

The boy started crying. He ran out of the classroom. He ran to an office and called his mother on the phone. He begged her to come and pick him up and take him home.

Did he handle his frustration

A. with fortitude,
or
B. not with fortitude?

946. A pioneer family worked very hard to build themselves a house from logs. They finally finished, and they loved having their new house.

Once they went to get some seeds to plant. This trip took them several days. They all went, so that they could all help.

When they got back, they found their house had burned down. They heard that there had been a lightning storm. Lightning had hit their house.

The father of the family stood for a minute and looked at the burned house. He said, "Well, if we built the house once, we can build it again. And this time, we'll put a lightning rod on it. Let's get to work." And they all started working right away.

Did they handle this frustration

A. with fortitude,
or
B. not with fortitude?

Good and Bad Reasons for Noncompliance

947. One of the sixteen skills and principles is compliance. It is good to be able to comply with reasonable, good directions given by a person who is in charge of something you are doing. But it is certainly not a good idea to obey everyone who tells us to do anything. There are times when our consciences should tell us that we must not obey. Sometimes people give commands to us that are wrong to follow. At other times, we feel the urge to disobey simply because we feel lazy or because we want pleasure.

Suppose an army officer is given an order to shoot innocent people in a village, and the officer disobeys the order. He is probably doing this out of a sense of right and wrong. He is probably following his conscience. On the other hand, suppose there is a teenager who is asked by his parent to take out the trash. He ignores this, and lies around and listens to music instead. He is probably failing to comply because he's feeling lazy. The stories that will follow will give you practice in deciding whether or not the person has a good reason not to comply.

Which is a better reason not to comply?

A. conscience
or
B. laziness?

948. An older boy says to a younger boy: "A girl lives in this house. Knock on her door. When she comes to the door, kiss her and run."

The younger boy says to the older boy, "I'm not doing that. I don't think she'd enjoy that, and it would be rude."

The younger boy does not comply with the older boy.

Does he have

A. a good reason,
or
B. not a good reason?

949. A teacher in a school has a problem with a student in class talking out too much. This teacher tells the student behind the talkative student, "Whenever he talks out, I want you to take some paint and smear it in his hair."

The student says, "I'm sorry. I'm not willing to do that. I don't think that's a good way of punishing him."

Is this student disobeying because of

A. a good reason,
or
B. not a good reason?

950. A parent tells a child, "It's time to go to bed now."

The child does not comply. He says, "I want to watch this television show instead. It's really funny."

Is this child disobeying because of

A. a good reason,
or
B. not a good reason?

951. Some army men have captured one of the enemy. They are trying to find out something from the captive. An officer orders a soldier, "Keep punching him until he tells us."

The soldier says, "I'm sorry. I'm not willing to torture this person."

Is this soldier disobeying because of

A. a good reason,
or
B. not a good reason?

952. A teacher assigns some children some homework. A child says, "I just don't feel it's right to do this homework on a night when I could go to a party instead."

Do you think this child feels like disobeying because of

A. a good reason,
or
B. not a good reason?

953. A parent says to some children, "It's time to leave the swimming pool, now." The children ignore her because they're having fun in the swimming pool.

Are they failing to comply because of

A. a good reason,
or
B. not a good reason?

954. A cross-country running coach asks the people on his team to run on a path through the woods. A couple of kids stop running as soon as they get out of sight of the coach. They sit around in the woods and chat. Then they take a short-cut back. They do this because they don't feel like running today.

Are they failing to comply because of

A. a good reason,
or
B. not a good reason?

955. A football coach is making the boys on his team run and practice in very hot weather without being able to get any water to drink. Finally, one boy on the team just walks over and gets some water. The coach yells at him, "I told you not to drink water!"

The boy says back to him, "I know it's not good for our bodies to sweat so much without being able to get water. It's not healthy. I know something about heat stroke. Someone could be harmed by the rule you're making, and I don't think it's right."

Is he failing to comply because of

A. a good reason,
or
B. not a good reason?

956. A boy is teasing another boy in a hurtful way. A teacher tells him to stop. The boy says, "I don't think I should have to. I think we should be able to tease each other all we want, without a grown-up telling us what to do."

Do you think he is failing to comply because of

A. a good reason,
or
B. not a good reason?

957. A boy is in a club. The people who are the older members of the club have a ritual for the people joining the club. The new members get hit with paddles. One of the people joining the club says, "I can take getting hit by a paddle, but I'm not going to. I don't believe in violence, and I don't want to join a club that has violence as part of its joining ceremony."

Do you think he is failing to comply because of

A. a good reason,
or
B. not a good reason?

958. A girl is picking up her food with her fingers and eating it. Her mom says, "Please don't pick it up with your fingers; please eat it up with your fork." The girl says, "But I don't feel like using my fork; I can get the food in faster with my fingers."

Do you think she is failing to comply because of

A. a good reason,
or
B. not a good reason?

959. A parent asks a boy to spray the whole house with insect poison. The boy says, "I'd like to wait on this until I can look up whether this type of insect poison is safe to use."

Do you think he is failing to comply because of

A. a good reason,
or
B. not a good reason?

960. A parent asks a boy to sweep the kitchen floor. He refuses because he'd rather play a computer game instead.

Do you think he is failing to comply because of

A. a good reason,
or
B. not a good reason?

961. A college student signs up to be in a study. A scientist is studying how people learn. The scientist tells the person, "Here is someone who is learning math facts. He has a wire strapped to his hand. When he gets a problem wrong, I want you to shock him. You turn the shock on this way. I want you to turn the shock up high, so it really hurts badly."

The college student says to the scientist, "I'm sorry, but I'm not going to shock anybody. You'd have to really convince me that some good came out of this that would justify hurting someone else. And you haven't done that yet."

The scientist says, "It will be worth it. Just do it, please. You'll mess up my study if you don't."

The college student says, "You'll have to deal with that however you want. But I don't believe in hurting people unless *I know* there's a really good reason to."

Do you think he is failing to comply for

A. a good reason,
or
B. not a good reason?

Locating Control

962. What can you control? What can you not control? When people feel they can control something, they are locating the control in themselves. When people feel that other people or luck controls something, they are locating the control in someone else or in luck. Sometimes control of things can be in several places. Things can have more than one cause.

The stories that follow will give practice in figuring out where people locate the control for how things turn out. You are figuring out where the person locates control. You are not trying to decide who really has control.

Suppose a boy goes to school. The teachers ask him to do work. He says, "No, that's no fun." They try in all sorts of ways to get him to work. But he will not do it. It turns out that he does not learn anything. His parents are angry. They sue the school. They say, "You should have taught him something."

Where are the parents locating control for what happened?

A. in the boy,
or
B. in other people?

963. A boy often annoys people at school, on purpose, because it is fun for him to do this. People start to dislike him. One day he passes some people, and one of them says something mean to him. He says, "People just treat me mean at school, for no reason. I haven't done anything to him. It's not fair."

Where is the boy locating control for how people treat him?

A. in himself,
or
B. in other people?

964. A boy is looking at a wild weasel in a cage. He sticks his finger into the cage. The weasel bites his finger. He thinks to himself, "I should have known better than to stick my finger into a wild animal's cage."

Where is the boy locating control?

A. in himself,
or
B. in luck?

965. Another boy is looking at a wild weasel in a cage, and he sticks his finger in and gets bit. He thinks to himself, "That darn weasel! He shouldn't have bit me!"

Where is this boy locating control?

A. in himself,
or
B. in someone else?

966. Another boy has the same thing happen. The boy's parents sue the people who own the weasel. The boy's

parents say, "You should have had a cage that no one could stick their fingers into."

Where are they locating control?

A. in the boy,

or

B. in someone else?

967. A person is walking down the street. Someone he does not know says to him, "Want to buy a laptop computer, cheap? You just have to give me cash." He buys it. A few days later the police come and tell him he bought a stolen computer.

He thinks to himself, "I should have suspected the computer was stolen. Next time I get an offer that sounds too good to be true, I'll suspect that it's stolen property."

Where is he locating control?

A. in himself,

or

B. in someone else?

968. A person picks some numbers and wins a lottery. The person thinks, "I was so smart to pick those numbers. I won because I was smarter than the other people who played."

Where is he locating control?

A. in himself,

or

B. in luck?

969. A man asks his brother to stop by a store and get something. It turns out there's a fire at that store just at the time the brother is there. The brother is harmed by breathing too much smoke. The man thinks, "This is my fault for asking him to go to the store."

Where is the man locating control?

A. in himself,

or

B. in luck?

970. A person doesn't do his homework throughout a college course. At the end of the course, he tries to make up all the homework he's missed. He can't get it in by the deadline the teacher has set. He asks the teacher to let him turn in the work later. The teacher says no. He fails the course. He thinks, "I failed that course because the professor was so mean."

Where is the man locating control?

A. in himself,

or

B. in someone else?

971. A teenaged boy is interested in a girl. One day he hasn't taken a shower. He smells bad. He walks up to the girl, who doesn't even know his name. Without introducing himself, he says, "Hey, can you go out with me?"

She says no.

He thinks, "She rejected me because she's so stuck up and snooty."

Where is the boy locating control?

A. in himself,
or
B. in someone else?

972. A man is able to concentrate and hold still and pay attention much better when he takes a certain medicine. He does really well at his work one day, and he thinks to himself, "I made a good decision to take the medicine, and I also made a good decision to try really hard at work."

Where is he locating control?

A. in himself,
or
B. in luck?

973. Another man is also able to concentrate and hold still and pay attention much better when he takes a certain medicine. He does really well at work one day, and he thinks to himself, "Whoever invented the medicine gets the credit for this, not me."

Where is he locating control?

A. in himself,
or
B. in someone else?

Handling Criticism

974. When someone says to us, "You are doing something wrong," or "You should do something differently, " or "You are a bad person," we are getting criticism.

When we get criticized, our natural tendency is to defend ourselves. To defend yourself means to try to persuade the other person that you are really OK, or that you are not to blame.

Suppose Jack says to Jean, "I wish you would put your things away more. You shouldn't be so sloppy."

Is Jack

A. criticizing,
or
B. defending himself?

975. Suppose Jean says back to Jack, "I can't help it. I've got too much other work to do."

Is Jean

A. criticizing,
or
B. defending herself?

976. When someone defends herself, the person who has criticized tends to argue back. For example, Jack might say, "What do you mean, too much work? You don't have any more than I do, and I put things away."

It's good to be able to give some answers to criticism other than defending yourself. Deciding when to answer in which way is very complicated. But our goal here is to learn some ways of answering that are new for many people. You will want to have these ways available to you, so you can use them when you decide to.

One of these ways of handling criticism is one you're already familiar with: the reflection.

Suppose Jean had said to Jack, "Sounds like it really irritates you when I don't put things away."

Is this

A. defending herself,
or
B. a reflection?

977. Another way of answering criticism is called agreeing with part of criticism. If Jean had said to Jack, "You're right; there are lots of times when I don't put things away," she would be agreeing with part of the criticism.

Another way is called asking for more specific criticism. If Jean had done this, she would have said, "Which of the things I've failed to put away bother you the most?"

Suppose Jean had said, "It's true. I should put my things away more."

Would this have been

A. agreeing with part of criticism,
or
B. asking for more specific criticism?

978. Suppose Jean had said, "I think I put my things away almost all the time, and you're just being picky."
    Would this have been

A. asking for more specific criticism,
or
B. defending herself?

979. Suppose Jean had said, "Please tell me more about the sorts of things I leave out that are most irritating to you."
    Would this have been

A. defending herself,
or
B. asking for more specific criticism?

980. Another way of responding to criticism is called planning to ponder or problem-solve. When you do this, you say that you'd like to think about this more, either by yourself or with the other person. Pondering means thinking, and problem-solving here means talking with the other person about how to solve the problem. If Jean had said, "Hmm. I'll think about what you've said," that would have been planning to ponder. If Jean had said, "Hmm. Let's see what options we can think of, to solve this problem," that

would have been planning to problem-solve.
    Suppose Jan says to Rick, "You are always late! It is so frustrating!"
    Suppose Rick were to say, "I am late very often, I'll have to admit."
    Is that

A. planning to ponder or problem-solve,
or
B. agreeing with part of criticism?

981. Suppose Rick were to say, "It sounds as if, when I'm late so much, it causes some big problems for you."
    Would this have been

A. planning to ponder or problem-solve,
or
B. reflection?

982. Suppose Rick were to say, "I want to figure out how not to frustrate you in that way. Let's think of how to solve this."
    Would this have been

A. planning to ponder or problem-solve,
or
B. defending himself?

983. Suppose Rick were to say, "What do you mean, always late? Was I late when I met you yesterday? No way."
    Would this have been

A. reflection,
or
B. defending himself?

984. Mary says to her daughter Lisa, "I'm afraid you're getting lazy. I don't want you to make yourself unhappy by getting too lazy."

Suppose Lisa says, "So you're worried that I might get too lazy and make myself unhappy that way?"

Is Lisa

A. defending herself,
or
B. doing a reflection?

985. Suppose Lisa says, "There are times when I don't feel like working, that's for sure."

Is she

A. asking for more specific criticism,
or
B. agreeing with part of criticism?

986. Suppose that Lisa says, "What are the things you would most like me to work on more?"

Is she

A. asking for more specific criticism,
or
B. agreeing with part of criticism?

987. Suppose Lisa says, "Let me think about this some. I'll try to figure out how much more I want to get myself to work."

Is she

A. asking for more specific criticism,
or
B. planning to ponder or problem-solve?

988. Maria says to her grown daughter Linda, "Linda, I think you're spoiling your son."

Linda says, "Sounds like you're worried that your grandson is going to become a brat, huh?"

Is she

A. reflecting,
or
B. defending herself?

989. Suppose Linda says, "It's true; there are times he does demand to get his way, all right."

Is she

A. agreeing with part of criticism,
or
B. asking for more specific criticism?

990. Suppose Linda says, "Please tell me more about what you've noticed, and what you think I should have been doing instead of what I did do."

Is she

A. reflecting,
or
B. asking for more specific criticism?

991. Suppose that, after Maria gives Linda more specific suggestions, Linda says, "I'll think about what you've said.

You've given me some ideas to consider."
    Is she

A. planning to ponder or problem-solve,
or
B. defending herself?

992. Suppose Linda had said, "I think I am one good mother. And if you don't like how I take care of my child, you can just keep it to yourself."
    Is she

A. planning to ponder or problem-solve,
or
B. defending herself?

993. Bert is playing baseball with his dad. His dad says, "Hey Bert, I think you'd hit more if you swung your bat more level."
    Suppose Bert says, "Hmm. I could use something to make me hit more, because I have been missing a lot, that's for sure."
    Is he

A. defending himself,
or
B. agreeing with part of criticism?

994. Suppose Bert says, "Could you show me how I've been doing it, and how I should do it?"
    Would this be

A. reflecting,
or

B. asking for more specific criticism?

995. Suppose Bert says, "I do swing level. I swing level every time. You just don't think I do."
    Would this be

A. defending himself,
or
B. planning to ponder or problem-solve?

996. Suppose Frank's dad says to Frank, "Son, if you want to stay married, you've got to be more polite to your wife. You've got to quit using the word *stupid* to describe anything she does."
    Suppose Frank says, "So you think I'm too insulting to her, huh?"
    Would this be

A. reflection,
or
B. defending himself?

997. Suppose Frank says, "Please tell me what else you've noticed that you think I should change."
    Would this be

A. agreeing with part of criticism,
or
B. asking for more specific criticism?

998. Suppose Frank says, "I guess I could be more gentle than I am sometimes."
    Would this be

A. planning to ponder or problem-solve,
or
B. agreeing with part of criticism?

999. Suppose Frank says, "You think I'm not polite! You should hear how she talks to me sometimes! My impoliteness is nothing compared to that! That's the only reason I do it."
Would this be

A. planning to ponder or problem-solve,
or
B. defending himself?

1000. Suppose Frank says, "I'll have to think about what you're telling me, Dad."
Is he

A. planning to ponder or problem-solve,
or
B. defending himself?

1001. Alex is playing chess against the computer, and Larry is watching. Larry says to Alex, "You just made a big mistake."
Alex says, "I do make mistakes sometimes, that's for sure."
Is he

A. defending himself,
or
B. agreeing with part of criticism?

1002. Suppose Alex had said, "Oh? Tell me what the mistake was, and what you think I should have done."
Is he

A. asking for more specific criticism,
or
B. doing a reflection?

1003. Suppose Alex had said, "OK, don't tell me any more, please, and let me see if when I think about it I can figure out something I missed."
Is he

A. defending himself,
or
B. planning to ponder or problem-solve?

Sixty-two Psychological Skills

1004. Do you remember the sixteen skills? They are really the sixteen skill groups. Most of these groups have several other skills in the group. For example, part of the skill of productivity is the skill of persistence and concentration. Another productivity skill is organization.

Part of joyousness is enjoying your own kind acts. Another joyousness skill is enjoying learning and discovery. Another is enjoying approval from other people.

Which group do you think the skill of enjoying other people's kind acts toward you falls into?

A. productivity
or
B. joyousness?

The following stories give examples of each of the skills. There are sixty-two skills in all.

1005. A boy went out into his neighborhood and met someone who teased him and was mean to him and tried to hurt him. The boy said, "I certainly can't trust this kid." He was tempted to feel that he couldn't trust anybody. But he decided this would be generalizing too much.

So he looked around and finally found another boy who told the truth and did things when he said he was going to do them, and was almost always nice. The boy got to be better and better friends with this person as time went on, and they had a lot of fun together.

A. Discernment and trusting. Deciding whom to trust and trusting them,
or
B. Habits of self-care. Having healthy habits: not smoking, not drinking alcohol, exercising and eating right foods

1006. A boy had lots of trouble with math. He couldn't figure out how to do a lot of the problems, and he found himself disliking math class. He thought about trying to get some help from someone. At first when he thought of this, he felt ashamed, and thought, "I shouldn't need any help."

But then he read something that convinced him that getting help when you need it is a brave thing to do, not a shameful thing. He talked with his mother about this, and she thought it was a great idea.

They found someone to help him with his math, and he started understanding things he'd never understood before. Gradually he started liking math and enjoying going to math class. After a lot of work, he was a good math student.

A. Depending. Asking for and accepting help when it's a good idea to do that,
or
B. Loyalty. Being loyal to someone or sticking by someone over a long time.

1007. A girl had an old friend. The girl got a new friend. She found herself wanting to be with the new friend so much that she was neglecting her old friend. But she said to herself, "My old friend is important to me. I don't want to drop her."

So the second girl made sure to keep on getting together with her old friend, and keep on being nice to her, even though she spent some time with her new friend too. And sometimes she spent some time with her two friends together. She said to herself, "I want to stick by people when they've been nice to me and not just drop them."

A. Loyalty. Being loyal to someone or sticking with someone over a long time,
or
B. Self-disclosure. Feeling OK telling someone about your innermost thoughts.

1008. A girl had a good friend she could trust very much. She got the urge to talk to the friend about some personal things, like how she felt when people she knew weren't kind to her, and some of her hopes about what her future would hold, and times when she didn't feel confident. She said to herself, "Why not? If the friend doesn't like

hearing about these things she will let me know."

So she talked about those things, and the friend also talked about lots of personal things that made a lot of difference to her. The girl and her friend felt a lot closer to each other when they found they could talk with each other about anything that was on their minds.

A. Handling rejection. Handling it when people don't accept you,
or
B. Self-disclosure. Feeling OK telling someone about your innermost thoughts.

1009. A girl saw another girl who was being teased by other people. She thought to herself, "If everybody were teasing me, I would really like someone to be friendly to me."

So the second girl started chatting with the girl, and invited her to do some things with her, and was very nice to her. After a while they got to be friends, and they both had fun doing things together.

A. Fortitude or Frustration tolerance. Handling it when you don't get what you want,
or
B. Kindness. Being kind and helpful to someone else.

1010. A boy got lost in the middle of the woods. Some people in that situation would have said to themselves,

"You dummy! How could you have done something like this?" But this boy decided to speak differently to himself.

He said to himself, "I can take care of myself. I can sit down and figure out what I'm going to do and then do it. I'm smart enough to solve this problem if I put my mind to it. It will take some time, but I can do it."

A. Gratitude. Expressing positive feelings to other people,
or
B. Self-nurture. Saying nice things to yourself when you think to yourself; self-nurturing.

1011. A person was walking somewhere, and asked someone for directions. The person gave him good directions. The person said, "I think I've got it. Thank you for your time. You've really helped me."

A. Compliance: Obeying someone who is good to obey,
or
B. Gratitude: Expressing positive feelings to other people.

1012. A boy was at a birthday party. He was not playing with anybody. He saw a group of children who were all trying to put some construction toys together. He got the urge to interrupt them and ask them to play kickball with him, but then he thought better of it.

So he went over and sat down by them and just watched what they were

doing. He figured out that two people were building something together, and the other two were building their own thing. He said to one of them, "It's getting pretty big."

The person said back to him, "It's a space station."

He watched some more. By this time he had figured out that there was a pile of construction pieces no one was using. He took some of them and said, "Do you want an antenna on your space station?"

The other person said, "Hey, that's a good idea."

A. Social initiations: Starting to talk or play with other people in a good way,
or
B. Awareness of emotions: Recognizing and talking about your own feelings.

1013. A boy was riding home on the bus when someone sat down beside him. He said to him, "I think I remember seeing you. We have a class together, don't we?"

The second boy said, "Yes, we're in Mr. Thompson's math class."

The first boy said, "That's right. Now I remember. Do you like Mr. Thompson?"

The second boy said, "Yes, I like him, and I have to work really hard for his class." They went on talking the whole rest of the way home, and had a nice time getting to know each other better.

A. Handling rejection. Handling it when people don't accept you,
or
B. Socializing. Having a good social conversation

1014. A boy wanted to tell his friend about a movie he had seen. But when he went up to tell his friend about it, the friend said to him, "Wait until you hear what happened to me today. I was so scared."

The boy got the urge to tell about the movie, but he thought he should pay attention to what his friend was talking about. So he said, "What was it that happened?"

The friend said, "A bunch of guys tried to jump me!"

The boy said, "Jump you? What do you mean? What did they do to you?"

The friend said, "There were about five or six of them, and I was riding my bike. I think they wanted to steal my bike. They started running after me, but I rode off on my bike. They almost caught me, but I got away."

The boy said, "I can see why you'd be scared. How old were they?"

The friend went on talking about what happened some more.

A. Listening. Being a good listener for someone else,
or
B. Independent thinking. Making your own decisions instead of blindly following a leader.

1015. A college guy went to a party. A guy who seemed to be the leader of lots of people at the party said, "OK, we're going to have a contest to see who can drink the most beer the fastest."

The college guy yelled out at him, "I think your game is a very bad idea, and anybody who plays along with it will be acting stupid."

Some people yelled at him, "What are you, a wimp?"

Other people said, "I'm glad to hear someone with some sense." The college guy met a nice woman and took a walk outside with her and didn't come back to the party. He didn't care what the leader of the drinking game thought about him.

A. Independent thinking. Making your own decisions instead of blindly going along with another person or a group,
or
B. Differential reinforcement. Reinforcing or rewarding other people's good behavior and avoiding reinforcing the negative.

1016. A boy had a girlfriend he liked very much and spent lots of time with. One day she told him her family was moving to a state two thousand miles away. The boy was very lonesome. He had the urge to mope around and not do anything but miss his friend.

But he said to himself, "I'll try to make myself less lonesome by keeping busy." He worked very hard on his schoolwork, and also worked at a job.

He used the money he made on his job to call his friend long distance sometimes, and he wrote letters to her very often.

He got together with his other friends a lot. He said to himself, "I still don't like it that she went away, but I can handle it."

A. Pleasure from approval. Feeling good when someone gives you a compliment,
or
B. Handling separation. Putting up with separating from someone you love or depend on.

1017. Jane had a good friend she spent a lot of time with. The friend met another friend, though, and didn't want to spend so much time with Jane. The friend invited her other friend to go with her to some nice place and didn't invite Jane.

Jane said to herself, "That hurts my feelings some, but I can handle it. If she doesn't want me to be her best friend, we can still be friends. And I'll find some other people to do more things with."

So she kept on being friends with her first friend and made lots more friends, too.

A. Handling rejection. Handling it when someone rejects you, a little bit or a lot,
or
B. Compliance. Obeying someone when it is good to obey.

1018. A boy went to class at school and was talking and playing with someone else while the teacher was trying to say something to the whole group. The teacher said to him, "Talking is a good thing, but not when I'm trying to talk to everybody. When you do that, you keep people from paying attention to what I am saying, and people learn less and have less fun that way. So from now on, save your talking until the times when you have permission."

The boy thought to himself, "I've gotten some criticism. Does the teacher have a good point, or not?" He decided that, if he were the teacher, he would have to ask the students to be quiet some of the time, too. So he practiced in his mind waiting to talk to his friends until later.

A. Handling criticism. Dealing well with criticism or disapproval,
or
B. Differential reinforcement. Recognizing and praising the part of someone else's behavior that is positive.

1019. A girl was given some work to do by herself in class. She felt a little lonely at first, and got the urge to talk to people when she should have been working. But she was able to handle not having anybody to talk with for a while.

She practiced enjoying being by herself. She found that when her mother was on the phone, she could say to herself, "I'll do something fun on my own," and do it, without bothering her mother.

A. Empathy. Recognizing what other people are feeling about something,
or
B. Enjoying aloneness. Having a good time alone, doing OK without attention.

1020. A boy had a little brother who was two-years old. When the boy played a board game with a friend his age, the little brother would come up and be curious about the things they were doing, and move the pieces around and ruin the game.

   The boy thought to himself, "What should I do? I could just let him do his thing and hope he doesn't come around too much. Or I could try to get my parents to punish him each time he does this. Or I could try to talk with him about it. Or I could go into a room and close the door, and put the game on a table high enough that he can't reach it, even if he does come in, instead of playing on the floor in the living room. I think I like that last idea best."

A. Rational approach to conflict. Deciding how to approach a conflict situation,
or
B. Pleasure from approval. Feeling good when someone gives you a compliment.

1021. A girl's sister liked to turn the television on and watch it very often.

The girl thought that, when the television was on, the other people in the family didn't get as much good stuff done and didn't do as many fun things with one another

   The girl sat down with her sister and her parents and said, "I've been thinking of several different options for this problem. One is, we could buy some of those earphones and plug them into the TV, so my sister could watch it without distracting everybody else. Another one is, we could move the TV out of the living room and into my sister's room, since she's the one who watches it the most, so that she could watch it by herself in there if she wants. Another is, we could all try not watching TV at all for one month and see if we're happier or not. What do you think?"

A. Option-generating. Thinking of good options for solving a two-person problem,
or
B. Pleasure from your own kindness. Feeling good when you do something kind for someone else.

1022. One time a man had a little tool shed made out of wood, on the edge of his property. One day a neighbor was burning some things, and while the neighbor wasn't looking, the fire spread and burned down the tool shed, and destroyed most of the tools in it.

   The neighbor went over to talk to this man. The neighbor said, "I realize the fire was my fault. How about if I get the same company that built your shed to build you a new one, and how about if I pay for new tools?"

The man thought about this for a while, and then said, "That sounds fair to me. Thank you for making that very fair offer."

A. Option-evaluating. Choosing reasonable options for solving a two-person problem,
or
B. Persistence and concentration. Keeping on paying attention to something for a long enough time to accomplish something.

1023. A boy was the president of a club at high school. He wanted to try to persuade the principal of the school to let his club use a certain room to meet in. The boy said to the principal, "We're looking for a room to have our meetings in. Do you have any thoughts on that, or would you like to hear our thoughts first?"

The principal said, "Tell me your thoughts."

The boy said, "We'd like to use the trophy room to have our meetings in. If we can do this, we will be sure to clean up the room after we've used it, if necessary, so that we'll leave it just as we found it. We also would promise that we wouldn't make noise in it that would bother anybody in the next rooms. We want to propose a trial period of a month, just to see whether there are any problems, and if there are, we can try to figure out some other plan. How does that sound to you?"

A. Rational approach to joint decisions. Deciding rationally on stance and strategies,
or
B. Handling rejection. Handling it when people don't accept you.

1024. A boy was with a friend. The friend said to him, "Here, light up this cigarette and smoke it and tell me what you think."

The boy said, "I don't need to smoke it to tell you what I think. I don't think it's smart to breathe in smoke of any sort."

The friend said, "But just try it. I want you to. Come on, do it."

The second boy said, "No way! I'm not interested."

The friend said, "You're just scared."

And the second boy just laughed and said, "If you want to damage your own lungs, feel free to. But I'm saving mine just in case I might need them to breathe with some day."

A. Assertion. Being able to stick up for your own ideas or stick up for what you want,
or
B. Conciliation or submission. Giving in or conceding to what the other wants when it is a good idea.

1025. A girl was at her house. She turned the television on. But instead of watching the show, she got interested in reading a book. So she sat and read the book, with the television still on.

Her brother came up and said, "I'm going to change the channel, OK?"

The girl thought for a minute and said, "Sure, change it to whatever you want to. I'm not really watching it anyway."

A. Conciliation, submission. Giving in or conceding to what the other wants when it is a good idea,
or
B. Pleasure from others' kindness. Feeling grateful when someone has done something kind for you.

1026. A boy had a little brother who would often yell really loud. Many times the boy had said, "Please don't be so loud." But it didn't work. The little brother kept yelling.

The boy tried something else. When his brother yelled, he left him alone for a few minutes and did not say anything to him. When the boy spoke in a normal tone, he tried to be very attentive to him. After a while he noticed that his brother yelled a lot less.

A. Habits of self-care. Having healthy habits: not smoking, not drinking alcohol, exercising, and eating right foods,
or

B. Differential reinforcement. Reinforcing or rewarding other people's positive behavior and avoiding reinforcing the negative.

1027. A girl had a friend visiting her at her house. She had the urge to say to the friend, "Come on, we're going to play first with something really fun," and then to say to the friend, "Stand here. No, not that way! Like this! Don't do it that way. Here, watch me! Now do it like that! . . . OK, that's enough. Now come over here, I've got something else I want you to do."

But even though the girl had the urge to act this way, she didn't do it. She said to her friend, "I'm glad you came over. Would you like to see some of the things I like to do?"

The girl showed her friend around, and her friend said, "Oh, look at that rope! Let's play with that!"

The girl at first thought to herself, "What fun things can anybody do with a bunch of rope?" But then she said to herself, "I'll try letting her do what she wants to do, and even do it with her." She said to her friend, "OK, let's play with the rope."

And she played with what her friend wanted to play with. The friend showed her all sorts of interesting games and tricks to do with the rope, and both of them had a very good time.

A. Conservation and Thrift. Not wasting, saving money, being thrifty,
or

B. Toleration. Putting up with or enjoying a wide range of other people's behavior, without needing to boss them around.

1028. A girl was teased by some other girls. She at first said to herself, "I'll never be friendly with them, ever, for the rest of my life."

But then she changed her mind about what to say to herself. She thought, "I don't like what they did. But people aren't perfect."

Three years later, one of the girls acted nice to her, and invited her to do something fun with her. The girl remembered how the girl had teased her three years earlier. She said to herself, "I'm glad that she's gotten to be friendly. It's nice that people can change." And she accepted the invitation and had a good time.

A. Forgiveness and anger control. Forgiving other people, stopping being angry at them,
or
B. Gleefulness. Playing, being gleeful, or having fun being silly.

1029. A boy entered a project in a science contest. He worked for many hours to set up a very interesting exhibit. He said to himself, "I'm sure mine will be the best, and I'll win first prize."

But he didn't win at all. He felt the urge to get very upset. But then he said to himself, "Well, even though I didn't win, I still had fun putting the project together." And he thought to himself, "I'm going to look very closely at the exhibits that did win, so I can learn some things that might help me next time."

A. Frustration tolerance. Handling it when you don't get what you want,
or
B. Imagination and positive fantasy rehearsal. Being able to use imagination well.

1030. A girl was doing some math problems. After she had done five or six of them, the teacher came to check them. The teacher said, "None of these are right!"

The girl thought, "I'm glad I found out so soon that I was doing something wrong. Now I'll have time to correct it." And she said to the teacher, "Show me what I was doing wrong, and how to do it right, please." And the teacher showed her.

The girl said to herself, "I'll try it again, and see how I do this time." And she finally got them right, and she felt good.

A. Carefulness. Recognizing and avoiding danger when it is really present,
or
B. Handling mistakes and failures. Handling it when you make a mistake or don't succeed at something.

1031. A boy's father came home with a new computer. It came with some very interesting things to do. The boy had two brothers.

The father said, "I want to show these things to each of the three of you, by yourself, without the others there. I'll do it with one of you tonight, one tomorrow night, and one the next night."

The boy thought to himself, "I hope I get to do it first!" The father rolled some dice to see who would get to do it in what order, and the boy got the third night.

The boy said to himself, "I wish I'd gotten to go first, instead of my brothers. But we can't all go first. I'm tough enough to put up with waiting."

A. Pleasure from approval. Feeling good when someone gives you a compliment,
or
B. Non-jealousy. Handling it when someone else gets what you wanted.

1032. One time a teacher said, "I have an interesting game I want to play with someone. Who wants to volunteer to come out in front of everyone else and play it with me?"

A girl felt a little nervous about getting up in front of many people. But then she thought to herself, "Hey, that sounds like it might be fun. What do I have to lose? The worst thing that could happen would be that I wouldn't be able to figure out how to do the game and I would look a little silly, but that wouldn't hurt me any. I'll give it a try."

A. Courage. Not letting fear get in the way,
or
B. Pleasure from your own kindness. Feeling good when you do something kind for someone else.

1033. A boy was riding in a car with an older brother of a friend. The brother who was driving the car was driving really fast—about eighty or nines miles an hour, down regular streets, not even on the freeway.

The boy thought to himself, "I'm scared this guy could kill us all." So when they came to a stop light, the boy hopped out of the car and said, "I'm getting out here; you're going too fast; good bye."

The driver yelled back at him, "Come back! Where are you going?" But the boy ran off. Later the older brother had a very bad wreck. The boy wasn't hurt, because he wasn't in the car.

A. Pleasure from discovery. Feeling good about discovering or learning something new,
or
B. Carefulness. Recognizing danger when it is really present.

1034. Dan was teasing Ted, a boy in his class. Dan said, "Your mother is bald-headed!" Ted looked really upset and hurt. When Dan saw this, he felt bad. He said, "I'm sorry. I didn't mean to hurt your feelings."

Ted told him his mother had died, and that while she was getting treated for cancer, her hair really had fallen out. Dan felt really bad.

Dan said to himself, "From now on, for the rest of my life, I'm going to be careful about saying hurtful things to people." And partly because he felt so bad, he really was much more careful from then on.

A. Conscience. Recognizing when you have hurt someone else, and feeling remorseful about it,
or
B. Pleasure from others' kindness. Feeling grateful when someone has done something kind for you.

1035. A girl who had to give a speech felt herself getting scared and nervous. She said to herself, "I'm feeling scared and nervous, but that's OK; I can handle it. It's natural to feel nervous sometimes. I'll give a good speech even though I am feeling nervous." And she went on feeling scared, but she gave a good speech anyway.

A. Painful emotion-tolerance. Handling feeling bad for a while, without feeling bad about feeling bad,
or
B. Humor. Enjoying funny things, finding funny things to say or think about.

1036. When a boy was very angry, for a few seconds, he wished his father were dead. But then a few minutes later he said to himself, "I had some pretty mean thoughts toward my father. I'm sorry about that. But I'm glad I didn't really do anything that hurt him. I didn't even say any angry words to him. So he was not harmed. I'm glad it just happened within my mind and nowhere else."

A. Fantasy-tolerance. Knowing the difference between a thought and an action,
or
B. Option-generating. Thinking of good options for solving a two-person problem.

1037. A girl was singing a song. Someone heard her and said, "Hey, that's nice singing!"

The girl felt good and said to herself, "Wow, that's really neat that this person likes my singing!" And she said to the other person, "Thank you!"

A. Pleasure from approval. Feeling good when someone gives you a compliment,
or
B. Delay of gratification. Doing without something fun now, to get something better later.

1038. Someone asked a boy a question about math, to see if he could answer it.

The boy figured out the answer to the question. He thought to himself, "Hooray! I figured it out! That feels good!"

A. Frustration tolerance. Handling it when you don't get what you want,
or
B. Pleasure from accomplishments. Feeling good when you accomplish something.

1039. A girl saw someone who didn't have any lunch to eat, so she shared some of her lunch with the other person. Later she thought to herself, "I did a good deed. I made someone happier, by acting kind. I feel good about that!"

A. Enjoying aloneness. Having a good time alone, doing OK without attention,
or
B. Pleasure from your own kindness. Feeling good when you do something kind for someone else.

1040. Jeff was reading a book, and he learned from the book how people first learned that the world was round.

Some other kids thought to themselves, "I wonder if the teacher will ask about this on the test. If so, I guess I have to remember it." And they didn't feel very good.

But Jeff thought to himself, "Isn't that interesting! It really makes sense to me! I never thought of it before! I'm glad I learned that today!"

A. Pleasure from discovery. Feeling good about discovering or learning something new,
or
B. Assertion. Being able to stick up for your own ideas or stick up for what you want.

1041. A boy had a mother who worked really hard at doing lots of things for the boy, including washing the boy's clothes so that he would have clean clothes to wear. Some other boys in the same situation never even gave this a thought, but just took for granted that there would be clean clothes in their drawers.

But this boy thought to himself, "I'm thankful my mother does this for me. She really works hard so I can have these clean clothes." And he felt good.

And he said to his mother, "I appreciate your putting so much work into doing things for me, like cleaning my clothes." She felt good too.

A. Pleasure from others' kindness. Feeling grateful when someone has done something kind for you,
or
B. Social initiations. Starting to talk or play with other people in a good way.

1042. A boy was very hot and sweaty and thirsty because he had been doing some hard work outside. He went inside and took a shower and went to the refrigerator and got some orange juice.

Many people wouldn't have said anything to themselves about this, and wouldn't have felt particularly good. But this boy said to himself, "I'm so glad that I live in a time and place where I can take a shower whenever I want. A long time ago no one had showers. It feels so good."

He also said to himself, "Wow, it's wonderful that I can have this cool orange juice. A long time ago, people could only have orange juice if they happened to live near where the orange trees grow, and then only during the time of year when the oranges get ripe. Hooray!" And he felt good.

A. Pleasure from blessings. Feeling good when something happened to turn out the way you want it,
or
B. Socializing. Having a good social conversation.

1043. A boy was about a year old. When his mother picked him up, he enjoyed it, and he hugged her.

A. Listening. Being a good listener for someone else,
or
B. Pleasure from affection. Feeling good about touching someone or being touched, when it is a good idea.

1044. A woman had a friend who was attracted to "tough guy" type men who were mean or hostile to others. These men treated the woman's friend in a mean way too.

But the woman herself wasn't attracted to this type of man. She was really turned off by guys who acted mean and hostile, and was very attracted to guys who were gentle and kind.

She found one who always treated her gently and kindly too, and she had a great time with him.

A. Handling criticism. Dealing well with criticism or disapproval,
or
B. Favorable attractions. Feeling romantic feelings about the right sort of situations and person.

1045. A boy sat down to do his homework. The work was not very interesting this particular night. He got the urge to watch a television show, but he said to himself, "I'll do my work now, and I'll be really glad later."

He got the urge to read a comic book instead, but he said to himself again, "I'll do my work now, so that I'll feel good about it after it's done."

He finished, and had some time to go outside and play some before he went to bed. The next day at school he felt very good that he had got his work done.

A. Self-discipline. Doing without something fun now, to get something better later,
or

B. Rational approach to joint decisions. Deciding how to approach a conflict situation: how much to give in, forgive the other person, give the other person something, stick up for your own way, punish the other person, or some other strategy.

1046. A boy said to his father, "May I go ice-skating today?" The father said, "You can, but you must always wear your helmet. You are not allowed to skate without your helmet on." The boy said, "OK."

When the boy got to the skating rink, he saw that almost no one else had a helmet on. A friend saw his helmet and teased him. The friend said, "Planning on falling on your head, huh?"

The boy was tempted to leave the helmet off. But he remembered what his father had said. So he left it on.

While he was skating, another kid was skating very fast and recklessly. This kid slammed into him. Both of them fell onto the ice. Both of them hit their heads. The helmet protected him from being hurt badly. The other boy was knocked out. He was taken to a doctor.

A. Pleasure from approval. Feeling good when someone gives you a compliment,
or
B. Compliance. Obeying someone when it is good to obey.

1047. A man found a note written in secret code. He thought the note would tell where some treasure was buried.

He started to work on figuring out what the note said. He sat down and worked on it for three hours without stopping. After three hours he had a clue about how to solve it, and then the next day he worked on it for five hours straight.

At the end of all that time, he had figured it out. He followed the directions and found the treasure.

A. Option-generating. Thinking of good options for solving a two-person problem,
or
B. Persistence and concentration. Keeping on paying attention to something for a long enough time to accomplish something.

1048. A man got into a pattern when he came home from work where he would lift weights for a little while, and then go out for a walk with each of his children, and then eat a lot of fruits and vegetables for supper. He avoided drinking alcohol and smoking. His doctor told him, "You're in fantastic shape."

A. Health habits. Not smoking, not drinking alcohol, exercising, and eating right foods,
or

B. Conciliation or submission. Giving in or conceding to what the other wants when it is a good idea.

1049. A boy found an axe and decided he would use it to cut down a tree. His parents saw that the tree was cut down, and they didn't know who did it. They were very upset.

His mom said, "Look what happened! That was the tree we were thinking would grow cherries for us next year! Somebody cut it down!"

His dad was very angry to see that it had been cut down. He asked the boy, "Do you know who did it?"

The boy said, "Yes, I did it. I'm sorry. I didn't think it was an important tree."

His parents were very angry at him. But afterward, they did think to themselves, "We can trust him. We have a truthful son. Some children would have lied to us, but he was brave enough not to."

A. Pleasure from others' kindness. Feeling grateful when someone has done something kind for you,
or
B. Honesty. Being honest or dependable even when it is hard to do this.

1050. A boy went to a school where the students were called on to read out loud to a group of other children. And at recess, they would play soccer. The boy wasn't very good at reading out loud, and he wasn't very good at soccer.

The boy said to himself, "I don't like being embarrassed by not reading or playing soccer very well. I'm going to work at it."

So he took his school reading books home, and practiced reading from them out loud. He would read by himself, and when he couldn't figure out a word, he would ask his mother or his older sister.

After he had done this for a while, he would go outside and practice kicking a soccer ball. He did both these things for hours and hours. Finally he got to be really good at both of them, and he enjoyed being at school a lot more than before.

A. Competence-development. Working at improving your abilities in schoolwork, games or sports, or work, or
B. Differential Reinforcement. Reinforcing or rewarding other people's positive behavior and avoiding reinforcing the negative.

1051. A boy got a job delivering newspapers. Other friends who made money from jobs spent their money on skateboards, expensive shoes and fast food places.

But this boy started a savings account in a bank, and when he had any extra money, he would put it in the bank. He did without expensive shoes and put the money in the bank instead.

He did this over many years. The bank paid him money called interest, just for keeping his money in the bank.

Finally he had saved up twenty thousand dollars. By that time, the bank was paying him one thousand dollars a year in interest, which he didn't have to work for.

A. Toleration. Putting up with or enjoying a wide range of other people's behavior, without needing to boss them around,
or
B. Conservation and Thrift. Saving money, being thrifty.

1052. A boy met people for the first time, he got very excited and nervous. He didn't enjoy the way he felt when that happened.

But he practiced relaxing his muscles, making them limp and loose, and sitting still. He practiced this a little bit every day. When he practiced, he imagined himself going to see someone new, and imagined himself getting very relaxed.

Then he did go and see someone new, and he practiced getting relaxed every few minutes or so. He had a very good time, and the person he visited enjoyed it too.

A. Forgiveness. Forgiving other people, stopping being angry at them,
or
B. Relaxation. Relaxing, letting the mind drift and letting the body be at ease.

1053. A girl went on the trip to a park with her friends. She ran around and said, "Wow, look at all there is to see and do!" And she picked up sticks and leaves and then pointed to the leaves and said to one of her friends, "Each one of these is a thousand dollar bill! I'm rich! Hooray!" And then she said, "I think I'll buy this car, and also that one, and that house over there."

And then the friend played that she was trying to steal the money from her, and they ran all over everywhere, laughing and having a good time.

Then they saw a puddle of water in which they could see the reflections of their faces, and they made very funny faces and laughed at each other.

A. Gleefulness. Playing, being gleeful, or having fun being silly,
or
B. Handling mistakes and failures. Handling it when you make a mistake or don't succeed at something.

1054. A boy had a friend over to play with him. The friend saw some toy people, and he started making up a real silly story about them and having them talk to each other with strange voices. The friend laughed at what he was making up. The second boy laughed at the silly story and added some more to it that was even sillier. They both had the toy people do very funny things, and they had a great time.

A. Humor. Enjoying funny things, finding funny things to say or think about,

or

B. Carefulness. Recognizing danger when it is really present.

1055. A girl had two babysitters. The girl went to her parents and said, "I like one babysitter, but I don't want the second one to come back." Her parents said, "Why not?"

The girl said, "She screams and yells at me, maybe thirty or forty times in an evening. She spends most of her time talking on the phone with someone else. If I start playing and having fun in any way, she seems to get irritated with me and to yell at me to stop doing something, even when I'm not doing anything wrong. The best times are when she falls asleep and leaves me alone to do my own thing."

The girl's parents took this seriously and did some investigating on their own and never had that babysitter back again. The girl said, "I'm glad I could talk well enough to tell them what I didn't like."

A. Fluency. Using words and language well,

or

B. Fantasy-tolerance. Knowing the difference between a thought and an action.

1056. It was a Sunday, and a girl had a sort of yucky feeling. She said to her sister, "I have this sort of yucky feeling. My body feels OK, but it's like I'm worried or scared about something, something that's going to happen."

Her sister said, "Can you think of anything that you have to worry about?"

The girl said, "I think I know! There's a report that I have to make in front of the whole class at school tomorrow, and I haven't even done it. That's what I'm dreading!"

So the girl got to work right away and did the report, and practiced it, and then she felt good again for the whole rest of the day.

The next day she had some fun giving the report. She felt glad she had figured out the nagging worrying feeling that he had felt.

A. Pleasure from your own kindness. Feeling good when you do something kind for someone else,

or

B. Awareness of your emotions. Recognizing and talking about your own feelings.

1057. A boy was playing with a younger boy, picking him up, swinging him around and chasing him. The little boy laughed at first. Then at one moment the little boy got scared and stopped having a good time. The second boy could tell it by looking at his face and hearing his tone of voice.

So he immediately stopped chasing him and just sat down and said, "I can tell you're starting not to like this; we won't play so roughly." The younger boy gradually walked back to him and started talking, and they had a good time.

A. Empathy. Recognizing what other people are feeling about something,
or
B. Assertion. Being able to stick up for your own ideas or stick up for what you want.

1058. A boy had two parents who were getting divorced and who were very angry at each other. He said to himself, "Is this something I can change, or is it something I don't have any control over?"

He thought and talked about this question some, and he finally decided, "Other than being as nice as I can to both of them, I don't think there's much I can do about their problems with each other."

The boy noticed that he was getting fat. He said to himself, "Is this something I can change, or is this something I don't have any control over?"

He read and talked about this question, and he decided he could lose weight if he wanted to badly enough. So he exercised for about two hours a day and lost enough weight that he wasn't at all fat.

A. Pleasure from others' kindness. Feeling grateful when someone has done something kind for you,

or
B. Awareness of control. Figuring out what things you can change, and what things you can't change.

1059. A boy was in high school. He started thinking a long time in advance about what he was going to do after high school. He read about different jobs, and he also read books about colleges. He read about what kinds of jobs college graduates can get, and what kind high school graduates can get. He read about how you can get scholarship money and loans to go to college. He talked with his teachers about what options they would suggest.

He finally decided to try to go to college. Then he read about different colleges. He listed about ten of them that interested him, and for each one of them he made a list of the advantages and disadvantages. He picked the one where the advantages most outweighed the disadvantages, and he went to it and liked it.

A. Decision-making. Systematically deciding something by defining the problem, getting information on it, thinking of some options of what to do, thinking ahead to what might happen with the different options, and then making a choice,
or
B. Non-jealousy. Handling it when someone else gets what you wanted.

1060. A boy was chasing a ball. The ball rolled out into the street, but the boy said to himself, "Wait a second. Let me think. I don't want to just run after it. There could be a car."

So the boy stopped at the street and watched and listened very carefully for a car. Sure enough, a car came by very fast and almost hit the ball. The boy said, "I'm glad the car didn't hit me!"

A. Thinking before acting. Letting thoughts mediate between situation and action,
or
B. Pleasure from my own kindness. Feeling good when you do something kind for someone else.

1061. A woman got lots of mail. She would put it in a big basket, and then once a week she would take each piece of paper and either save it in folders in a file cabinet, or throw it away, or do something with it like pay a bill.

When she made an agreement to see someone at a certain time, she would write it down in a little appointment book she kept with her. Every day she would look at her book and see what things she had already agreed to do, and she would also plan what she wanted to do and write it down in the little book. Then she would check off each thing as she did it. She got lots more things done than most other people.

A. Pleasure from others' kindness. Feeling grateful when someone has done something kind for you,
or
B. Organization. Being organized, making and following plans, in how to use time or money or where to put papers or objects.

1062. A boy went skiing for the first time with some friends. When he saw the people coming down the side of the mountain, just as he had seen them on television, he thought, "I'm sure I can do that! In fact, I will be able to do it better than anyone else here!" But before he rode up to the top of a very hard trail, he thought again.

He said to himself, "I've never done this before, so I shouldn't expect to do very much today. But I read a book about how to ski, and if I start at the very easiest hill, and work on the things I read, I'll bet I can learn a lot today."

So he put the skis on, and at first it was hard for him to get around. But he tried the things he learned in the book, and he got some tips from some other people, and gradually he learned. By the end of a few hours, he was able to ski under control, although he still didn't want to go too fast. He said to himself, "I'm still no expert, but I can learn."

A. Awareness of your abilities. Figuring out accurately how skilled you are at something, rather than tricking yourself to think you're better or worse at it than you really are,

or
B. Empathy. Recognizing what other people are feeling about something.

1063. A girl joined an acting club. She said to herself, "I wonder how good the acting coach will be?" At first he made her feel confident, and she said to herself, "It's nice to feel confident. That's one sign of a good acting coach."

She started to think the acting coach was the greatest person she had ever met, but she caught herself and thought, "Wait a minute. Let's not go overboard. I don't know this person well yet."

Then the acting coach criticized her, in a not very nice way, for how she acted on a certain part. She said to herself, "He wasn't very tactful in criticizing me. Being tactful and nice is something the perfect acting coach should do. But nobody's perfect. And he did make some good points, which I can learn from."

A. Conservation and Thrift. Saving money, being thrifty,
or
B. Discernment and trusting. Figuring out accurately how well someone else can do something, rather than tricking yourself into thinking they're better or worse at it than they really are.

1064. A boy was afraid of giving speeches to people. He said to himself, "I guess I should practice giving speeches to people more, if I want to get over being scared." But he didn't have a chance to give speeches very often.

Then one day he got an idea. "I know! I'll practice giving speeches by pretending." So he imagined he was in a big auditorium, and there were lots of people sitting and listening to him. He practiced reading out loud a speech he would be giving some day, and he imagined the people listening.

At first, it would make him nervous to do this, even in his imagination, but then it got easier and easier for him. When it came time for him to give his speech in real life, he was confident, and he did a great job. He said to himself, "I'm glad I could use my imagination to practice."

A. Imagination and positive fantasy rehearsal. Being able to use imagination well,
or
B. Frustration tolerance. Handling it when you don't get what you want.

1065. A little boy played with some older boys, while his mother did something else. Every once in a while, the boy would get lonesome for his mother. He got the urge to get hurt or start crying to get his mother's attention.

But then he said to himself, "I don't need to make something bad happen in order to get her attention." So he would get a big smile on his face and run back to her and say, "Hooray that you're my mommy! I want a hug from my mommy!"

His mother would laugh and pick him up and hug him, and then he would go back and play with the other boys.

A. Pleasure from discovery. Feeling good about discovering or learning something new,
or
B. Positive aim. Aiming toward making things better, rather than trying to get pity or attention or something else by making things worse.

1066. A man was driven by a goal to help people learn to read better. He taught reading to children and also to adults who hadn't learned to read.

Then this man was in a car accident that left him unable to move his arms or his legs. He was very sad, and he said to himself, "This will get in the way of my teaching reading to people."

But then he said to himself, "I can still teach reading, as long as I can talk, even if I can't move. My students can move their papers and books, and can even move me around when I need to be moved."

And he also said to himself, "In addition to teaching people to read, I can also be an example to other people who have been hurt badly and show them that they can accomplish things."

So he set up a schedule of teaching people to read, from early in the morning till nightfall. They would come to him, and he would speak to them and explain to them how to pick up the books and how to run the computer programs and how to move him.

He taught lots of people to read, and he said to himself, "I don't like not being able to move my arms and legs, but life is still very much worth living."

A. Purposefulness. Feeling a sense of purpose that lets effort toward that purpose feel fulfilling,
or
B. Conscience. Recognizing when you have hurt someone else, and feeling remorseful about it.

1067. A person formed an organization that works to prevent people from shooting or hurting one another. The person figured out all sorts of different programs that could help in this cause, and he worked tirelessly to bring about the result he envisioned – a more peaceful world.

A. Awareness of your abilities. Being honest and brave in assessing your strengths and weaknesses,
or
B. Nonviolence. Being committed to the principle of nonviolence and working to foster it.

1068. A person was teaching guitar lessons. He had told his students several times how to hold their hands. But one student still was holding his hands wrong.

The teacher got the urge to say, "Can't you understand English? I told you not to hold your hands that way!"

But he caught himself. He thought, "I don't want to make my student feel bad." So he said to the student, "Let me model how to hold your hands, and see if you can do it the same way, OK? Take a picture in your mind. Now try it. That's better! Look one more time at me, and imitate this picture. Now try again. You did it!"

A. Non-jealousy. Handling it when someone else gets what you want,
or
B. Respectful talk, not being rude. Being sensitive to words that are accusing, punishing, or demeaning, and avoiding them unless there is a very good reason.

1069. A father kept nagging his teenaged daughter to study hard for school. He would always say, "It's time to start working! Why are you goofing off! You need to study more! You are too lazy!" But the more he said these things, the more his daughter rebelled. She got mad at him. She chose not to study, just to spite him. He got mad at her, too.

The father talked to a friend. The friend said, "Do you remember the old story by Aesop? The sun and the winter wind saw a traveler walking along the road, wearing a heavy coat. They decided to have a contest, to see who could get the man's coat off. The winter wind tried first. He tried to blow the man's coat off him. But the harder the wind blew, the more tightly the man clutched the coat around him. Finally the winter wind gave up. Next it was the sun's turn. He came out and shone warmly upon the man. The man got warm enough that he himself took his coat off. The sun won the contest."

The father thought about the friend's story. He decided that he would stop nagging his daughter. He decided that he would do fun things with her, and have nice chats with her. He decided that he would say nice things when she did well in school work, and he would not get mad when she did not do well.

The father and his daughter got along better and better. After a while, the daughter started working harder at her studies. The father was very happy.

A. Toleration. Non-bossiness. Tolerating a wide range of other people's behavior
or
B. Honesty. Being honest and dependable, especially when it is difficult to be so

Appendix: Psychological Skills Axis

Group 1: Productivity

1. Purposefulness. Having a sense of purpose that drives activity
2. Persistence and concentration. Sustaining attention, concentrating, focusing, staying on task
3. Competence-development. Working toward competence in job, academics, recreation, life skills
4. Organization. Organizing goals, priorities, time, money, and physical objects; planfulness

Group 2. Joyousness

5. Enjoying aloneness. Having a good time by oneself, tolerating not getting someone's attention
6. Pleasure from approval. Enjoying approval, compliments, and positive attention from others
7. Pleasure from accomplishments. Self-reinforcement for successes.
8. Pleasure from your own kindness. Feeling pleasure from doing kind, loving acts for others
9. Pleasure from discovery. Enjoying exploration and satisfaction of curiosity
10. Pleasure from others' kindness. Feeling gratitude for what others have done
11. Pleasure from blessings. Celebrating and feeling the blessings of luck or fate
12. Pleasure from affection. Enjoying physical affection without various fears interfering

13. Favorable attractions. Having feelings of attraction aroused in ways consonant with happiness
14. Relaxation. Calming oneself, letting the mind drift pleasantly and the body be at ease
15. Gleefulness. Playing, becoming childlike, experiencing glee, being spontaneous
16. Humor. Enjoying funny things, finding and producing comedy in life

Group 3: Kindness

17. Kindness. Nurturing someone, being kind and helpful
18. Empathy. Recognizing other people's feelings, seeing things from the other's point of view
19. Conscience. Feeling appropriate guilt, avoiding harming others

Group 4: Honesty

20. Honesty. Being honest and dependable, especially when it is difficult to be so
21. Awareness of your abilities. Being honest and brave in assessing your strengths and weaknesses

Group 5: Fortitude

22. Frustration-tolerance. Handling frustration, tolerating adverse circumstances, fortitude
23. Handling separation. Tolerating separation from close others, or loss of a relationship

24. Handling rejection. Tolerating it when people don't like or accept you or want to be with you

25. Handling criticism. Dealing with disapproval and criticism and lack of respect from others

26. Handling mistakes and failures. Regretting mistakes without being overly self-punitive

27. Magnanimity, non-jealousy. Handling it when someone else gets what I want

28. Painful emotion-tolerance. Tolerating feeling bad without having that make you feel worse

29. Fantasy-tolerance. Tolerating unwanted mental images, confident that they will not be enacted

Group 6: Good decisions
   6a: Individual decision-making

30. Positive aim. Aiming toward making things better. Seeking reward and not punishment

31. Reflectiveness. Thinking before acting, letting thoughts mediate between situation and action

32. Fluency. Using words to conceptualize the world: verbal skills

33. Awareness of your emotions. Recognizing, and being able to verbalize one's own feelings

34. Awareness of control. Accurately assessing the degree of control one has over specific events

35. Decision-making. Defining a problem, gathering information, generating options, predicting and evaluating consequences, making a choice

   6b: Joint decision-making, including conflict resolution

36. Toleration. Non-bossiness. Tolerating a wide range of other people's behavior

37. Rational approach to joint decisions. Deciding rationally on stance and strategies

38. Option-generating. Generating creative options for solutions to problems

39. Option-evaluating. Justice skills: Recognizing just solutions to interpersonal problems

40. Assertion. Dominance, sticking up for oneself, taking charge, enjoying winning

41. Submission: Conciliation, giving in, conceding, admitting one was wrong, being led

42. Differential reinforcement. Reinforcing positive behavior and avoiding reinforcing the negative

Group 7: Nonviolence

43. Forgiveness and anger control. Forgiving, handling an insult or injury by another

44. Nonviolence. Being committed to the principle of nonviolence and working to foster it

Group 8: Not being rude (Respectful talk)

45. Not being rude, respectful talk. Being sensitive to words, vocal tones and facial expressions that are accusing,

punishing or demeaning, and avoiding them unless there is a very good reason

Group 9: Friendship-Building
46. Discernment and Trusting. Accurately appraising others. Not distorting with prejudice, overgeneralization, wish-fulfilling fantasies. Deciding what someone can be trusted for and trusting when appropriate
47. Self-disclosure. Disclosing and revealing oneself to another when it is safe
48. Gratitude. Expressing gratitude, admiration, and other positive feelings toward others
49. Social initiations. Starting social interaction; getting social contact going.
50. Socializing. Engaging well in social conversation or play
51. Listening. Empathizing, encouraging another to talk about his own experience

Group 10: Self discipline
52. Self discipline Delay of gratification, self-control. Denying oneself pleasure for future gain

Group 11: Loyalty
53. Loyalty. Tolerating and enjoying sustained closeness, attachment, and commitment to another

Group 12: Conservation
54. Conservation and Thrift. Preserving resources for ourselves and future

generations. Foregoing consumption on luxuries, but using resources more wisely. Financial delay of gratification skills

Group 13: Self-care
55. Self-nurture. Delivering assuring or care taking thoughts to oneself, feeling comforted thereby
56. Habits of self-care. Healthy habits regarding drinking, smoking, drug use, exercise and diet
57. Carefulness. Feeling appropriate fear and avoiding unwise risks

Group 14: Compliance
58. Compliance. Obeying, submitting to legitimate and reasonable authority

Group 15: Positive fantasy rehearsal
59. Imagination and positive fantasy rehearsal. Using fantasy as a tool in rehearsing or evaluating a plan, or adjusting to an event or situation

Group 16: Courage
60. Courage. Estimating danger, overcoming fear of non-dangerous situations, handling danger rationally
61. Independent thinking. Making decisions independently, carrying out actions independently
62. Depending. Accepting help, being dependent without shame, asking for help appropriately

Index